GENESIS

The Storyteller's Companion to the Bible

Michael E. Williams, editor

VOLUME ONE

GENESIS

Abingdon Press
Nashville

GENESIS

Copyright © 1991 by Abingdon Press

This book is printed on recycled acid-free paper.

Library of Congress Cataloging-in-Publication Data

Williams, Michael.
    Genesis / Michael E. Williams, editor ; John Holbert, contributor. p. cm. -- (A Story-
    teller's companion to the Bible ; v. 1)
    Includes index.
    ISBN 0-687-39670-0 (alk. paper)
    1. Bible. O.T. Genesis–Paraphrases, English. 2. Bible stories, English–O.T. Genesis. I.
Williams, Michael E. (Michael Edward), 1950-   . II. Title. III. Series.
BS1235.7.H655   1991
222'.1109505–dc20   90-26289
                                                  CIP

Scripture quotations in "The Story" section of each chapter are from The Revised English Bible. The Delegates of the Oxford University Press and the Syndics of the Cambridge University Press 1989. Used by permission.

Those in the "Comments on the Story" section of each chapter are the author's own translations.

Selections from *Genesis Rabbah* are paraphrased from *Midrash Rabbah*, copyright © 1939, with the permission of Soncino Press, Ltd., 123 Ditmas Avenue, Brooklyn, NY 11218.

99 00 01 02—10 9 8

MANUFACTURED IN THE UNITED STATES OF AMERICA

As always
for
Margaret
and now
for
Sarah

Contributors

Michael E. Williams, editor of The Storyteller's Companion to the Bible series, is the author of *Friends for Life: A Treasury of Stories for Worship and Other Gatherings.* He serves as Director of Preaching Ministries, General Board of Discipleship, The United Methodist Church.

John C. Holbert, Assistant Professor, teaches courses on the Old Testament and Preaching at Perkins School of Theology, Southern Methodist University. He is author of the forthcoming book *Preaching Old Testament: Proclamation and Narrative in the Hebrew Bible* for Abingdon Press in 1991.

Contents

Acknowledgments

When you work with traditional stories that were told for generations before being written down, there are many people to thank. First, I am eternally grateful for the ancient tellers who kept these words alive and the writers who saved them for later generations. I must not neglect to mention those who keep the stories alive today by telling them: pastors, teachers, parents, grandparents, and all who continue to tell Bible stories.

Several persons and groups deserve special thanks. First, John Holbert, a fine storyteller as well as scholar, agreed to contribute to this book when it was still a dream. Without him it might never have come to be. John Miller gathered a group of laity and clergy together at Olmstead Manor Retreat Center in Pennsylvania to "try out" portions of this companion. Their telling and their enthusiasm for the project were proof that such a volume would, indeed, help people to tell Bible stories.

Natalie Houghtby arranged for early versions of the companion to be shared with youth leaders in Long Beach, California. Her efforts and the courage of those leaders to tell Bible stories to teenagers reinforced my belief that stories are truly for all ages. The people of Belmont United Methodist Church in Nashville, Tennessee, heard me retell several of these stories from Genesis (including midrashim) at their all-church retreat. Their responses confirmed for me that midrash has a place in biblical storytelling.

Paul Franklyn, my editor and friend, has believed in this project all along, but more than that he has worked to see that it found its way into print in the most appropriate and helpful form. Linda Allen went beyond the call of duty as a copy editor by reading the manuscript and proclaiming it "interesting."

Finally, for Margaret, whose companionship undergirds all that I do, and for Sarah, who brought deep delight into both our lives, there are not words to express my gratitude.

Michael Williams
October 28, 1990

A Storyteller's Companion

Michael E. Williams

This book is for anyone who is interested in telling Bible stories, specifically the stories from Genesis. Many of us in the Church find occasions when we are called upon or feel moved to tell someone else one of the foundational stories of our faith. Pastors who are preparing sermons or Bible studies and church school teachers who are planning for their classes are constantly aware of times that a lesson or sermon could be brought to life by simply telling a story from the Bible. Parents and grandparents may feel the desire to introduce younger members of their families to biblical characters through telling their stories.

The stories from Genesis and other books in the Bible are our stories. They are not just a collection of ancient narratives about people who lived long ago and far away. They are stories of human beings (sometimes too much like us for comfort) who are striving to know who they are and who God is. They often failed, just as we do, but the stories told about their struggle help us to live and grow in our own relationship to God and our neighbors.

The stories of biblical characters are family stories for Jews and Christians. Adam and Eve, Abraham and Sarah, Jacob and Esau, Rachel and Leah, and the numerous other characters of Genesis are our forebears, and their stories help us to remember that we belong to God and to God's family despite our wanderings and failures. Ours is a family story that reaches back through history and around the world.

So this book is intended to help you tell these family stories. It is meant to be put to use, not simply read. It provides for the would-be storyteller everything you need to begin or to continue telling Bible stories. In this companion you will find:

The Stories

While this book does not cover every word of Genesis, it does provide helpful storytelling information for the vast majority of stories from the book that opens our Bible. All the passages that appear in all the various current lectionaries (including the proposed revisions of the *New Common Lectionary*) are covered. In addition, we have added certain other passages that simply could not be left out.

11

One thing you will discover as you use this companion is that the insights and information that help you tell one part of a story apply to the other parts as well. For example, we do not cover every portion of the Joseph saga, but much of the help given for the portions we do include will assist you as you tell the entire story.

The translation from which the printed texts in this companion are taken is *The Revised English Bible.* You may wish to compare the readings here with your favorite translation or several others. It enriches the telling of biblical stories, especially for those who do not read the original language, to work from various translations.

Comments on the Stories

Dr. John Holbert, who teaches both Old Testament and preaching at Perkins School of Theology, Southern Methodist University, provides information and insights related to each passage that are intended to be of help to everyone who wishes to tell these stories. He does not tell you how to tell the story; that is something only you can decide, based on your knowledge of the needs and experiences of those who will be hearing the story. He simply offers historical, cultural, and literary insights to ensure that your telling of the story can be done with integrity and understanding.

While only you can know the places in the lives of your class, congregation, or family where a particular Bible story will strike a chord, turn on a light or heal a hurt, John Holbert points you toward the significant aspects of the Bible passage itself that will inform your telling. Unlike other biblical commentaries this companion is intended to assist you in telling Bible stories in a way that honors both the original texts and your listeners. For more information on how to shape a story so that it will speak to your specific group of hearers see "Learning to Tell Bible Stories: A Self-directed Workshop" in this volume.

Retelling the Stories

There is no one right way to retell a Bible story. Your telling will depend on your own life experiences, the life experiences of your hearers, and the understanding of the Bible you both bring to the story.

This companion includes sample retellings related to each biblical passage. Some will tell the entire story, while others will relate only a portion. These are not intended to be memorized by you and repeated. They are simply examples of one way to retell a given story. These retellings are intended to spark your imagination and help you to discover how you will tell the story.

Sometimes a passage will be retold pretty much the way it appears in Genesis. At other times a retelling will be from one character's point of view, even told in that character's voice. The variety of approaches to retelling a Bible story included in this companion will give you a taste for the many ways you will wish to tell these stories. Each approach to retelling a story carries with it the possibility of your hearing the story fresh, as if for the first time. John Holbert retold the even-numbered stories and I retold the odd-numbered ones.

Midrashim

One of the most time honored ways of interpreting the Bible is to tell stories about its stories. Certain events in the Old Testament are told more than once, with each telling being different. Some of these retellings are ways of interpreting an old story for a new time. Even those who wrote the texts of the biblical narratives interpreted and commented on those stories by telling other stories.

Most of us are used to interpreting a story by telling what it means in the form of a message or moral or by listing the three (Why always three?) things a passage has to say for us today. Jewish teachers of Jesus' time and in the centuries following taught and preached the Scriptures in a different way. The rabbis who interpreted the stories of the Bible often did so by telling stories about them. Each story is called a *midrash* (plural, *midrashim*) and the collections of the stories are also called *Midrash*.

The most unique contribution that this companion makes to the retelling of Bible stories is that it included a number of these midrashim with the retelling of each story. The retelling appears at the end of each section while the midrashim related to each story are in shaded boxes in the text. Each midrash is placed next to the portion of the story with which it most closely relates. This is also the place in the story you may wish to insert one of these story interpretations when retelling that particular story. (For more information see "What Are Midrashim, and What Are They Doing Here?" on pages 19-21.)

You will probably not want to read this companion from front to back as you would most books. It was really not designed to be read that way. One way to use this volume effectively would be to read John Holbert's introduction to his comments on the stories and the introduction to midrash. Then choose a story that you wish to tell from the table of contents. This may be a story for an upcoming Sunday of the lectionary or the church school curriculum, or it may simply be a story that captures your interest. Once you have chosen the story work through the short workshop on storytelling using the story you chose as your content.

Use the retelling provided with the story as a guide, but do not feel obligated to simply repeat it. Tell the story for your hearers in your own way. You may choose to include the midrashim with your retelling, or you may tell them afterward. In any case you are about to take part in one of the most ancient experiences of our faith: offering the gift of God's story so that it touches our stories today.

13

Reading the Narratives of Genesis

John C. Holbert

A revolution is occurring in the reading of biblical narrative, and this book is in part a result of that revolution. Many scholars are taking with far greater seriousness the fact that the narratives of the Bible are precisely what they appear to be: stories. Thus some scholars are asking questions of these texts that are rather different from the questions that critical scholars have been asking. Those questions include: What is the plot of this story? Why is it ordered in the way that it is? How are the characters described? How can I learn from what they say and what they do? What effect does the point of view of the narration have on my understanding of it? Does it make a difference who tells the story or on what character the storytelling is focused? These are the questions of *poetics,* questions that literary critics have asked of secular stories for most of this century. Biblical critics are, in one sense, catching up.

Our readings of the stories in Genesis ask these kinds of questions first. We by no means avoid questions of history when they are pertinent, but we attempt to solve difficulties in the text, first by reference to the literary shape of the text at hand and by a careful look at the broader literary context, rather than by comparing it to other extra-biblical texts of a similar or somewhat related kind. The same type of questions could be asked of several other particularly thorny texts of Genesis (see, for example, 4:23-24 and chap. 34). We thereby assume that the collectors of the stories in Genesis had some goal in mind as they shaped their material, and that they were not hack writers, haphazardly tossing materials together in some sort of confusing salad.

To be sure, there are times when the texts are not easily harmonized (see the problem of who sold Joseph into Egypt in Gen. 37 and 39). But more often than not, the stories of Genesis have a kind of literary relational logic that can be uncovered if enough careful attention is given to the questions, which we now unpack.

Plot

Plot may be defined as the dynamic, sequential element in narrative literature. To have plot, a narrative must have some action, it must be dynamic, and it must be sequential; random materials do not make a plot in any sort of recognizable sense. An example of the importance of plot may be seen in the following overview of the long cycle of Jacob stories, found in Genesis 25–50. There is considerable pleasure as we observe the wily Jacob trick Esau and then Laban in turn. We expect that Jacob, upon his return as Israel, after his confrontation with the mysterious *man* at the Jabbok river, and his tearful meeting with a surprisingly forgiving Esau, will at last drop his trickster identity and join his brother in a new-found harmony. After all, he does announce that to see Esau is to "see the face of God" (Gen. 33:10).

But we are surprised to hear that though Jacob promises to follow Esau to Seir (33:14), he in fact journeys alone to Succoth (33:17), adding this small lie to the many he has told before. My possible expectations for the results of lying behavior—some sort of "come-uppance"—are not satisfied by the end of chapter 33. But the story is not over. In the subsequent account of the rise of Joseph, Jacob is cruelly lied to and tricked by his own sons, not the least of whom is Joseph, his favorite. Joseph's game of cat and mouse with his brothers inevitably leads to the heart-rending decision on the part of Jacob to relinquish his new favorite, Benjamin, into the less than trustworthy hands of his sons, who themselves plotted the demise of Joseph so long before. When Jacob says, "You will bring down my gray hairs with sorrow to Sheol" (42:38), the reader gets the feeling that Jacob's earlier behavior has had its agonizing consequences after all. Careful attention to plot and its dynamic sequence can give meaning to materials across a long narrative distance, and across materials that in their origins had little to do with one another. You will find many such examples in our readings of the stories of Genesis.

Character and Characterization

Biblical narrative provides very little description or interior monologue in the modern sense. No individual character is described in any real sense, either in terms of physical descriptions or in terms of motivations for particular behaviors. The biblical narrators use instead the actions of characters and what those characters say in order to develop the characters for the readers.

Consider our reading of Genesis 22. Abraham, earlier in his cycle of stories, was not always a reliable character; in several instances he lied and was indecisive. By his resolute actions of following the strange command of his God, he demonstrates his willingness to perform the command. And his words match those decisive actions. For example, to his son's question about the absence of a sacrificial animal, Abraham answers quite simply that "God will provide." There is here no irresolution, no lying for self-gain; Abraham is going to be obedient, he will pass the test of God.

As we read this great chapter, we raise very few questions of history or archaeology. We do not ask after the origin of the text or its literary sources.

We attempt to see the story as the climax of a series of stories concerning Abraham. To do that, we paid attention especially to the character of Abraham, revealed to us by action and speech, the character who stands always at the very heart of the narrative.

Point of View

A narrative artist controls the reader's relationship to the story by the way the artist handles the sources of the story's telling. Reading pleasure arises from insight into the disparity between knowledge of the story as reader and the knowledge, or lack of knowledge, demonstrated by various characters in the story.

For example, in the prologue to the book of Job, the readers are allowed to see both levels of the drama unfold. We see Job as an absolutely righteous man who loses everything in a terrible series of events. However, we are also witnesses to the mysterious scene in heaven between God and Satan, which in ways not altogether clear has triggered the choice of Job for the test. When Job's friends come on the scene, they do not possess the knowledge that we have been given; they see only the miserable Job. From their incomplete knowledge, which they claim to be complete, they conclude dogmatically that Job is a sinner, because only sinners end up on ash heaps. But we, the readers, know them to be hopelessly wrong; Job is not on the heap because of some sin.

Job knows only that he is not worthy of this terrible punishment, but he knows nothing of the heavenly wager. In summary, we know all, thanks to the narrator. And Job knows his own experience, which is less than we know. But the friends are completely in the dark about Job and his relevant circumstances. We then are in the marvelous position of being able to make judgments of the rightness or wrongness of the various positions in the debate. The narrator creates this pleasure for us by manipulating the point of view: Who knows what, when, and how? As you tell the stories of Genesis, you need to examine the narratives with an eye on who is telling the story and on whom the story itself is focused and not focused.

This brief introduction only scratches the surface of intensely complex topics. Still, we think that you can begin to see that attention to the poetics of texts can lead to deeper understanding about just how those texts "work," what makes them tick. Once you have grasped these detailed building blocks of the text, keys to preaching and teaching can leap off the page. Poetics can keep you focused when you tell a biblical story, because you understand far better just how the story "works." Poetics is a way to a richer, fuller, and more faithful presentation of the story.

What Are Midrashim, and
What Are They Doing Here?

Michael E. Williams

Midrash (the plural in Hebrew is *midrashim*) comes from a Hebrew word meaning "to go in search of" or "to inquire." So, midrashim resulted when the ancient rabbis went in search of (inquired into) the meaning of the Scriptures for their lives. Midrash is also the name for the process of inquiring into the Scriptures for their meaning.

We might say that midrash is both our encounter with the biblical stories as we seek their meaning for our lives and times, and the stories that emerge to express that meaning. Often midrashim do take the form of stories or pieces of stories (at least the ones we will focus on here do). These stories seek to answer questions about and to fill gaps in the biblical stories.

The midrashim drawn from for this volume come from the period 400–1200 C.E. (what is sometimes called A.D.). They were told, in part, to make the stories of Genesis relevant to a Jewish community that had no homeland, could not hold citizenship in other countries, and experienced hostility and persecution from the outside, including from Christian authorities. Most of these midrashim originated in sermons preached in synagogues, based on the prescribed weekly readings from the Torah (the first five books of the Bible). Others emerged from the popular and folk traditions of the Jewish communities. Though they were collected and written during that eight-hundred-year period, there is no way of knowing how long the midrashim had been circulating by word of mouth before someone wrote them down. Some are attributed to rabbis living at the time of Jesus. In fact, certain scholars find evidence that this way of interpreting the Bible has its roots intertwined with the texts of the biblical stories themselves.

I see three basic functions for the midrashim I have selected to be included in this book. The first might be called "filling the gaps." These stories and story fragments answer questions about the biblical stories that the Scripture leaves unanswered. For instance, where did the dust come from to make the first human being? How high did the Tower of Babel rise before God decided to do something about it? When the rabbis answered such questions, they revealed both their fertile imaginations and their own understanding of God and human beings. Sunday school teachers and college professors will also have encountered these imaginative questions.

The second function of midrash is to draw an analogy. These stories begin with "This may be compared to. . . . " Then the rabbi would tell a contemporary story that exhibited a situation and characters like the biblical story under consideration. You may notice that sometimes these stories bear a resemblance to the parables of Jesus and the *mashal* (parable) form of Jewish teaching.

The third function is to describe an encounter. In these stories someone comes to a rabbi with a question, and the rabbi's response interprets both the biblical story and the situation from which the question emerged. For example, when someone asked a rabbi how it is that we know that Joseph didn't attack Potiphar's wife, the rabbi reads two other stories of graphic sexual disobedience (Reuben and Bilhah, Judah and Tamar) from the Torah and asks, "If the Bible is so brutally honest about these two, would it not tell us the truth about Joseph?" (*Genesis Rabbah* 87.6).

Why did I choose a predominantly Jewish form of interpretation in this book? First, Christians have too often ignored this ancient and time-honored way to interpret the Bible. Given our Jewish roots and Jesus' heritage, midrash is at least as directly related to our tradition as the Greco-Roman philosophy on which we have depended so heavily for ordering our questions and structuring our theological doctrines.

Second, midrash provides us with a way of interpreting the Bible that involves the imagination and speaks to our experience. It is also, according to certain scholars, the way the Bible interprets itself.

Third, midrash provides a model for a community-based, inclusive (even children can imaginatively participate in stories), nonprofessional (you don't have to be a trained theologian) way of interpreting the Bible for our times. In short, we can learn the stories the rabbis told about the scriptures to interpret them for their time. In addition, we can follow the example of the rabbis and learn to tell stories about Bible stories that interpret them for our time.

This is just the first step to reclaiming midrashim for modern tellers of Bible stories, but it is a step. If you want to learn more about midrashim related to the stories of Genesis you may wish to read the volumes from which those included here were paraphrased. The citiations following the paraphrases are to the books listed below, in which you may read the original midrashim.

Genesis Rabbah in *Midrash Rabbah,* trans. H. Freedman (London: Soncino Press, 1939) is a ten-volume translation of midrashim on a variety of books of the Bible. The first two volumes are *Genesis Rabbah* and deal with the stories of Genesis. The references here are to chapter and section. The third edition of this work was published in 1983.

Volume one in Louis Ginzberg's classic collection of stories related to biblical texts, *The Legends of the Jews,* trans. Henrietta Szold (Philadelphia: The

Jewish Publication Society, 1909 & 1937), still in print, draws from a wide number of sources, including Christian and Islamic traditions. Here this work is listed as Ginzberg, followed by the volume and page number.

Another collection that draws from a wide range of sources is Robert Graves and Raphael Patai, *Hebrew Myths: The Book of Genesis* (New York: Anchor Books, 1964). Here it is listed as Graves and Patai, followed by the page number.

A good general Jewish commentary on the Torah is Gunther Plaut, ed., *The Torah: A Modern Commentary* (New York: Union of American Hebrew Congregations, 1981). Here this work is listed as Plaut, followed by the page number.

One more word on midrash: For any given passage of Scripture several stories or interpretations of various rabbis are presented side by side in collections of midrashim. Those who collected these stories saw no reason to decide which was the one right interpretation. This is also true, we might mention, of those who assembled the canon of the New Testament, who saw no reason to choose among the four very different stories about Rabbi Jesus. The understanding behind these choices is that there need be no single correct interpretation. The Bible is viewed as being so inclusive that it could apply to a range of possible life situations. Therefore, we would expect a variety of interpretations to speak to a variety of life situations. Not only the Bible, but also all of its many possible interpretations are encompassed by the expansive imagination of God. In fact, Solomon, the wisest of all humans is reputed by the rabbis to have known three thousand stories for every verse of Scripture and one thousand and five interpretations for every story.

Learning to Tell Bible Stories

A Self-directed Workshop

1. Read the story aloud at least twice. You may choose to read the translation included here or the one you are accustomed to reading. I recommend that you examine at least two translations as you prepare, so you can hear the differences in the way they sound when read aloud.

Do read them *aloud*. Yes, if you are not by yourself, people may give you funny looks, but this really is important. Your ear will hear things about the passage that your eye will miss. Besides, you can't skim when you read aloud. You are forced to take your time, and you might notice aspects of the story that you never saw (or heard) before.

As you read, pay special attention to *where* the story takes place, *when* the story takes place, who the characters are, *what* objects are important to the story, and the general *order of events* in the story.

2. Now close your eyes and imagine the story taking place. This is your chance to become a playwright/director or screenwriter/filmmaker because you will experience the story on the stage or screen in your imagination. Enjoy this part of the process. It takes only a few minutes, and the budget is within everybody's reach.

3. Look back at the story briefly to make sure you haven't left out any important people, places, things, or events.

4. Try telling the story. This works better if you have someone to listen (even the family pet will do). You can try speaking aloud to yourself or to an imaginary listener. Afterwards ask your listener or yourself what questions arise as a result of this telling. Is there information you need about the people, places, things, or language in the story? Is it appropriate to the age, experiences, and interests of those who will be hearing it? Does the story capture your imagination? One more thing: You don't have to be able to explain the meaning of a story to tell it. In fact, those of the most enduring interest have an element of mystery about them.

5. Read the "Comments on the Story" that John Holbert has provided for each passage. Are some of your questions answered there? You may also wish to look at a good Bible dictionary for place names, characters, professions, objects, or words that you need to learn more about. *The Interpreter's Dictio-*

nary of the Bible (Nashville: Abingdon Press, 1962) is still the most complete source for storytellers.

6. Read the "Retelling the Story" section for the passage you are learning to tell. Does it give you any ideas about how you will tell the story? How would you tell it differently? Would you tell it from another character's point of view? How would that make it a different story? Would you transfer it to a modern setting? What places and characters will you choose to correspond to those in the biblical story? Remember, the retellings that John and I have provided are not meant to be told exactly as we did them. They are to serve as springboards for your imagination as you develop your telling.

7. Read the midrashim that accompany each retelling. Would you include any of these in your telling? You could introduce them by saying, "This is not in the original story, but the rabbis say. . . . " Do these midrashim respond to any of your questions or relate to any of your life situations or those of your listeners? If so, you might consider using them after the retelling to encourage persons to tell their own stories, which hearing the Bible story has brought to mind. You may even wish to begin creating some modern midrashim of your own or with your listeners.

8. Once you have gotten the elements of the story in mind and have chosen the approach you are going to take in retelling it, you need to practice, practice, practice. Tell the story aloud ten or twenty or fifty times over a period of several days or weeks. Listen as you tell your story. Revise your telling as you go along. Remember that you are not memorizing a text; you are preparing a living event. Each time you tell the story, it will be a little different, because you will be different (if for no other reason than that you have told the story before).

9. Then "taste and see" that even the stories of God are good—not all sweet, but good and good for us and for those who hunger to hear.

The First Account of Creation

This is the first of two accounts of creation. In this one the focus is on the entire universe and on the creation, which takes place in seven days.

The Story

In the beginning God created the heavens and the earth. The earth was a vast waste, darkness covered the deep, and the spirit of God hovered over the surface of the water. God said, 'Let there be light,' and there was light; and God saw the light was good, and he separated light from darkness. He called the light day, and the darkness night. So evening came, and morning came; it was the first day.

God said, 'Let there be a vault between the waters, to separate water from water.' So God made the vault, and separated the water under the vault from the water above it, and so it was; and God called the vault the heavens. Evening came, and morning came, the second day.

God said, 'Let the water under the heavens be gathered into one place, so that dry land may appear'; and so it was. God called the dry land earth, and the gathering of the water he called sea; and God saw that it was good. Then God said, 'Let the earth produce growing things; let there be on the earth plants that bear seed, and trees bearing fruit each with its own kind of seed.' So it was; the earth produced growing things: plants bearing their own kind of seed and trees bearing fruit, each with its own kind of seed; and God saw that it was good. Evening came, and morning came, the third day.

God said, 'Let there be lights in the vault of the heavens to separate day from night, and let them serve as signs both for festivals and for seasons and years. Let them also shine in the heavens to give light on earth.' So it was; God made two great lights, the greater to govern the day and the lesser to govern the night; he also made the stars. God put these lights in the vault of the heavens to give light on earth, to govern day and night, and to separate light from darkness; and God saw that it was good. Evening came, and morning came, the fourth day.

God said, 'Let the water teem with living creatures, and let birds fly above the earth across the vault of the heavens.' God then created the great sea-beasts and all living creatures that move and swarm in the water, according to their various kinds, and every kind of bird; and God saw that it was good. He blessed them and said, 'Be fruitful and increase; fill the water of the sea, and let the birds increase on the land.' Evening came, and morning came, the fifth day.

God said, 'Let the earth bring forth living creatures, according to their various kinds: cattle, creeping things, and wild animals, all according to their various kinds.' So it was; God made wild animals, cattle, and every creeping thing, all according to their various kinds; and he saw that it was good. Then God said, 'Let us make human beings in our image, after our likeness, to have dominion over the fish in the sea, the birds of the air, the cattle, all wild animals on land, and everything that creeps on the earth.'

> God created human beings in his
>   own image;
> in the image of God he created
>   them;
> male and female he created them.

God blessed them and said to them, 'Be fruitful and increase, fill the earth and subdue it, have dominion over the fish in the sea, the birds of the air, and every living thing that moves on the earth.'

God also said, 'Throughout the earth I give you all plants that bear seed, and every tree that bears fruit with seed; they shall be yours for food. All green plants I give for food to the wild animals, to all the birds of the air, and to everything that creeps on the earth, every living creature.' So it was; and God saw what he had made, and it was very good. Evening came, and morning came, the sixth day.

Thus the heavens and the earth and everything in them were completed. On the sixth day God brought to an end all the work he had been doing; on the seventh day, having finished all his work, God blessed the day and made it holy, because it was the day he finished all his work of creation. This is the story of the heavens and the earth after their creation.

Comments on the Story

It may prove peculiar to begin a storyteller's companion with a look at a passage that is by no one's reckoning a story in the normal sense. This first account of creation has been described as poetry, liturgy, poetic theology, a proclamatory sermon, and as many other forms of literature.

Though this passage is different from the narratives we will encounter in much of the rest of Genesis, nevertheless certain features of this text are at least storylike. God does speak; in fact, speaking is the defining characteristic of God in chapter 1. What characters *say* is one of the biblical authors' chief ways of teaching us about those characters. The fact that God is the *only* speaker in this passage indicates that God is the chief actor and should be the focus of any retelling of the story for preaching or teaching. God, like any good storyteller, speaks creation into being; and when God speaks, things happen.

Another storylike feature of this passage is that there is a recognizable plot—that is, a dynamic sequence of action, moving through the seven days of creation. As the main character of this plot, God begins the action with the spoken command of 1:3 and concludes the action with a divine rest in 2:2. At one level, God's rest can be taken quite literally; the work of creation has been

26

exhausting, and even God needs a break from all that labor. Indeed, one role this passage has played is in the understanding shared by both Judaism and Christianity that a "sabbath" (Hebrew for "rest" or "to cease activity") was necessary for God and is necessary for us as well.

The seven-step plot of this passage has prompted several important questions. I will note three of them here.

First, God calls for the creation of light on the first day; yet, the sun (note that it is called only "the greater light," rather than its quite familiar Hebrew *shemesh*) is not made until day four. Now any Hebrew knows, as well as you and I, that the sun is the giver of light. What is this "light of God" on the first day?

Second, God, in the creation of the human creatures on day six, uses the second-person plural pronoun three times in one verse (1:26). With whom is God speaking here? To whom is God referring with these plural pronouns? The structure of the plot gives us a clue to the context; look at what comes before and after the statement for a possible answer. On the previous day God created the animals, both wild and domesticated. Is God then speaking to them, or perhaps speaking about them in the second-person plural pronouns of verse 26? Some midrashim suggest other answers.

Third, God gives the human beings "dominion" over the freshly created world and demands that they "subdue it." The verb used here is a very forceful one, meaning to "tread on grapes" (see also Joel 3:13) and to "dominate an enemy" in war (see Num. 24:19 and Ps. 72:8-9). What is the nature of God's gift of dominion and power to the human beings in the light of our modern devastation of the natural environment?

Other questions intrude as we read. God speaks into "the deep" (1:2; the word is *tehom* in Hebrew) to call the creation into being. Where does *tehom* come from? There is no mention of *tehom* or the deep being created by God.

According to this account all animals, including humans, in God's creation are vegetarians (1:29-30). Why do we and the Hebrews eat meat? This is a passage that raises as many questions as it answers.

There are two features of the language of this passage that add to the movement of the plot. In the first six days of creation, the commands of God follow two patterns: "let there be" on days one, two, and four; and "Let the waters/earth" on days three, five, and six. Verse 26 breaks the pattern. The command here is phrased "let us make." Here God's involvement in this part of creation is far more direct. By using repeated phrases and then altering them, the author highlights the uniqueness of human beings in creation. A storyteller can use the same technique of repetition and alteration in retelling.

The second feature of the language of this passage is the use of the word *good*. In verses 4, 10, 12, 18, 21, and 25 God calls the creation "good." Finally, God surveys all of the creation and pronounces it "very good." That judgment covers all of the preceding creations (including the "great sea monsters" of verse 21!) and at the same time raises in our minds the question: If all that comes from God's hands is very good, then what happened? In this way the author urges us to read on. We can celebrate God's creation as good, but we cannot deny the fact that good is not the only word we would use now, nor that the Hebrews used then, to describe the creation.

In certain respects, anyone wishing to retell this story can see that Genesis 1:1–2:4*a* is a storylike passage with character and plot. It certainly must be said that it introduces the longer story of Genesis chapters 1–11 and ultimately the whole book.

This passage is *not* science. We recall a memorable statement of Karl Barth. In a 1965 letter to his grandniece, he wrote: "Has no one explained to you in your seminar that one can as little compare the biblical creation story and a scientific theory like that of evolution as one can compare, shall we say, an organ and a vacuum cleaner?" (*Karl Barth Letters 1961-1968*, trans. Geoffrey W. Bromiley [Grand Rapids, Mich.: Eerdmans, 1981], p. 184). What do you suppose he meant by this comparison?

With whom did God consult when beginning to create the universe and all that is in it? Some rabbis said that, like a builder consulting an architect's drawings before beginning construction on a building, God consulted the Torah (the first five books of the Bible) before speaking the universe into being. Apparently this record of the relationship between God and human beings was much more than a book. The rabbis saw it as a living, breathing design for living that had assisted God in creation. This is similar to the role described for wisdom in Proverbs 8:22-31. Could this be the "we" God refers to later when humans are about to be created? (*Genesis Rabbah* 1.1)

Retelling the Story

Before the beginning of the beginning of anything that ever was there was God and there was nothing. The emptiness was emptier than anyone could imagine, and the loneliness was lonelier than anyone could imagine.

So God began to tell the story that became the universe, saying, "Once upon a time there was light." And there *was* light. Then God named the light day and the darkness night, the first two characters in the story. And at the end of the first day God said, "This is great."

Then God continued the story, "Once upon a time there was a sky that sat upon the water." And that took care of the second day.

"And once upon a time there was dry land surrounded by oceans, and the land sprouted all kinds of trees and bushes and plants and flowers, all with seeds to reproduce themselves." And at the end of the third day God said, "This is great!"

On the fourth day God continued, "Once there were two lights, a greater one to look over the day and a lesser one to guard the night. We'll call the greater one the sun and the lesser one the moon." And so it was. Then God said, "This is really great!"

On the fifth day God said, "Once there were fish and birds and other creatures of the sea and sky, and they were blessed by giving birth to others of their kind and filled the oceans and the heavens." And when God saw the colors of the fish sparkling in the water and how the birds graced the sky, the Creator sighed, "This is truly great."

The sixth day was a very busy one as God moved toward the completion of the story. "Then there were wild animals in the forests and jungles and tame ones on the pastures and plains." But the story was still not complete. Then God had a flash of insight as sometimes happens in stories. "Let's put a character in this story who is just like us to take care of all the other characters and things in this story. This character could pick up the story and tell it just as I have."

Whom did God speak to when saying "Let us. . . "? Some rabbis say it was the ministering angels to whom God spoke and that there was some strong disagreement over whether the human should be created at all. The angel of love supported God's creation of the human because of all the acts of compassion that would enter the world through human beings. The angel of truth opposed the human because of the lies that humans would tell. The angel of righteousness was for the human, since humans would do many righteous deeds, but the angel of peace was against the human because humans would start wars. While the angels were arguing among themselves, God created the humans, male and female, and told the angels to be quiet: "It's too late to argue; humans are a fact of life now." (*Genesis Rabbah* 8.4)

So God told of a character who would be the very image of the divine story-teller. The character was like God and came in two styles, male and female. God told the new creatures to care for everything else in creation and gave the green plants of the earth for the human creatures and all the other animals to eat. So God's story that spoke the world into being came to a close. When God looked at all the wonderful parts of this divine story, the Creator's voice boomed across the entire creation like a strong wind, "Now this is really great."

Then on the seventh day God rested from telling the story of creation and blessed the day, setting it aside for rest.

The Sabbath came to God and said, "Everything in creation has a partner, but I have none. Who shall be my partner?" And God replied, "The people of Israel, those who remember you and keep you holy will be your partners." (*Genesis Rabbah* 11.8)

To this day we humans still gather on the day of rest to tell God's stories and to bless the day, each other, and creation.

GENESIS 2:4*b*-25

The First Humans

The second story of creation focuses on the first human beings, their relationship to God, and the creatures who surround them in the garden.

The Story

When the Lord God made the earth and the heavens, there was neither shrub nor plant growing on the earth, because the Lord God had sent no rain; nor was there anyone to till the ground. Moisture used to well up out of the earth and water all the surface of the ground.

The Lord God formed a human being from the dust of the ground and breathed into his nostrils the breath of life, so that he became a living creature. The Lord God planted a garden in Eden away to the east, and in it he put the man he had formed. The Lord God made trees grow up from the ground, every kind of tree pleasing to the eye and good for food; and in the middle of the garden he set the tree of life and the tree of the knowledge of good and evil.

There was a river flowing from Eden to water the garden, and from there it branched into four streams. The name of the first is Pishon; it is the river that skirts the whole land of Havilah, where gold is found. The gold of that land is good; gum resin and carnelians are also to be found there. The name of the second river is Gihon; this is the one which skirts the whole land of Cush. The name of the third is Tigris; this is the river which flows east of Asshur. The fourth river is the Euphrates.

The Lord God took the man and put him in the garden of Eden to till it and look after it. 'You may eat from any tree in the garden,' he told the man, 'except from the tree of the knowledge of good and evil; the day you eat from that, you are surely doomed to die.' Then the Lord God said, 'It is not good for the man to be alone; I shall make a partner suited to him.' So from the earth he formed all the wild animals and all the birds of the air, and brought them to the man to see what he would call them; whatever the man called each living creature, that would be its name. The man gave names to all cattle, to the birds of the air, and to every wild animal; but for the man himself no suitable partner was found. The Lord God then put the man into a deep sleep and, while he slept, he took one of the man's ribs and closed up the flesh over the place. The rib he had taken out of the man the Lord God built up into a woman, and he brought her to the man. The man said:

'This one at last
is bone from my bones,
flesh from my flesh!
She shall be called woman,
for from man was she taken.'

That is why a man leaves his father and mother and attaches himself to his wife, and the two become one.

Both were naked, the man and his wife, but they had no feeling of shame.

Comments on the Story

In this second chapter of Genesis we enter into the realm that is clearly story. In sharp contrast to the quite general descriptions of the world at the beginning of God's creation in chapter 1 (the formless void, the great darkness, the vast cosmic ocean, and the great wind of God), in the first sentence of this story we find a specific description of a large barren plain. On this plain, no plant or field shrub grows because God has not yet brought rain; besides, there is no person available to till the ground. The only sign of life, which in the Middle East is closely tied to the presence of water, is a mysterious mist (vs. 6) or dew that waters the face of the ground. We find then a huge desert, completely empty, yet kept moist not by the natural presence of rain water, but by the apparently supernatural ground water of no certain origin. I think of certain parts of the Mojave desert in southwestern California when I read this description.

From that unpromising desert God "forms" an 'adam. The verb used to mean "form" here portrays God as an artist, since this word is usually employed to describe the life and work of a potter (see II Sam. 17:28; Isa. 29:16, 30:14, 41:25; and Jer. 18:2-4). We may thus see God with dirty hands and knees, clay caked under the divine fingernails, toiling over the potter's wheel, carefully shaping bits of moist earth into the 'adam. The word 'adam means "human being" and should not be identified as a male figure, which many translations imply. One scholar suggests the reading "earth creature" to avoid the question of gender. You might call this clay figure "Dusty."

God then animates Dusty with the "breath of life," that distinctive gift of the holy God that makes a living being out of all of us bits of useless clay. Turning from Dusty, God then forms a garden in Eden (Hebrew for "pleasant") and puts Dusty right in the middle of the garden. Then from the ground God makes every tree, each growing "pleasant to the sight and good for food." The author focuses our attention on two trees in particular: the tree of life and the tree of the knowledge of good and bad. This latter tree, the one we will hear much more of, is, in effect, the tree of the knowledge of everything. With this special attention on the two particular trees the author breathes life into the plot of the story. How will Dusty and the trees relate? What is Dusty's task in this garden of God? We shall see.

After an important announcement that the rivers are in place to distribute water to the world and that their source is God's own garden we receive an answer to our second question about Dusty's role. Dusty is to "till" (or "serve") and to "keep" (or "guard") the garden. In effect, Dusty is the chairperson of the garden property committee. Dusty's role is not simply to guard the garden but to work it, to make it better than when it was received from the hand of God. But while guarding and serving, Dusty is not allowed to enter one part of the garden; it is strictly off limits. Every tree *save one* (compare this with the first story of creation, where every tree without restriction is given for food) is available for food. On the very day that the fruit of that tree is eaten, says God, the eater will surely die. The command seems clear enough.

Then God announces that it is simply not good that *'adam* be alone, and so God decides to "make a companion who is like him [Dusty]." Those translations that suggest that God is in search of a "helper fit for him," or some sort of assistant "suitable to his needs," are badly off the mark. The Hebrew word is "helper," to be sure, but the fact that the most common reference for the word in the Hebrew Bible is God (about 75 percent of the time) indicates that the word hardly suggests any kind of male dominance over the female. The literal translation of the end of verse 18 is "like in relationship to him (or it)."

God first attempts to find an appropriate companion among all the animals, who were also formed on the divine potter's wheel. In verse 19 God proudly parades all these new creatures in front of Dusty, who dutifully gives each of them a name. However, among all the barks, growls, and screeches "there was not found a companion who was like him." So God goes back to the drawing board (or the operating table), abandoning the potter's wheel, and gives Dusty a divine anesthesia. While Dusty is out, God takes a part from Dusty's "side" (the traditional reading is "rib"), and after closing over the hole with flesh, "builds" a woman from that piece of Dusty.

Upon seeing her, Dusty, who is now clearly "a man," breaks into joyous song. "This *at last* [the implication is that God got it right this time!] is bone of my bone and flesh of my flesh. She shall be called *ishah,* because she was taken out of *ish.*" The author concludes that this is the very reason why men and women seem so anxious to be married to each other, because at one time they really were one person, whom we have been calling Dusty. This is called an etiology—namely, a story that explains the origin of a custom, place, or name. The Bible is filled with such etiologies.

So the appropriate companion has been created, and the two now can live together in God's garden. The author concludes by saying that both of them are "naked but not ashamed." By saying this, the author clearly distinguishes this wonderful garden from the place where we live. Our nakedness, both physical and psychological, leads almost unfailingly to shame. Thus we are left with at least two questions: What about that forbidden tree of the knowledge of everything and, perhaps more pressing, why don't we live in such a place anymore? The story is far from over.

> When God decided to make the first human, dust was brought from the four corners of the earth. This was so that if a person from the east should die in the west the earth would receive him or her. Or if anyone from the north should die in the south he or she might be buried there. Since we are from the earth, no matter where we die, the earth will take us in.
> (Ginzberg, vol. 1, p. 55)

Retelling the Story

Light. Space. Wind. Dust. Emptiness. As far as new eyes could see. It (he? she? they?) was alone. The horizon swept on to nowhere. When the sky's burning ball had gone to its unknown place and the gentler ball appeared, something wet came with it. Dew or mist, at least something, the only other something that it could see. But how do you talk to a mist? What does the mist have to say? Alone.

But things changed. Suddenly, there was a green place to break the monotony of the dust. The green place, when it looked closer, had individual green and brown things in it (trees?). Two of the trees stuck out right in the middle of the green place (a garden, it turns out). One was the tree of life, and the other was the tree of knowledge, whatever those things are.

Then with a mighty roar, a giant stream of the mist rumbled out of the ground and cascaded to the far horizon, branching as it went. But before it could plunge itself into the inviting water, it was lifted up and dropped rather unceremoniously right next to the trees of life and knowledge. And the one who did the lifting and the dropping told it to serve the garden and guard it. For what reason? From whom? Alone.

And the unseen lifter suddenly found a voice. "It is not good that you are alone. I will make a companion who is like you." Now we are getting somewhere, thought Dusty. Dusty? Well, it was better than "it," at least, and the name reminded Dusty of its roots in the soil and the dust and the mist. So the great lifter got out a potter's wheel (had Dusty been made like that?) and began to make; the great lifter was in fact a great maker, too. Shapes began to fly off the wheel, strange and miraculous. After the wheel slowed and the shapes ceased, the maker brought all the shapes to Dusty and invited it to give names to them. At first, it was a delightful game: horse, duck, platypus (what else could you call such a thing?), pig, mosquito, roach, lion, tiger, and bear; oh my, it was exhausting work, and finally boring. There was no companion here who was like Dusty! Still alone!

The maker put the wheel away, and Dusty grew very sleepy. While sleeping, Dusty thought it saw all the newly shaped things coming toward it, growling and mewing and hissing and scratching for Dusty's attention, somehow all slightly threatening. A new creature awoke with a start. What he saw (Dusty was a "he" now) was a new shape. But there was a companion who was like him.

The man broke into excited song. Looking at the maker, who had a somewhat sheepish expression, Dusty sang, "This at last (you got it right this time!) is my bone and flesh. She is woman, because she was taken out of man." And he and she got together as men and women have been doing ever since. They were both stark naked, but felt not a shred of shame. Sure not like you and me! But like you and me, it is not at all good that anyone be alone. And he and she were never completely alone again.

Someone asked a rabbi, "Why did God steal a rib to make a companion for Adam?" The rabbi answered, "Would you call it theft if someone took one piece of silver during the night and returned the next morning and returned twelve pieces of silver?" (*Genesis Rabbah* 17.7)

Certain traditions have it that Adam had a wife before Eve whose name was Lillith. While her history is too long and involved to recount here, you may be interested to read about her in Graves and Patai (pp. 65-69.) Others suggest that the first earth creature was made having both male and female features, facing in opposite directions. God simply took the female face and added a body to it to make the two earth creatures. (Graves and Patai, p. 66).

Leaving the Garden

The second story of creation continues as the first real complication of the plot occurs when the serpent appears.

The Story

The serpent, which was the most cunning of all the creatures the LORD God had made, asked the woman, 'Is it true that God has forbidden you to eat from any tree in the garden?' She replied, 'We may eat the fruit of any tree in the garden, except for the tree in the middle of the garden. God has forbidden us to eat the fruit of that tree or even to touch it; if we do, we shall die.' 'Of course you will not die,' said the serpent; 'for God knows that, as soon as you eat it, your eyes will be opened and you will be like God himself, knowing both good and evil.' The woman looked at the tree: the fruit would be good to eat; it was pleasing to the eye and desirable for the knowledge it could give. So she took some and ate it; she also gave some to her husband, and he ate it. Then the eyes of both of them were opened, and they knew that they were naked; so they stitched figleaves together and made themselves loincloths.

The man and his wife heard the sound of the LORD God walking around in the garden at the time of the evening breeze, and they hid from him among the trees. The LORD God called to the man, 'Where are you?' He replied, 'I heard the sound of you in the garden and I was afraid because I was naked, so I hid.' God said, 'Who told you that you were naked? Have you eaten from the tree which I forbade you to eat from?' The man replied, 'It was the woman you gave to be with me who gave me the fruit from the tree, and I ate it.' The LORD God said to the woman, 'What have you done?' The woman answered, 'It was the serpent who deceived me into eating it.' Then the LORD God said to the serpent:

'Because you have done this you are cursed alone of all cattle and the creatures of the wild.

'On your belly you will crawl,
and dust you will eat
all the days of your life.
I shall put enmity between you and the woman,
between your brood and hers.
They will strike at your head,
and you will strike at their heel.'

To the woman he said:

'I shall give you great labour in childbearing;
with labour you will bear children.
You will desire your husband,
but he will be your master.'

And to the man he said: 'Because you have listened to your wife and have eaten from the tree which I forbade you,

on your account the earth will be
cursed.
You will get your food from it only
by labour
all the days of your life;
it will yield thorns and thistles for
you.
You will eat of the produce of the
field,
and only by the sweat of your brow
will you win your bread
until you return to the earth;
for from it you were taken.
Dust you are, to dust you will
return.'

The man named his wife Eve because she was the mother of all living beings. The LORD God made coverings from skins for the man and his wife and clothed them. But he said, 'The man has become like one of us, knowing good and evil; what if he now reaches out and takes fruit from the tree of life also, and eats it and lives forever?' So the LORD God banished him from the garden of Eden to till the ground from which he had been taken. When he drove him out, God settled him to the east of the garden of Eden, and he stationed the cherubim and a sword whirling and flashing to guard the way to the tree of life.

Comments on the Story

"The man and his wife were both naked (*'arummim*), but they were not ashamed." That sentence closes the first part of the story of the garden (2:25), and it is followed by this: "Now the snake was more clever (*'arum*) than any wild creature that Yahweh had made." By punning the two words *naked* and *clever*, the author draws the reader's attention to the possible relationships between the snake and the nakedness of human beings. One author suggests that a possible translation for the two words could be "nude" and "shrewd," which plays the same sound game we hear in the Hebrew.

Immediately, dialogue begins. In this story dialogue is particularly important. As we listen to what the characters say to each other, we learn more specifically what the characters want. The translation of the snake's first comment to the woman is ambiguous. It is usually read as a question: "Did God really say that you could not eat from any tree of this garden?" It might also be translated: "So! God really said that you could not eat from any tree of this garden." Either way, the sentence is understood as some sort of challenge, because the woman responds, "From the fruit of the garden's trees we may eat, but from the fruit of the tree in the middle of the garden, God said we must not eat from it, nor touch it, lest we die." Neither the snake nor the woman has accurately reported what God said. (Look back at 2:16-17.) The snake insinuates that God has denied *all* trees to the human beings, while the woman in setting the snake right adds that the special tree cannot even be *touched*, much less have its fruit eaten.

The woman is under attack, and she responds defensively by hardening the command of God. However, by saying that they cannot even touch this one

37

special tree, the woman implies that the tree is much on her mind, and the snake goes on to loosen her objections to getting the fruit that apparently she wants so badly. To answer her fear of dying the snake simply says that they will *not* die. Quite the contrary! The snake asserts that God *knows* that death will not result from eating the fruit of the tree, in fact, instead they will attain knowledge, specifically the knowledge of good and bad, the knowledge of everything. In this, says the snake, the humans will become "like God." That promise stops the dialogue, and the eyes of the woman are riveted on the tree (vs. 6). The author has moved us inside of her mind so that we overhear how she convinces herself to get the fruit.

After eating, she hands some to her husband (the Hebrew text includes the small phrase "with her," suggesting that perhaps he has been standing there throughout the preceding dialogue), "and he eats." That is all that he does. At least the woman, confronted with the possibility of eating, has a discussion about it; and the man just eats! After *both* of them have eaten, the consequences are presented. First, "their eyes are opened"; the snake promised that would happen. Could it be that they are now in fact like God? Second, they do gain knowledge; "they *knew* that they were naked" (*'arummim*). This simple fact, the source of no shame before, now leads to a whirlwind of activity all designed to solve what is now a problem. Nakedness must now be covered; shame directs all of their actions. Third, "they sewed figleaves together and made themselves aprons." Have you ever felt a figleaf? At certain points in their cycles of growth, they feel like medium-grade sandpaper; wearing a figleaf while stark naked is a long way from the comfort of cotton. I can imagine that whenever this story was told in homes and around campfires, this scene brought forth great peals of laughter from the listeners.

So the newly clothed pair hear the sound of the Lord God walking in the garden for the breezes of the day (the Hebrew implies that this stroll is a regular one for God), and they rush off to hide, no doubt scratching themselves all the way. Upon reaching the spot where conversation is anticipated, God calls out "to the man" (in surprise?) "Where are you?" The man's response is a long one: "I heard the sound of you in the garden. I was afraid, because I was naked. I hid myself." The man might have responded more simply, "I'm over here!" His reply seems calculated to reveal facts, but to conceal reasons. In any case, it does not satisfy God's curiosity. "Who told you that you were naked? Have you eaten from the tree which I commanded you not to eat?" The second question demands a yes or no answer, which is precisely what the man refuses to give: "The woman, whom you gave to me, she gave me the fruit of the tree, and I ate." It is a craven passing of the buck. "The woman did it," says the man then rushes on to blame God. "After all, you, God, gave her to me!" And to complete the picture of the pair's refusal to take responsibility, when God asks the woman about it, she blames the snake!

Thus at the end of verse 13 the harmonious picture of 2:25 has been shattered. Man, woman, snake, and God are separated from one another, and the curses of verses 14-19 seal the separation. The snake is first cursed to crawl on its belly and to be in perpetual struggle with the descendants of the woman. Then the woman is said to be subject to the man, while her sexual desire for him will lead to painful childbirth. Last, the man is cursed to work the rocky soil, which will yield "thorns and thistles" as often as edible crops. And at the end of their lives they will return to the dust from which they were made. We hear in these curses more examples of etiologies, telling why things were the way they were in the time of the story's telling.

Two important verses follow this grim portrait of life after the eating of the prohibited fruit. First, the man affirms that he and his wife will live on in the face of a harsh existence; "Eve" (related to the word *life, living*) will be the mother of life. It is a statement of human will and determination. Second, God responds to such determination with the gift of animal skins. In effect God says, "Take off those stupid figleaves and try something that will really work!" It is a clear sign of the grace of God; God will not abandon these erring children.

Nevertheless, they can no longer live in the garden, because they just might eat from that *other* tree, the tree of immortality, and live forever. So they are driven out of the garden and prevented from returning by a monstrous cherubim with a whirling sword. Would you choose to live forever a life defined by the curses imposed upon the humans? Hardly! Thus in this story death is God's gift so that the harshness of life will find an end.

The avalanche of sin has begun with the eating of the fruit. It will gain momentum in the next story. Still, this story describes not simply a "fall," however deeply that word has rooted itself into the traditions to which the story belongs. The Hebrews knew that knowledge is crucial for life and growth; we cannot live without knowledge. What this story warns against is the knowledge that leads to figleaf aprons, that leads us to think that we are God. Who knows better than we, whose aprons have become nuclear ones, and whose knowledge always threatens to outrun our judgment?

Retelling the Story

The children had a question. They knew that creation was a wondrous thing and that God had called it good. But if everything in the world is so great, why are there things like broccoli and Brussels sprouts and homework?

> The rabbis say that God created human beings so that they share four qualities with the angels and four with animals. Like the angels, humans walk upright, speak, and have understanding and peripheral vision. Like the animals, humans eat and drink, reproduce, excrete waste, and die. (*Genesis Rabbah* 8.11 and 14.3)

What was the fruit that Adam and Eve ate? The Bible doesn't say, and many today assume that it was an apple. That is not so for the sages. Some of them say that it was wheat, while others say citron, and still others say it was a fig. (*Genesis Rabbah* 15.7)

The old woman told them this story.

In the garden there was a trickster named Snake. This Snake was the shrewdest of all the creatures. One day the woman was walking when she happened to encounter Snake. "Do you mind if I ask you a question?" the trickster hissed. And before she could answer yes or no, he continued, "Why did God put you in such a beautiful garden and then tell you not to eat fruit from any of the trees?"

"Oh, we can eat fruit from any of the trees but one, the one that stands in the middle of the garden. If we take a bite of that fruit, or even touch it for that matter, we will die."

A slow serpentine smile crept across Snake's face, "You won't die. God was just afraid that if you ate from that tree you would be like gods yourself, knowing good from evil and making your own decisions. Go on, try it."

Well she ate, and her husband ate, and immediately she knew that everything was different. It was something in the way her husband looked at her. For the very first time she felt that she should cover herself; she felt shamed by the way he leered at her. In response to her glances, he began to cover himself, too. She was just looking at him, and he began to cover his nakedness. Naked! Her husband was nude, and she had never even noticed before. You would think a person might immediately observe something as important as being naked.

When women were on the birthstool, the rabbis noticed, they often shouted, "I'll make sure this never happens again!" Or to their husbands they cried out, "You did this to me, see if you ever do it again." Afterwards, though, they would be so delighted by this new life that there would be more children in that family, sometimes many more. The rabbis said that it was God who whispered that desire back into their hearts. (*Genesis Rabbah* 20.7)

Having no experience of making clothes, the two chose figleaves from which to make aprons. As soon as they put the aprons on, she knew they had made the wrong choice. The figleaves were rough and uncomfortable. Then, shamefaced and scratching, they went into hiding.

When God came walking through the garden in the cool of the evening and called for them, they were afraid to answer. Before they answered, God knew what was wrong. Her husband blamed her, and she blamed Snake. They all felt that God was at least a little responsible for putting them all there.

Snake got off easy, it seemed to her. All he had to do was crawl on his belly and watch so that neither she nor her children crushed his head. Now her husband would farm, and the earth would not be as cooperative as before. But she would come to know the pain of birth and the even greater pain of a child's leaving (but that is another story).

Now they had to make their own decisions, because now they knew good from evil. And they would never be able to return to the comfort and security of the garden again.

But, she told the children, before we left God came, bringing us something for our new life. As your mothers make you clothes as you face the excitement and terror of starting school, the Creator of the universe made garments for us. They were soft and warm (unlike our figleaf aprons) and were always reminders of the comfort we had known in the garden."

What kind of clothing did God make for Adam and Eve? The story doesn't specify. Some rabbis suggested goat skin or rabbit skin or skin with the wool still attached. Some said that God made garments that could be worn next to the skin, and these were made from Circassian wool (in which firstborn children were dressed at a later time), camel hair, or rabbit hair. Others took it one step further and suggested that it was fine linen from Bethshean. (*Genesis Rabbah* 20.12)

The First Murder

Here we meet the sons of the first couple, and the tragic impact of the humans' newfound knowledge of good and evil is played out in the first murder.

The Story

The man lay with his wife Eve, and she conceived and gave birth to Cain. She said, 'With the help of the LORD I have brought into being a male child.' Afterwards she had another child, Abel. He tended the flock, and Cain worked the land. In due season Cain brought some of the fruits of the earth as an offering to the LORD, while Abel brought the choicest of the first-born of his flock. The LORD regarded Abel and his offering with favour, but not Cain and his offering. Cain was furious and he glowered. The LORD said to Cain,

'Why are you angry? Why are you scowling?
 If you do well, you hold your head up;
 if not, sin is a demon crouching at the door;
 it will desire you, and you will be mastered by it.'

Cain said to his brother Abel, 'Let us go out into the country.' Once there, Cain attacked and murdered his brother. The LORD asked Cain, 'Where is your brother Abel?' 'I do not know,' Cain answered, 'Am I my brother's keeper?' The LORD said, 'What have you done? Your brother's blood is crying out to me from the ground. Now you are accursed and will be banished from the very ground which has opened its mouth to receive the blood you have shed. When you till the ground, it will no longer yield you its produce. You shall be a wanderer, a fugitive on the earth.' Cain said to the LORD, 'My punishment is heavier than I can bear; now you are driving me off the land, and I must hide myself from your presence. I shall be a wanderer, a fugitive on the earth, and I can be killed at sight by anyone.' The LORD answered him, 'No: if anyone kills Cain, sevenfold vengeance will be exacted from him.' The LORD put a mark on Cain, so that anyone happening to meet him should not kill him. Cain went out from the LORD's presence and settled in the land of Nod to the east of Eden.

Then Cain lay with his wife; and she conceived and gave birth to Enoch. Cain was then building a town which he named Enoch after his son. Enoch was the father of Irad, Irad of Mehu-jael, Mehujael of Methushael, and Methushael of Lamech.

Lamech married two women, one named Adah, the other Zillah. Adah gave birth to Jabal, the ancestor of tent-dwellers who raise flocks and herds. His brother's name was Jubal; he was the ancestor of those who play the harp and pipe. Zillah, the other wife, bore Tubal-cain, the master of all coppersmiths and blacksmiths, and Tubal-cain's sister was Naamah. Lamech said to his wives:

'Adah and Zillah, listen to me; wives of Lamech, mark what I say: I kill a man for wounding me, a young man for a blow. If sevenfold vengeance was to be exacted for Cain, for Lamech it would be seventy-sevenfold.'

Comments on the Story

The harmony of the "very good" creation of God has been shattered by the events in the garden. The man and woman have been expelled and are doomed to work and to reproduce in pain and struggle; their eventual death is certain. Immediately, the darkness of the story begins to manifest itself.

The woman conceives and gives birth to a son, Cain (*qayin*, "spear" in Hebrew). She cries out, "I have gotten (*qanah*) a man with the Lord," making a sound pun on the name of the child. In short order, she gives birth to another son, Abel (*habel*, "breath," "wind" in Hebrew—see Eccles. 1:1 for the most famous use of this word). In the names of the two boys the reader senses an ominous note, spear over against breath.

The action moves quickly. After a time, offerings are made to God by the two. Cain's offering is described by one small Hebrew word that means "some." He brings as his offering "some of the fruits of the earth." Abel offers to God, too, but his offering is given a lengthy description. He brought some of "the firstborn of his flocks, that is their fattest portions." The reaction to these offerings is that God "has regard for" (more literally "looked at") Abel and his offering, but God has no regard for Cain and his offering. The result of God's disregard for Cain and his offering is that Cain "was angry and his countenance changed" (literally, "his faces fell").

It is common in reading this story to say that no reason is given for God's acceptance of Abel and rejection of Cain. Or it is suggested that the offering of blood is more acceptable than the offering of fruit of the ground. Or it is said that we find here an ancient tale that revolves around the old antagonism between farmers and ranchers, and that God decides for the latter. After all, the ground was cursed, and whatever comes from it must bear that same curse. The first interpretation pleads ignorance, implying that there is no evidence in the text to provide an answer to the riddle. The second interpretation moves outside the story altogether for an answer, assuming that no answer is forthcoming from the text. The third interpretation takes the story seriously, but ultimately goes beyond the text for its answer.

I believe there is an answer in the text. Cain's offering is "some," while Abel's is the very best he has. Thus God rejects the former and accepts the latter. Cain's anger results from his own decision, not from the result of arbitrary divine actions. This helps to make sense of what God says to Cain in the face of his anger. "If you do well, there is a lifting up [as opposed to the fallen countenance of Cain], but if you do not do well, sin is crouching [like an animal about to spring] at the door. Its desire is for you, but you must master it." The refusal to do one's best opens one up for the assaults of sin, which, like a crouching tiger, is ever ready to attack. And the attack is not long in coming.

Cain invites his brother to the field, and once they are alone, Cain kills his brother. Immediately, God asks a question of Cain: "Where is Abel, your brother?" We are reminded of the question God first asked the man in the garden: "Where are you" (3:9)? Cain lies; sin has indeed overpowered him. "I do not know. Am I my brother's keeper?" The word translated "keeper" is the same word used when God created the human beings in the first place; they were to "work" and to "guard" (keep) the garden (2:15). Cain has not guarded the creation of God; he has done precisely the opposite by destroying it.

God cries out (partially in anguish?), "What have you done? The voice of the blood [*dam*] of your brother [an *'adam*—that is, a "human being"; the Hebrew for "brother" is *'ah.*] is crying to me from the ground [*'adamah*]." In a terrible series of puns, God announces that the separations of the garden have now been extended to the awful separation of fratricide, a heinous crime with the most ancient of roots. After the garden episode, the ground is cursed; Cain is now himself cursed off of the ground. He has made the blood of his brother one with the ground in death. Cain will be separated from the ground, the source of his life and livelihood, in life.

Now Cain cries out that his "punishment [the word can also mean "iniquity"] is more than I can bear" (4:13). Cain fears that his rootless existence will bring death at the hands of whomever he meets. But God marks Cain, both to save him from being murdered and to keep him alive in order that his wandering punishment can continue to work. Like the animal skins of the garden, the mark of Cain is at least in part a sign of the grace of God. So marked, Cain goes to live in the land of Nod. But, because Nod means "wandering," it is clear that Cain in effect lives no where at all.

Cain now leaves the garden and bears offspring. The fact that the first city is built for the son of Cain, the notorious committer of fratricide, may suggest the fear and even loathing of cities that nomadic peoples often share. After a quick move through several generations of the family of Cain (v. 18), Lamech is born. Four children are born to his two wives, and these children are noted for their occupations, each of which is crucial to the lives of ancient semi-nomads. They are Jabal, the ancestor of all who have tents and cattle; Jubal, the ancestor of all musicians, the historians of the tribe; and Tubal-cain, the ancestor of all metalworkers, a crucial job in any ancient economy. In short, 4:17-22 includes a brief lesson in ancient sociology.

Genesis 4:23-24 returns us to the main theme of the ongoing story—namely, the continuing movement away from the harmony of the garden. I will first translate the poem as literally as I can:

> Lamech said to his wives:
> "Adah and Zillah, hear my voice;
> wives of Lamech, give ear to my speech:
> Surely, a man I have killed for wounding me,
> a young boy for touching me!
> If Cain is avenged seven times,
> then Lamech seventy-seven times!"

See what God's world has become now! Lamech, the direct descendant of Cain, boasts to his wives that he kills for wounds, which might have some rationale to it, but he goes on to say that he also kills "young boys" (probably under the age of ten) for touching him. This Lamech is a cruel and angry man. But there is more. Lamech says that if the revenge for a possible murder of his ancestor Cain was to have been sevenfold, then if Lamech is killed, he demands that the vengeance not stop until seventy-seven are killed. Because seven is a number of completeness in the Hebrew Bible, Lamech seems to imply that his death should bring on the wholesale slaughter of an incredible number of people. In other words, this poem indicates that God's world has descended nearly to the level of beasts. From fruit-eating to fratricide to wholesale vengeance, the world of God is on a slippery slope to disaster. Such a disaster is not long in coming.

A tiny note of hope concludes the chapter. To Seth, the child born to Adam and Eve after the murder of Abel, is born a child named Enosh, who "then began to call on the name of the Lord" (one possible translation of the last phrase of vs. 26). It is a small hope, but it is hope, and in this deteriorating story, the reader grabs for any hope at all.

Retelling the Story

It was a day like any other day. The brothers arose early, one to check on his herd, pastured quietly not too far distant, while the other continued the exhausting work of weeding his wheat field. Both were up before the sun to complete the bulk of their work before the searing heat became unbearable.

But before work could be begun, sacrifice must be performed; they had learned that lesson from their father, who seemed especially concerned to perform proper sacrifice to the God I AM. It was as if their father had some terrible dark sin for which he had to atone, and the family never missed the morning sacrifice. So as the sun peeped over the horizon, casting a cool light over the land, quite unlike the later blast furnace to come, Adam brought his family to the high place.

After the prayers, spoken always by the head of the family, mother Eve was the first to lay her gift on the earthen altar, a loaf of her finest bread, fresh from the brick-lined oven; her sons were not the only ones up before the sun. Then the patriarch laid a fresh pile of fig leaves on the altar, as he did every day. It was an odd gift, and the old man always smiled broadly as he moved away from the altar and caught the eye of his wife who always seemed to be suppressing a laugh. The brothers never knew what the joke was. Then came Abel, the secondborn, the owner of several fine flocks of goats and sheep. Proudly, he laid upon the sacred altar the succulent flank of his most prized animal. It was without doubt the very finest gift he could have given, and his parents nodded and murmured their approval. Finally, the firstborn son, Cain, who always concluded the morning ritual with his gift, moved lazily toward the altar and dropped a rather moldy looking, none too fresh shock of wheat right next to the superb meat offering of his brother.

Adam grunted his displeasure, Eve sucked in her breath in startled dismay, and Abel made a little clucking sound, a sound of disgust to the ears of Cain. He looked at each member of his family one at a time with defiance, his glance telling them in no uncertain terms that he had done precisely what he had intended to do. Ominous thunder split the leaden sky, promising rain in the season without rain.

> At first, sin is as weak as the strand of a spider's web, but later it becomes as strong as a stout rope. At first, sin is a stranger passing by a house, then a guest in the house, and finally it comes to rule the house. (*Genesis Rabbah* 22.6)

> What did the brothers quarrel about? Well, they both owned land, and each wanted the Temple built on his land, according to the rabbis. That religious dispute was the beginning of the situation that led to the first murder. (*Genesis Rabbah* 22.7)

Adam and Eve left the high place, mumbling to each other. The eyes of the brothers remained locked in nonverbal combat. They exchanged no words as the rain began to fall, but each knew what was about to happen. Silently, they moved down from the sacred hill and toward the open field that lay between Abel's flocks and Cain's gardens. The wind increased, and the rain washed down from the boiling sky, slashing the brothers with knives of water.

In the maelstrom of the deafening storm, Cain shouted something to his brother, but what he said was swallowed by the tempest. The dark act was hidden by the rain—a rain unearthly in its fury, a rain that might never stop until the whole world were destroyed.

It did stop this time, but as the wind died and the rain ceased, only one brother left the field, while the other mingled his blood with the saturated earth. Cain did not look back at his deed, but set his face eastward, moving away from the flocks, the gardens, and his parents. From the sky came a loud crash of thunder, heralding the passing of the storm. But to the brother-killer, it sounded rather more like the beginning of judgment.

God's Disappointment

This story recounts God's disappointment in the violence of the inhabitants of the earth and the decision to save one family and a selection of animals to start all over again.

The Story

Lamech was one hundred and eighty-two years old when he begot a son. He named him Noah, saying, 'This boy will bring us relief from our work, from the labour that has come upon us because of the LORD's curse on the ground. . . .'

The human race began to increase and to spread over the earth and daughters were born to them. The sons of the gods saw how beautiful these daughters were, so they took for themselves such women as they chose. But the LORD said, 'My spirit will not remain in a human being for ever; because he is mortal flesh, he will live only for a hundred and twenty years.

In those days as well as later, when the sons of the gods had intercourse with the daughters of mortals and children were born to them, the Nephilim were on the earth; they were the heroes of old, people of renown.

When the LORD saw how great was the wickedness of human beings on earth, and how their every thought and inclination were always wicked, he bitterly regretted that he had made mankind on earth. He said, 'I shall wipe off the face of the earth this human race which I have created— yes, man and beast, creeping things and birds. I regret that I ever made them.' Noah, however, had won the LORD's favour.

This is the story of Noah. Noah was a righteous man, the one blameless man of his time, and he walked with God. He had three sons: Shem, Ham, and Japheth. God saw that the world was corrupt and full of violence; and seeing this corruption, for the life of everyone on earth was corrupt, God said to Noah, 'I am going to bring the whole human race to an end, for because of them the earth is full of violence. I am about to destroy them, and the earth along with them. Make yourself an ark with ribs of cypress; cover it with reeds and coat it inside and out with pitch. This is to be its design: the length of the ark is to be three hundred cubits, its breadth fifty cubits, and its height thirty cubits. You are to make a roof for the ark, giving it a fall of one cubit when complete; put a door in the side of the ark, and build three decks, lower, middle, and upper. I am about to bring the waters of the flood over the earth to destroy from under heaven every human being that has the spirit of life; everything on earth shall perish. But with you I shall make my covenant, and you will go into the ark, you with your sons, your wife, and your sons' wives. You are to bring living creatures of every kind into the ark to keep them alive with you, two of each kind, a male and a female; two of every kind of bird, beast, and creeping thing are to come to you to be kept alive. See that you take and store by you every kind of food that can be eaten; this will be food for you and for them.' Noah carried out exactly all God had commanded him.

The LORD said to Noah, 'Go into the ark, you and all your household; for you alone in this generation have I found to be righteous. Take with you seven pairs, a male and female, of all beasts that are ritually clean, and one pair, a male and female, of all beasts that are not clean; also seven pairs, males and females, of every bird—to ensure that life continues on earth. For in seven days' time I am going to send rain on the earth for forty days and forty nights, and I shall wipe off the face of the earth every living creature I have made.' Noah did all that the LORD had commanded him. He was six hundred years old when the water of the flood came on the earth.

So to escape the flood Noah went into the ark together with his sons, his wife, and his sons' wives. And to him on board the ark went one pair, a male and a female, of all beasts, clean and unclean, of birds, and of everything that creeps on the ground, two by two, as God had commanded. At the end of seven days the water of the flood came over the earth. In the year when Noah was six hundred years old, on the seventeenth day of the second month, that very day all the springs of the great deep burst out, the windows of the heavens were opened, and rain fell on the earth for forty days and forty nights. That was the day Noah went into the ark with his sons, Shem, Ham, and Japheth, his own wife, and his three sons' wives. Wild animals of every kind, cattle of every kind, every kind of thing that creeps on the ground, and winged birds of every kind—all living creatures came two by two to Noah in the ark. Those which came were one male and one female of all living things; they came in as God had commanded Noah, and the LORD closed the door on him.

The flood continued on the earth for forty days, and the swelling waters lifted up the ark so that it rose high above the ground. The ark floated on the surface of the swollen waters as they increased over the earth. They increased more and more until they covered all the high mountains everywhere under heaven. The water increased until the mountains were covered to a depth of fifteen cubits. Every living thing that moved on earth perished: birds, cattle, wild animals, all creatures that swarm on the ground, and all human beings. Everything on dry land died, everything that had the breath of life in its nostrils. God wiped out every living creature that existed on earth, man and beast, creeping thing and bird; they were all wiped out over the whole earth, and only Noah and those who were with him in the ark survived.

When the water had increased over the earth for a hundred and fifty days, God took thought for Noah and all the beasts and cattle with him in the ark, and he caused a wind to blow over the earth, so that the water began to subside. The springs of the deep and the windows of the heavens were stopped up, the downpour from the skies was checked. Gradually the water receded from the earth, and by the end of a hundred and fifty days it had abated. On the seventeenth day of the seventh month the ark grounded on the mountains of Ararat. The water continued to abate until the tenth month, and on the first day of the tenth month the tops of the mountains could be seen.

At the end of forty days Noah opened the hatch that he had made in the ark, and sent out a raven; it continued flying to and fro until the water on the earth had dried up. Then Noah sent out a dove to see whether the water on the earth had subsided. But the dove found no place where she could settle because all the earth was under water, and so she came back to him in the ark. Noah reached out and caught her, and brought her into the ark. He waited seven days more and again sent out the dove from the ark. She came back to him towards evening with a freshly plucked olive leaf in her beak. Noah knew then that the water had subsided from the earth's surface. He waited yet another seven days and, when he sent out the dove, she did not come back to him. So it came about that, on the first day of the first month of his six hundred and first year, the water had dried up on the earth, and when Noah removed the hatch and looked out, he saw that the ground was dry.

By the twenty-seventh day of the second month the earth was dry, and God spoke to Noah. 'Come out of the ark together with your wife, your sons, and their wives,' he said. 'Bring out every living creature that is with you, live things of every kind, birds, beasts, and creeping things, and let them spread over the earth and be fruitful and increase on it.' So Noah came out with his sons, his wife, and his sons' wives, and all the animals, creeping things, and birds; everything that moves on the ground came out of the ark, one kind after another.

Comments on the Story

We left the world populated by people like Lamech, breathing out threats of wild vengeance on anyone who would dare touch him. But we also saw the tiny hope of the family of Seth, who began to call upon the name of the Lord. Genesis 5 gives us the long genealogy of the family of Seth, which concludes in verses 28-29 with the birth of Noah. Noah's father's name is, ironically, Lamech. Surely, this Lamech is a far cry from the monster of the preceding story.

This new Lamech names his son Noah (*noach*; "rest" in Hebrew), because, he says, "this one will bring us rest (*yenachamenu*—the name *Noah* is constructed from this verb) from our work and from the toil of our hands on the ground which the Lord has cursed." Noah's role is to reverse the curse of the ground, which occurred in 3:17. Our expectations for this man are quite high as the new story begins.

The strange interlude of 6:1-4 has been much discussed, but if it is placed in its context, it can be seen to play an important role in the ongoing story. With the earth filled with Lamech-like characters, who are now multiplying on the face of the ground, certain divine beings ("sons of God") begin to mate with the daughters of these human beings. God's initial response to this mating is to limit the life of the human offspring to 120 years, effectively denying again the possibility of immortality to the human creatures (see Gen. 3:22-24). However, the offspring of these divine-human marriages were indeed mighty, men of renown, literally "men of the name." What can this peculiar story mean in the context? I would say that the stain of evil, so pervasive in the earth, is now being transmitted into the entire cosmos. What began as the eating of fruit has evolved into a nearly universal disaster. God must act to stop this disaster.

Genesis 6:5 is crucial to our understanding of the story of the flood: "God saw that the evil of humanity was immense in the earth, and that every inclination of the thoughts of their hearts was only evil all day long." That sentence is filled with universal language: "every," "only," "all day long." The indictment of humanity is complete; there are no redeeming circumstances to be found. The judgment must come, and it must be complete. The absolute evil must be stopped.

In two other flood stories from the ancient Near East, the reasons given for the coming of the flood are instructive. In the Sumerian account, the gods send the flood to wipe out humanity because the humans are too loud at night and the gods cannot sleep! In the later Babylonian story, the gods decide to destroy humanity because the humans are becoming too self-sufficient, too big for their britches. How different is our Genesis story! God's flood comes as a result of human evil; it is a question of divine justice. In fact, in 6:11-12, the words *corrupt* and *violence* are used to describe the human disaster, two words that are often found in the Hebrew Bible in contexts of social injustice and oppression (for "violence," *chamas,* see, for example, Amos 3:10, 6:3; Jon. 3:8; Mic. 6:12; for "corrupt," *shachath,* see, for example, Gen. 18:28; Jer. 6:5; Amos 1:11). God brings the flood as a result of the activity of divine justice. This is a remarkable theological reworking of the ancient story by the Hebrew authors.

Yet, this God does not bring the flood joyously, nor does God find sadistic delight in the deluge. Quite the contrary! God "is sorry" and "grieved" in the divine heart. The wonderful creation described in chapters 1 and 2 has come to this, a place of violence, corruption, and evil worthy only for obliteration. "But Noah found grace in the eyes of the Lord." Even in the midst of a universal judgment, the grace of God remains alive and active; much like God's Spirit, it moves wherever it wills. The evaluation of Noah as "righteous" and "blameless" (vs. 9) says little about his character, but a great deal about God's grace, which finds in him the literal new Adam who will start everything over again.

At God's request, Noah builds a huge ark (see Exod. 2:3-5 for the same word), about 450 feet long, 75 feet wide, and 45 feet high. He builds three decks into his ark and takes with him his family, his wife, his sons, and their wives. And, according to one tradition of the story (6:19-20), he is also to take "two of every kind of living flesh," "male and female," into the ark. (This language is reminiscent of Gen. 1:12, 21, 27.) The author of that first creation account seems to have had a hand here as well: "Noah did this; he did all that God commanded him" (6:22).

But another tradition intrudes in Genesis 7:2-5. Now Noah is asked to take with him "seven pairs of all clean animals, and one pair of all unclean animals." This author is most concerned that when Noah is saved at the end of the flood he will have appropriate, clean animals to sacrifice to God.

Genesis 7:11 provides a portrait of a reverse creation. First, the "fountains of the great deep burst open" (61:22, 28). It was the "great deep" (*tehom*) that God first tamed at the very beginning of creation (Gen. 1:2). Next, the "windows of the skies are opened." In Genesis 1, the control of water made creation possible. Water is now out of control as the world returns to its pre-creation condition, with the notable exception of the little ark, bobbing rudderless on the vast ocean. All flesh dies (7:21-22), and only Noah and those with him on the ark are left (7:23).

But creation occurs again (8:1-2), as God "remembered Noah" and brings a "wind to blow over the earth" (see Gen. 1:2). The waters subside, while the fountains of the deep and the windows of the skies close. After the ark finally finds rest on the "mountains [note the plural] of Ararat," Noah opens the window and sends out a "raven," which goes "to and fro until the waters are dried up." This raven is probably a literary reference from the earlier Babylonian account of the flood, which features ravens exclusively at this point in the story. The raven plays no role in the Noah story. Noah then sends out a dove, but the dove can find no dry ground and returns to the ark. After seven days, Noah sends the dove again, and this time the bird returns with an olive branch in its beak, indicating dry ground somewhere. After another seven-day wait, Noah sends the bird again; the bird this time does not return.

So at the command of God (Gen. 8:15-17), Noah leaves the ark. He and the creatures with him are given the same command from God that was heard at the first creation: "Be fruitful and multiply on the earth" (Gen. 1:22, 28). By all accounts, the world is to begin afresh; Noah seems to be the new Adam. The stain of humanity has apparently been washed away.

Retelling the Story

Noah's wife speaks:

"Every time I hear the rain begin to fall in the night or smell the odor of damp earth that precedes a summer shower the memories return. I thought at first that Noah had gone mad. 'I have married and born sons to a crazy man!' I said to myself when he began to build the ark. 'What now, you're going to take up fishing maybe? You're six hundred years old; it's time you retired.' The man's name is supposed to mean 'rest,' but in all the time I've known him he's never given my nerves a rest.

"So I asked him, 'Why the big boat?' He said God told him to build it. 'What? The creator of the universe needs a yacht?' 'It's not for God,' Noah told me, 'it's for us.' 'And what do we need a boat for? A house at the beach, *that* we could use, but there's not a beach for miles in any direction.'

"So Noah sat by the fire in his rocking chair one night and told me the whole story. God had come and said that the whole creation would be destroyed by flood because it hadn't turned out the way it was intended. I started to say, 'So why should God's projects turn out any different from mine?' But before I could finish, Noah said that God expects divine projects to turn out right. It's just part of God's perfectionism. Well, when people kept taking whatever they wanted whether it belonged to them or not and kept settling every disagreement with a rock to the head or a knife between the ribs, God just got fed up. The whole creation project was a wash-out (so to speak), and God was going to clean up everybody's act with a bath like you've never seen. 'Didn't you try to change God's mind?' I asked, since the cure seemed at least as bad as the disease. 'No,' Noah told me, 'it was just that God's voice sounded so sad, so very disappointed.' Besides, if God doesn't know when to call it quits, then who does? I must admit he had a point.

The rabbis say that God mourned for creation for seven days (the traditional period of mourning for a close family member) before beginning the flood. In fact, they compare God's grief to the grief of King David over the death of his son Absalom (II Sam. 18:31–19:4). (*Genesis Rabbah* 32.7)

The rabbis told this story to demonstrate the kind of justice that was dispensed by the courts before the flood. Alexander of Macedon went to visit King Kazia (the king of the city at the end of the world) to see what sort of justice he dispensed. As they sat together two men came to the king. One had bought a pile of manure from the other and found a treasure in it. They disputed to whom the treasure belonged. The king asked if they had children. One had a daughter and the other a son. King Kazia said that they should arrange for the two to be married and for the treasure to belong to both families.

The king noticed a look of astonishment on Alexander's face. "Have I not ruled well? What would you have done?" Alexander answered, "I would have had both killed and taken the treasure for myself." King Kazia asked, "Does the rain fall on your country?" "Don't be silly," Alexander replied, "Of course, it does." Then the king asked, "Do you have sheep and goats in your country?" "Yes," said the visitor impatiently. "Well, it must be for the sake of the animals that God sends rain on your country, since it is certainly not because of the justice that humans dispense." (*Genesis Rabbah* 33.1)

The people at the time of the flood knew that if they stole less than the amount of the smallest coin they could not be prosecuted. So when someone would bring goods to the marketplace the people passing by would each take less than the value of the smallest coin from the basket. Thus the seller could take none of them to court, though the basket of goods was empty. Perhaps the people thought that in stealing so little they were not stealing at all. God, however, saw their smallest theft as an injustice, and that was one of the reasons for the flood. (*Genesis Rabbah* 31.5)

" 'Why you?' I asked, 'Why us?' And Noah said he didn't know for sure, since he didn't seem to be any different from anyone else. But there Noah was wrong, you see, or just being modest. Noah wouldn't hurt a flea, which isn't such a compliment coming from someone who had to share the voyage with fleas. He wouldn't take a thing that didn't belong to him. He even paid cash for all the supplies for the ark, even though he knew that before the bill would come due the store where he bought them would be under water. He's a good man at heart, a little crazy, but decent. A man who could even feel sorry for God.

"So it wasn't long before the beautiful variety of hills and valleys became nothing but gray sky and dark water. When my grandchildren ask how long our voyage was I tell them, "Forever." To this very day when the clouds roll in dark and thick and the smell of rain is in the air the old feelings come rushing back. That's when memories come flooding back like the springs of the deep bursting. Then I am carried along like a single ship on an ocean of time stretching in all directions."

God's Covenant

God makes a covenant with all creation through Noah and his family.

The Story

Noah built an altar to the LORD and, taking beasts and birds of every kind that were ritually clean, he offered them as whole-offerings on it. When the LORD smelt the soothing odour, he said within himself, 'Never again shall I put the earth under a curse because of mankind, however evil their inclination may be from their youth upwards, nor shall I ever again kill all living creatures, as I have just done.

'As long as the earth lasts,
seedtime and harvest, cold and
    heat,
summer and winter, day and night,
they will never cease.'

God blessed Noah and his sons; he said to them, 'Be fruitful and increase in numbers, and fill the earth. Fear and dread of you will come on all the animals on earth, on all the birds of the air, on everything that moves on the ground, and on all fish in the sea; they are made subject to you. Every creature that lives and moves will be food for you; I give them all to you, as I have given you every green plant. But you must never eat flesh with its life still in it, that is the blood. And further, for your life-blood I shall demand satisfaction; from every animal I shall require it, and from human beings also I shall require satisfaction for the death of their fellows.

'Anyone who sheds human blood,
for that human being his blood will
    be shed;
because in the image of God
has God made human beings.

Be fruitful, then, and increase in number; people the earth and rule over it.'

God said to Noah and his sons: 'I am now establishing my covenant with you and with your descendants after you, and with every living creature that is with you, all birds and cattle, all the animals with you on earth, all that have come out of the ark. I shall sustain my covenant with you: never again will all living creatures be destroyed by the waters of a flood, never again will there be a flood to lay waste the earth.'

God said, 'For all generations to come, this is the sign which I am giving of the covenant between myself and you and all living creatures with you:

my bow I set in the clouds
to be a sign of the covenant
between myself and the earth.
When I bring clouds over the earth,
the rainbow will appear in the
    clouds.

Then I shall remember the covenant which I have made with you and with all living creatures, and never again will the waters become a flood to destroy all creation. Whenever the bow appears in the cloud, I shall see it and remember the everlasting covenant between God and living creatures of every kind on earth.' So God said to Noah, 'This is the sign of the covenant which I have established with all that lives on earth.'

The sons of Noah who came out of the ark were Shem, Ham, and Japheth; Ham was the father of Canaan. These three were the sons of Noah, and their descendants spread over the whole earth.

Noah, who was the first tiller of the soil, planted a vineyard. He drank so much of the wine that he became drunk and lay naked inside his tent. Ham, father of Canaan, saw his father naked, and went out and told his two brothers. Shem and Japheth took a cloak, put it on their shoulders, and, walking backwards, covered their father's naked body. They kept their faces averted, so that they did not see his nakedness. When Noah woke from his drunkenness and learnt what his youngest son had done to him, he said:

'Cursed be Canaan!
Most servile of slaves
shall he be to his brothers.'

And he went on:

'Bless, O LORD,
the tents of Shem;
may Canaan be his slave.
May God extend Japheth's boundaries,
let him dwell in the tents of Shem,
may Canaan be his slave.'

After the flood Noah lived for three hundred and fifty years; he was nine hundred and fifty years old when he died.

Comments on the Story

As Noah steps off of the ark into what appears to be a fresh new world, he offers sacrifice to God, using only the clean animals for the sacrifice, in line with the expressed concerns of Genesis 7:2-3. At this point in the older Babylonian story, Utnapishtim, the Babylonian Noah, also offers sacrifice after the ordeal of the flood. The Babylonian text proclaims that upon seeing the sacrifice, the gods, who brought the flood in order to destroy the human beings, "gathered around the sacrifice like flies." Once again the Hebrew authors have altered the ancient story. Here God "smells the pleasing odor." (The Hebrew sentence is a long sound pun on the name *Noah—noach. wayarah 'adonai 'eth re'ach hanichoach*.) In the older story the gods cannot survive without the sustenance of meat sacrifice; in the Hebrew story, God finds pleasure in the sacrifice, but is surely in no physical need of it.

But what is most theologically significant for the Hebrew flood story occurs as God reflects, alone, on the entire experience. "I will certainly never again curse the ground because of the human beings, because (or "even though") the inclinations of the hearts of the human beings are evil from their youth" (8:21). This is a remarkable phrase. We must remember that the very reason for the coming of the flood in the first place was precisely the fact that "the *inclination* of the thoughts of the *hearts of the human beings* was only *evil* all day long" (6:5). Now, *after* the flood, God announces that the human beings have not changed at all! The flood has not functioned to alter the reality of human evil, and the first extended story about Noah, the so-called hero of the flood, will make that fact certain.

Who changes because of the flood, then? What is the effect of the near-universal cataclysm? The answer can only be: God changes. It is God who changes because of the flood, or, perhaps better said, our perception of God as offered to us by the Hebrews' changes. If the God who brought the flood did so as a direct reaction to the evil of humanity, an evil portrayed to us from the garden to Cain to Lamech to the divine-human marriages, that same God, still quite convinced of the existence of human evil after the flood, now refuses to act merely on the basis of strict justice. In short, God's grace now appears to be a grace that motivates God to forbear punishment rather than to act to bring punishment on the sinners who so richly deserve it. God will never again destroy all flesh. "While the earth remains, seedtime and harvest, cold and heat, summer and winter, day and night, shall not cease" (8:22). The constant and cyclical change of seasons is itself a sign that the God we worship is a God of grace rather than only a God of justice. Winter's inevitable change to spring tells us that God does not give us merely what we deserve, and to that reality, I utter a heartfelt, "Thank God!"

Any thought that this post-flood world is only a new garden of Eden is finally dispelled in 9:1-7. The command is reiterated to be fruitful, multiply, and fill the earth, but that earth is no longer an Eden. Now, the relationship between the human creation and the animal creation is characterized by "dread and fear" (9:2). Humans may now eat meat; no longer are they the vegetarians implied in 1:30. And, perhaps most terrible of all, is the fact that capital punishment is now a reality in the world. Shed blood demands shed blood (9:6). The flood in no way reestablishes the harmony of God's original creation. Both the eating of meat and the existence of capital punishment are certain signs that the world of Noah is not the world that God had in mind. Rather than rejoice when a society feels called upon to kill one of its members in punishment, perhaps that society ought to weep, knowing that once again it has given evidence that it is far from the way God wanted it to be.

Nevertheless, God proceeds to make covenant with this less than perfect world, and a most interesting covenant it is. First, it requires *no* response on the part of the human beings at all; there are no stipulations in this covenant. God simply announces, "I establish my covenant with you and your descendants after you"(9:8). Second, the sign of the covenant, God's bow in the cloud, is a sign intended for *God,* not primarily for humanity. God's "bow" (*kesheth,* the bow of war) now becomes the very symbol of God's peace with the earth. When the bow appears in the clouds, "I will remember my covenant," says God (9:15). "When the bow is in the clouds, I will look upon it and remember my everlasting covenant," says God (9:16). We may rejoice at the sign of the rainbow, but it is, in effect, a string tied around the finger of God in order that God will never forget the covenant. This covenant, too, like the refusal of God to act only with justice toward the world, is a sign of the unmerited grace of God.

With God's grace pouring down on the earth, the family of Noah sets about the task of repopulating the world. Immediately, there is another crisis. Noah plants a vineyard and becomes completely drunk on the wine from his own vineyard, so drunk that he passes out, stark naked, on the floor of his tent. In effect, Noah's nakedness is a recapitulation of the nakedness of the garden— he, too, is defenseless; he, too, has chosen a dangerous path that will lead to disaster. Ham, father of Canaan, wanders into his father's tent and sees his father naked. He goes outside and tells his brothers what he has seen. The great patriarch, naked and passed out cold, is a shameful sight; he is completely vulnerable and weak, and for his son to see him compromises the father's power in the family.

Shem and Japheth very carefully walk backwards into their father's tent in order not to see him naked, and they cover him. When Noah has slept off his drunkenness, he discovers "what his youngest son had done to him," and he curses Ham to be a slave to his brothers. The obvious reason for the story is to portray the evil origin of the Canaanites (the children of Ham) and to justify why they should be the slaves of the Israelites. It is, in that way, a pro-Israelite piece of propaganda, but in the context of the ongoing story of Genesis, there is more here than that. Noah's actions are the reason for the separation of his family; however much he would blame Ham, the sin is his own. Just as Adam and Eve chose poorly and were driven from the garden of God, so also Noah chooses badly and causes whatever harmony there may be in the new world to disappear again. The promise of Noah was that he would bring rest (5:29), but the world receives no rest at the hands of Noah. The post-flood world seems little different from the pre-flood one, and God is right about human beings: "the thoughts of their hearts are evil from their youth." The last story of the so-called Israelite pre-history will bear out God's judgment.

Retelling the Story

The infernal rocking of the boat had finally stopped. With a sharp thud, the massive vessel had landed on a high mountain peak, and the humans in the boat could not wait to get out of the thing. To be sure it was their salvation from death, but it had become more like a floating casket, so long had they been cooped up inside. And the beasts! Their growling, snarling, baying, barking, even the cooing, had become unbearable. The ramp was only half-way down when Ham, Shem, and Japheth were scrambling for the open air.

All looked with wonder at the new-washed earth. Even the camels ceased their swaying gait and gazed longingly at the dew-splashed sunrise. Noah, however, was far too busy to fall into reverie; he had but one thing on his mind. It was time to sacrifice to the One who had saved them from certain death, and because only appropriate animals could be used, Noah rushed about, capturing some of the older creatures.

After the creatures were captured and ritually slaughtered, Noah gathered his family around the carefully built earthen altar, an altar just like the one Noah's ancient ancestor, Cain, had defiled so long ago when he had murdered his brother, Abel. Noah thought, as he prepared to sacrifice the animals out of his love for the great I AM, that this was really a new beginning for the earth. Perhaps *this* time the Great One of the mountains would be pleased with the creatures.

The smoke of the whole-burnt offering rose lazily into the sky. The eyes of Noah and his family were fixed on that smoke, the symbol of their thanks. Noah imagined the great divine nose, resting above the eternal smile, as it sniffed up the savory smell of the meat. And he imagined that the I AM was pleased, so pleased that Noah was convinced that the watery inferno he had just survived was never to happen again.

> When Noah was instructed to exit the ark he hesitated. "Am I supposed to go out and start this all over again, just to have you wash everything away the next time you get mad or disappointed?" That was when God promised never to destroy the earth again. (*Genesis Rabbah* 34.6)

Yes, he thought, a new beginning. A new Eden. New harmony and peace for the earth of God. But suddenly a thought crossed his mind, a thought he had certainly never had before. He wanted a taste of this meat that was being burnt for God! He was startled at the craving he had. He knew that only the green plants were to be eaten, that was the command of the I AM, but now he wanted meat. Greedily, he tore off a piece of the flesh and thrust it into his mouth. Quickly, his family members did the same, the juices running down their faces.

> The rabbis are not too complimentary of Noah. They said that God's choosing Noah was like someone going to the wine-cellar and choosing a barrel that was going sour instead of one that was already vinegar. The reason he found grace was for the sake of his descendants. (*Genesis Rabbah* 29.5; 30.9)

And then Noah remembered Cain and his murder of Abel; Noah thought that Cain's banishment was too little punishment for such a terrible deed. Cain should have paid with his life! Life for life, thought Noah, that should be the way of the world of evil humanity. Noah looked at his sons, the heirs of his promise from God. How he loved them! But he noticed that Ham and Shem were arguing about something and that Japheth was out exploring the land, looking for the choicest spot for himself and his family. Well, at least that was still the same! Two brothers fought, while the third was getting the best of them!

The rabbis say of God's description of humans as "evil in the imaginations of their hearts" that it must be pretty bad bread if the baker says it's awful, or that it must be a pretty poor plant if the gardener says it's bad.

Then when does the evil urge enter us? At the same time that the soul does, when we enter the world from our mother's womb. (*Genesis Rabbah* 34.10)

And then Noah noticed that his mouth was dry; he needed a drink in the worst way. He knew he had trouble with drink in the past, but this was the new world, and besides, it was a day for celebration. One can hardly celebrate properly without wine and plenty of it. He could hardly wait to plant those vineyards; yet, it would be *years* before wine would flow from those grapes. Fortunately, he had squirreled away a secret cache under the floorboard of the boat. He rushed toward the spot, making certain that his wife was not watching. His mouth ached for the cooling buzz of the wine, desperately needed to wash down the new taste of meat. He grabbed the skin and splashed a great gulp down his eager throat. Ah, now this was living! Meat to eat, wine in abundance eventually, laws to avenge the slaughter of humans. Well, it wasn't quite a return to Eden after all, but the wine made up for whatever had been lost. As Noah sank into the familiar stupor, he caught just the glimpse of a rainbow in the fresh sky. Yes, everything was going to be fine, he thought, as his wine-soaked brain closed shop for the night.

The Rise and Fall of the Tower of Babel

This interlude between the prehistory of the world and the calling of Abraham seems to explain why people live scattered across the world and speak different languages. It is an ancient story, but the human motivations described here are still with us.

The Story

There was a time when all the world spoke a single language and used the same words. As people journeyed in the east, they came upon a plain in the land of Shinar and settled there. They said to one another, 'Come, let us make bricks and bake them hard'; they used bricks for stone and bitumen for mortar. Then they said, 'Let us build ourselves a city and a tower with its top in the heavens and make a name for ourselves, or we shall be dispersed over the face of the earth.' The LORD came down to see the city and tower which they had built, and he said, 'Here they are, one people with a single language, and now they have started to do this; from now on nothing they have a mind to do will be beyond their reach. Come, let us go down there and confuse their language, so that they will not understand what they say to one another.' So the LORD dispersed them from there all over the earth, and they left off building the city. That is why it is called Babel, because there the LORD made a babble of the language of the whole world. It was from that place the LORD scattered people over the face of the earth.

Comments on the Story

Our hopes for Noah as one who would bring us rest and freedom from the curse of the ground have not been fulfilled. Neither has the great flood of God washed away the evil of the human beings. We seem to have progressed little, if at all, from the problem of the garden. Chapter 10 gives a long genealogy, a so-called table of nations, that offers a glimpse of the makeup of the world known to the collector of these stories. For the purposes of this reading of the story, 10:32 is important. "These are the families of the children of Noah by means of their genealogies, in their respective nations. From these the nations spread abroad after the flood."

Though the evil of the world has not been expunged, at least the peoples are "spreading abroad" in fulfillment of the repeated command of God (Gen. 1:28; 8:17). But the story of the tower of Babel calls even that into question. Immediately, human unity is emphasized: "Now the whole earth had one language consisting of few words." A reader could imagine that this linguistic unity might be the harbinger of a return to the harmony of God's creation. This people then migrate to a "plain in the land of Shinar," a place connected in the tradition to the site of Babylon (see 10:10). They then begin to make plans.

"Come! Let us make bricks, firing them with fire. They had brick instead of stone and pitch instead of mortar." That is the first very important verse in the story. This account was composed by Israelites, living in the land of Israel. One of the most obvious features of the land of Israel is its enormous quantity of stone and its lack of any other good material for building. Even today in Israel, every new building must be made out of stone, which is the only appropriate material for building. In Babylon, it was quite different. Huge structures were made out of sun-dried brick, which was a material well suited to the hot and dry climate of the lands just north of the Persian Gulf. But for an Israelite, no fool would make anything out of brick. Well, perhaps a Babylonian fool would!

Not only that, the tower builders tried to bind their foolish bricks together with a water-based pitch, instead of using the best mortar, the material of choice for stone builders. In short, the Israelite author of this story is satirizing these ridiculous builders for their choice of materials. Not unlike Adam and Eve in the garden, who attempted to solve their problem of nakedness by sewing fig leaves together for clothes, these new creators have chosen the wrong material with which to create.

And what do they want to create? "Come, let *us* build *ourselves* a city, and a tower with its top in the sky, in order that *we* make for *ourselves* a name, lest *we* be scattered abroad upon the face of the whole earth." Five first-person plural pronouns set the tone for the desires of these human beings. Their building is designed only for their own glory, to fulfill the clear desire that they avoid being "spread abroad on the earth" in direct contradiction of the repeated command of God. The fact that they propose to attempt that great engineering feat by using mud brick and pitch gives added force to the portrait of human arrogance and the stupidity arising from it.

Verse 5 provides a telling comment on the project: "And the Lord came down to see the city and the tower which the human beings had built." The builders thought that their mighty tower would reach clear into the sky, up to the very heaven of God. But, in fact, God could not even *see* the tower where God dwells, and had to come down to have a look! The mighty tower is far less than mighty.

All of these facts of the story are crucial for the correct appreciation of God's statement in verse 6: "Look! They are one people, with one language. This is only the beginning of what they will do; nothing that they decide to do will be impossible for them." The context suggests that God's reason for stopping the work of the human beings is not fear that they will somehow contrive to take over heaven. These, after all, are people who think they can build on their own a tower into the sky out of mud brick and pitch, a tower that is not even visible from the place of God. God is not afraid of these humans; God must step in to prevent them from any further mischief. Why, they might attempt next a mud-brick bridge over the Mediterranean!

Thus, God says, "Let us [note the plural again as in 1:26] go down [again the great emphasis on the vast gulf between God and the tower], and there confuse [*balah*] their language so that they may not understand one another's speech." So "God scattered them," which was the original goal of God, and the people stopped their mud-brick project.

The story ends with an etiology (v. 9): "That is why its name is Babel, because there the Lord confused [*balal*] the language of all the earth." It is a simple sound pun on the familiar name of Babylon. For the Hebrew author, it is a great treat to know that the infamous city was born in literal confusion, built by arrogant and stupid people who for their efforts were scattered throughout the earth by a God who is not mocked. In reality, the word *Babylon* is probably related to the word *babel,* or "door of God."

Retelling the Story

One day a reporter from the *Celestial Times* came to God and asked, "Have you seen what those people are doing down on the plain of Shinar?"

"Why, no," God answered. "Why should I be aware of something so far from my home?"

"Well you may want to go take a look at their silly little project. You see, they think that they can build a tower so tall that it will reach up here to your place. And, get this, they are building it out of mud bricks and using pitch for mortar."

At that God gave forth with a hearty laugh that made the whole house shake, then replied, "Let's go on down there and see what games these children are playing. It is a long way, but worth it if I can get another laugh like that."

So God and the reporter made the journey to the plain of Shinar to see the tower. "Now tell me," God whispered

Certain of the rabbis said that the word meaning "dwell" or "settle" used here really meant that the people had it a little too easy. They had gained too much with too little effort and took their life and its comforts for granted. This complacency was the fertile ground in which the idea of the tower that would reach heaven came to grow. (*Genesis Rabbah* 38.7)

One tradition says that Nimrod and his hunters were behind the building of the tower. When it was taller than any other tower they had ever seen, the hunters would stand on the top and shoot arrows toward the sky. Angels would catch the arrows and send them back with blood on their tips. When Nimrod and his hunters saw the blood, they proclaimed, "We have conquered even the hosts of heaven." (Sepher Hayashar 22-31; Tanhuma Noah 18, 19 in Graves and Patai, p. 126)

Some say that the tower was so tall that it took a year to carry a brick that had been made at its base to the top. This meant that bricks became very precious. They were valued so highly that if a brick fell from the top and shattered there was mourning and crying. But if a worker fell and died, people hardly noticed (Midrash ha-Gadol 11.3 in Plaut, p. 85)

to the reporter so that the humans would not hear, "is this a tall tower by human standards?"

The reporter said with a grin "The tallest they have ever seen. They think that any day now they will arrive on your doorstep. The joke's on them, eh?"

"Let's have a little fun," said God with a playful gleam in the divine eyes. "They want to stay in one place and work together rather than scattering like I said. Let's see them do it if they all speak different languages." So God caused the workers to speak different languages. When work began again one worker would greet the others with "Good morning," and another would respond "Guten morgen" and another "Buenos dios." That wasn't so bad, but later when one of the workers would ask for bricks they were likely to get a handful of pitch. Or when they wanted the bucket of pitch they would be tossed a brick—often striking them on the side of the head. Finally everything became so confused that the tower project was abandoned and the people scattered across the earth.

Oh yes, God and the reporter had a good laugh on the long journey back.

They say that this is the reason that the place is called Babel, because God turned the peoples' market research and planning into babble. Perhaps God only showed it up for what it really was all along.

When God said that the languages of the workers would be "confused" some rabbis interpreted that to mean "I will see that their own lips will be their destruction." On one occasion a worker asked for water and another responded with a cup of dirt. Then the first worker attacked the second, splitting the skull of the second worker. And when one worker asked for an axe, the second brought a shovel, whereupon the first split the second's skull. And so the workers began to destroy each other. (*Genesis Rabbah* 38.10)

The rabbis say that the remains of the tower still stand, though one-third was destroyed by fire and one-third sank into the earth. And if you should think that the remaining third is small, they say that if you climb to the top the palm trees below look the size of grasshoppers. (*Genesis Rabbah* 38.8)

The Call of Abram and Sarai

The family story of the Israelites begins with God's calling of Abram and Sarai and their following God's call.

The Story

The LORD said to Abram, 'Leave your own country, your kin, and your father's house, and go to a country that I will show you. I shall make you into a great nation; I shall bless you and make your name so great that it will be used in blessings:

those who bless you, I shall bless;
those who curse you, I shall curse.
All the peoples on earth
will wish to be blessed as you are
    blessed.'

Abram, who was seventy-five years old when he left Harran, set out as the LORD had bidden him, and Lot went with him. He took his wife Sarai, his brother's son Lot, and all the possessions they had gathered and the dependants they had acquired in Harran, and they departed for Canaan. When they arrived there, Abram went on as far as the sanctuary at Shechem, the terebinth tree of Moreh. (At that time, the Canaanites lived in the land.) When the LORD appeared to him and said, 'I am giving this land to your descendants,' Abram built an altar there to the LORD who had appeared to him. From there he moved on to the hill-country east of Bethel and pitched his tent between Bethel on the west and Ai on the east.

He built there an altar to the LORD whom he invoked by name. Thus Abram journeyed by stages towards the Negeb.

The land was stricken by a famine so severe that Abram went down to Egypt to live there for a time. As he was about to enter Egypt, he said to his wife Sarai, 'I am well aware that you are a beautiful woman, and I know that when the Egyptians see you and think, "She is his wife," they will let you live but they will kill me. Tell them you are my sister, so that all may go well with me because of you, and my life be spared on your account.'

When Abram arrived in Egypt, the Egyptians saw that Sarai was indeed very beautiful, and Pharaoh's courtiers, when they saw her, sang her praises to Pharaoh. She was taken into Pharaoh's household, and he treated Abram well because of her, and Abram acquired sheep and cattle and donkeys, male and female slaves, she-donkeys, and camels. But when the LORD inflicted plagues on Pharaoh and his household on account of Abram's wife Sarai, Pharaoh summoned Abram. 'Why have you treated me like this?' he said. Why did you not tell me she was your wife? Why did you say she was your sister, so that I took her as a

wife? Here she is: take her and go.'
Pharaoh gave his men orders, and they
sent Abram on his way with his wife
and all that belonged to him.

Comments on the Story

At the end of the primeval history, the world is in an appalling state. Human beings are separated from one another, having been scattered all over the earth as a result of their stupid and arrogant attempt to create a culture without God (11:4). Their isolation and separation are symbolized by the literal babble of languages they speak after the disaster of the tower.

Time passes in the story, as the genealogy of 11:10-32 demonstrates. There are two notable facts in this genealogy. First, at verse 31, a short description of the migration of the family of Terah is given. They leave "Ur of the Chaldeans" on their way to the land of Canaan, but on the journey they come to Haran and decide to settle there instead. This movement, from the lower end of the Mesopotamian valley—site of the ancient city of Ur—up the course of the Euphrates river to Haran, traces a very old trade route and thus mirrors the wanderings of peoples from the most distant times. Also, the origins of what became the people of Israel are firmly fixed in the Mesopotamian valley.

The second important fact of this genealogy is found in 11:30. "Now Sarai was barren; she had no child." This easily overlooked statement will drive the story of Abram and Sarai for the next ten chapters and will shed doubt about the promise and purpose of God. Notwithstanding the couple's inability to have a child, God speaks to Abram anyway in memorable words: "Go [literally "take yourself"; see Gen. 22:2] from your land and your near relations and your father's house to the land that I will show you. I will make you a great nation, I will bless you, and I will make your name great so that you will be a blessing. I will bless those who bless you, and those who curse you I will curse. All the families of the ground will be blessed because of you" (12:1-3).

These verses are a major turning point in the entire story of the Bible, both Old and New Testaments. The world of the tower-builders has been addressed by God, and God has called a couple through whom God promises to bless the whole earth. Abram and Sarai have one function in the plan of God: to "be a blessing to all the families of the ground" (*'adamah*). The more typical translation, "families of the earth" or "peoples of the earth," obscures a crucial concern for the story. All human beings are created from "dust of the *ground*" (2:7). It is the *ground* to which all life will return in death (3:9). It is the *ground* that opened its mouth to receive the blood of the murdered Abel, and it is the *ground* from which the murderer Cain is cursed (4:10-11). Noah, it was hoped, would bring rest from this curse of the *ground* (5:29), but from the *ground* he received the wine that led to his drunken nakedness and the dissolution of his family (9:20). Thus when Abram is called to be a blessing to *all* of the families of the *ground,* we hear the call of Abram and Sarai for what it is: a new attempt on the part of God to reconstitute the harmony of the creation. This is a missionary call and will be echoed throughout the biblical story (see, for example Isa. 49:6 and Matt. 28:19).

Abram and Sarai go to the land promised by God, stopping at various places along the way to offer sacrifice to the God who called them; Shechem and Bethel are famous sanctuaries throughout the history of Israel. But a crisis is not long in coming, and the promise of God through the couple is soon in jeopardy.

A famine strikes the land of promise, and the couple resolve to go to Egypt, the bread basket of the ancient Near East; with the regular inundations of the Nile river, Egypt was often spared the worst ravages of famine during periods of drought. On the way to Egypt, Abram does some thinking—about himself and his future. He says to Sarai, "I know that you are a beautiful woman, and when the Egyptians see you, they will say, 'This is his wife'; then they will kill me and let you live. Say you are my sister, that it may go well with me because of you, and that my life may be spared on your account" (12:11-13). Abram's little plan is completely self-serving; he gives no thought to Sarai and, just as certainly, no thought to the plan of God. The chosen one has faced his first test and has failed miserably. In order to save his own skin, he is ready and willing to sacrifice his wife, the vessel of the promise. God's new plan to provide blessing for the earth has gotten off to a most ignominious beginning!

Sarai says nothing to this repulsive plan, and all happens as Abram has hoped. The beautiful Sarai is taken into the harem of Pharaoh, and because Abram is her "brother," Pharaoh showers many gifts on him, a literal king's ransom of sheep, oxen, donkeys, slaves, and camels. Abram must feel that his cleverness has saved him and gotten him riches in the bargain. A nice day's work!

But the promise, forgotten by Abram, has not been forgotten by God, who proceeds to send great plagues upon Pharaoh and his household "because of Sarai, Abram's wife." Pharaoh calls the culprit to him and chides Abram for his lie. "What have you done to me? Why didn't you tell me she was your wife? Why did you say, 'She is my sister,' so that I took her for my wife?" These are all very good and just questions, but Abram has no answer to give to any of them. Pharaoh throws Abram and Sarai out of the country, and they leave far richer materially than when they came.

This story leaves a sour taste in the mouth. I suppose certain Israelites would find a kind of perverse pleasure in the tricking of old Pharaoh, but the fact remains that the man of the promise, Abram, the very choice of God to be a blessing to the world, has acted in positively disgusting ways. Far from being a blessing, he has brought the plague of God down on an innocent man and his house through a bold-faced lie. What sort of judgment has God shown in choosing Abram? Besides, there is that little matter of Sarai's inability to have children. What could God have been thinking when Abram's number came up? Once again, the story is far from over.

Retelling the Story

A nice day's work, I must say! Look at all these camels—not the common, scruffy Palestinian camels, but the very finest of camels, bred from Pharaoh's private herd. This is to say nothing of the sheep (such wool!), the donkeys, and the wonderful servants, both male and female. They could do a day's work without complaining and still set a masterful table in the evening after I had spent a hard day toting up my new-found riches. It was a glad day, indeed, when that famine came into our land.

I hadn't been glad at the time, but the decision to go to Egypt had really been no decision at all. Where else did one go when there was no food to be had? I knew that the land of famine was special to the God who had called me to go there in the first place, but surely that God had not wanted me to starve. Besides, now that I look at those camels, I am persuaded that God probably had this in mind for me from the very beginning.

It was only one lie, and not a very big one at that. Well, I was afraid, and I had every right to be. Sarai could not have children, but she was a very beautiful woman. I am not nearly as stupid as I look. One peek at her, and the pharaoh's men would have killed me in a flash and taken her into the harem. So I thought I would beat them to the punch. I would appeal to their special concern for brothers and sisters (I had heard that they even married off brothers and sisters to each other regularly) by saying that Sarai was in fact my sister and not my wife at all. This had the added advantage of the appearance of legality. Pharaoh could take her with a clear conscience, and I could get rich and retire happy in the greatest country on earth. A delightful plan! And just look at those camels.

> When Abram was entering Egypt, he had Sarai hidden in a box. When he arrived at the border, he was asked to pay a tax on whatever he was carrying. The guard asked, "Do you have clothes in that box?" Abram answered, "I'll pay the clothes tax." "I'll bet you have precious silks in there," the guard responded. "I'll pay the silk tax," said Abram. "And I suppose there is some jewelry in there, too," continued the guard. "All right, what's the tax on that?" "No," said the guard, "you'll have to open the box and let us see what is really inside." Well, when Abram opened it and Sarai emerged, the entire land of Egypt was made beautiful by basking in her radiance. (*Genesis Rabbah* 40.5)

Oh, I had not completely forgotten what God had said to me, although I was doing my best to get it out of my mind. "You I will make a great nation," God had said, and I assumed that had meant Sarai, too. Yet, I did not completely trust the sort of God who would pick an infertile couple (out of all those who could have been picked) to do such a job. I mean, a great nation of two is not what I would call great! Maybe I just had misunderstood God at first. I mean with camels like these, even God could see the good in my cleverness.

> When Pharaoh even approached Sarai's shoe, she fell on her face and cried out to God, "Abram followed your instructions and left our home, and I followed, too, because I believed you. But now Abram is free and wealthy, and I am imprisoned in Pharaoh's harem. How is that fair?" And God answered, "All the terrible things that are happening to Pharaoh's household are for your sake, to secure your release. When the story is told, it will be remembered that I did this for you." (*Genesis Rabbah* 41.2)

What's that you say? Plagues in Pharaoh's house? He's on his way here right now? Sarai's with him? Well, prepare food and drink for him. I am surely rich enough to treat even a pharaoh well.

Hmm. He seems upset. What *have* I done to him, anyway? He got what he wanted, a beautiful Hebrew, and I got what I wanted, riches and comfort. Oh, he knows she is my wife and not my sister. I wonder how he found out? I guess the plagues tipped him off that something was not quite right in his house. Why did I lie and say that she was my sister? Get out of Egypt? Oh, no, I thought, and leave all these camels? Oh, I get to *keep* the camels! Well, I feel better already. Of course, I didn't say anything to him; what could I say? He had me dead to rights. Okay, okay, I'll leave. Servants, round up those camels, we are going back home. Don't leave anything now, or I'll tan your hides. What? Did you say something, my dear?

The Covenant with Abram and Sarai

Though it looks hopeless that Abram and Sarai will ever have a child, God reaffirms the promise that their descendants will be like the dust of the earth and the stars of the sky. First, however, there are two stories of Abram's parting from Lot and Abram's meeting with Melchizedek.

The Story

From Egypt Abram went up into the Negeb, he and his wife and all that he possessed, and Lot went with him. Abram had become very rich in cattle and in silver and gold. From the Negeb he journeyed by stages towards Bethel, to the place between Bethel and Ai where he had earlier pitched his tent, and where he had previously set up an altar and invoked the LORD by name. Since Lot, who was travelling with Abram, also possessed sheep and cattle and tents, the land could not support them while they were together. They had so much livestock that they could not settle in the same district, and quarrels arose between Abram's herdsmen and Lot's. (The Canaanites and the Perizzites were then living in the land.) Abram said to Lot, 'There must be no quarrelling between us, or between my herdsmen and yours; for we are close kinsmen. The whole country is there in front of you. Let us part company: if you go north, I shall go south; if you go south, I shall go north.' Lot looked around and saw how well watered the whole plain of Jordan was; all the way to Zoar it was like the Garden of the LORD, like the land of Egypt. This was

before the Lord had destroyed Sodom and Gomorrah. So Lot chose all the Jordan plain and took the road to the east. They parted company: Abram settled in Canaan, while Lot settled among the cities of the plain and pitched his tent near Sodom. Now the men of Sodom in their wickedness had committed monstrous sins against the LORD.

After Lot and Abram had parted, the LORD said to Abram, 'Look around from where you are towards north, south, east, and west: all the land you see I shall give to you and to your descendants for ever. I shall make your descendants countless as the dust of the earth; only if the specks of dust on the ground could be counted could your descendants be counted. Now go through the length and breadth of the land, for I am giving it to you.' Abram moved his tent and settled by the terebinths of Mamre at Hebron, where he built an altar to the LORD.

In those days King Amraphel of Shinar, King Arioch of Ellasar, King Kedorlaomer of Elam, and King Tidal of Goyim went to war against King Bera of Sodom, King Birsha of Gomorrah, King Shinab of Admah, King She-meber of Zeboyim, and the king of Bela, which is Zoar. These kings joined forces in the valley of Siddim, which is now the Dead Sea. For twelve years they had been subject to Kedor-laomer, but in the thirteenth year they rebelled. . . .

. . . On Abram's return from defeating Kedorlaomer and the allied kings, the king of Sodom came out to meet him in the valley of Shaveh, which is now the King's Valley.

Then the king of Salem, Melchizedek, brought food and wine. He was priest of God Most High, and he pronounced this blessing on Abram:

'Blessed be Abram by God Most High,
Creator of the heavens and the earth.
And blessed be God Most High, who has delivered your enemies into your hand.'

Then Abram gave him a tithe of all the booty. . . .

. . . After this the word of the LORD came to Abram in a vision. He said, 'Do not be afraid, Abram; I am your shield. Your reward will be very great.' Abram replied, 'Lord GOD, what can you give me, seeing that I am child-less? The heir to my household is Eliezer of Damascus. You have given me no children, and so my heir must be a slave born in my house.' The word of the LORD came to him: 'This man will not be your heir; your heir will be a child of your own body.' He brought Abram outside and said, 'Look up at the sky, and count the stars, if you can. So many will your descen-dants be.'

Abram put his faith in the LORD, who reckoned it to him as righteous-ness, and said, 'I am the LORD who brought you out from Ur of the Chaldees to give you this land as your possession.' Abram asked, 'Lord GOD, how can I be sure that I shall occupy it?' The LORD answered, 'Bring me a heifer three years old, a she-goat three years old, a ram three years old, a turtle-dove, and a young pigeon.' Abram brought him all these, cut the animals in two, and set the pieces opposite each other, but he did not cut the birds in half. Birds of prey swooped down on the carcasses, but he scared them away. As the sun was going down, Abram fell into a trance and great and fearful darkness came over him. The LORD said to Abram, 'Know this for certain: your descen-dants will be aliens living in a land that is not their own; they will be enslaved and held in oppression for four hundred years. But I shall punish the nation whose slaves they are, and afterwards they will depart with great possessions. You yourself will join your forefathers in peace and be buried at a ripe old age. But it will be the fourth generation who will return here, for till then the Amorites will not be ripe for punishment.' The sun went down and it was dusk, and there appeared a smoking brazier and a flaming torch which passed between the divided pieces. That day the LORD made a covenant with Abram, and said, 'I give to your descendants this land from the river of Egypt to the Great River, the river Euphrates, the territory of the Kenites, Kenizzites, Kadmonites, Hittites, Perizzites, Rephaim, Amorites, Canaanites, Gir-gashites, and Jebusites.'

Comments on the Story

God has chosen the childless couple, Abram and Sarai, to be the progenitors of the great nation that is to be a blessing to all the families of the ground. They already have two strikes against them. First, and most obviously, their inability to have children throws a definite crimp in the plan for the founding of a great nation; a nation of two hardly seems great by any normal standard of measurement. Second, the man of the promise has taken the first occasion of crisis recorded to lie about his wife and thus to throw the promise into desperate jeopardy. This picture is not designed to inspire confidence in the plan of God to bring back the harmony of creation.

Two stories precede the covenant with Abram in chapter 15. In chapter 13, Abram allows Lot, his nephew, to select the part of the land in which he wishes to live. Lot chooses the "well watered plain of the Jordan (13:10), a fine section of the land. Unfortunately, two of the major cities of that place turn out to be Sodom and Gomorrah, whose infamy will bring them to prominence later on. In 13:14-16, God appears to Abram and announces that all of the land he can see, in every direction, will be his. Also, Abram's descendants will be as "the dust of the earth." Such an announcement may sound grand, but to a man in a childless marriage, dust may sound more like ashes.

In the second, rather more enigmatic, story, Abram is forced to assemble a small rescue team to save Lot, who has been captured by a coalition of eastern kings (Gen. 14). After the victory, Abram meets the king of Sodom in the valley of Shaveh as well as "Melchizedek, king of Salem," who presents Abram with "bread and wine." Melchizedek is not only king, but he is also "priest of the Most High God." He blesses Abram with a formal blessing in the name of the Most High God (*el elyon*), and in response Abram gives him a tenth of everything. When Melchizedek offers to take the captured enemies but to allow Abram to keep all of the spoil of the battle, Abram refuses, saying that he has sworn by the Most High God not to take anything that belongs to Melchizedek, lest Melchizedek be able someday to say that Abram owed him all of his riches.

The effect of these two stories, appearing before the covenant account, seems to be in part to provide another portrait of Abram, the shameful liar of chapter 12. In chapter 13, he magnanimously allows his nephew first choice of land, after which God reiterates the promise of land and progeny to Abram, and in chapter 14 he saves the captured Lot in a feat of bravery and refuses to take any goods from the owner's hand. His refusal to accept goods is a far cry from the marvelous gifts he accepted from Pharaoh for the hand of his supposed sister. The Abram of chapters 13 and 14 is brave, forthright, and magnanimous, traits notably lacking in chapter 12. Thus the author begins to flesh out a more complex Abram for the reader.

Then God speaks to Abram in a vision and says, "Don't be afraid! I am your shield! Your *reward* will be very great" (15:2). The word translated "reward" nearly always means "wages," payment given for work done. Abram's response is full of doubt: "O Lord God, what will you *give* me, for I continue childless?" God speaks of reward, while Abram decries the absence of the *gift* of a child, which will make the promise possible. Abram goes on to complain that a household slave, Eliezer of Damascus, is his only heir. With that complaint Abram brings to the surface the absurdity of God's choice of just *this* couple. God may promise until the divine face turns blue, but the fact remains that there is no heir and none in the offing.

But God's promise is persistent. "This man shall not be your heir; your own son will be your heir." As a visible symbol of the greatness of the future, God leads Abram outside to attempt to count the stars. They are innumerable, and so shall Abram's descendants be (15:5). "And he believed in the Lord, and the Lord considered it to be righteousness." This line appears to imply that Abram, at least at this time in his life, believed in the promise of God despite the lack of any real evidence for it. Such belief, says the author, is indeed righteousness—that is, a correct stance in relationship to God. Unfortunately, for Abram such belief will be short-lived! Fortunately, such belief will return again.

God then reiterates briefly that Abram has been brought from Ur precisely to possess the land of promise. But Abram still asks for proof: "How am I to know that I shall possess it?" In response to Abram's request for proof, an ancient covenanting ceremony is described. Abram is asked to bring as offering several animals, appropriately cut in two, and to lay the halves next to one another with space in between. Birds of prey dive onto the bloody carcasses, but Abram drives them away.

As the sun sets, in the expectant atmosphere of twilight, God brings a deep trance upon Abram. The usual translation "deep sleep" hides the religious context of this word. This trance is what fell upon the *'adam* before God took the material from which God made the woman (2:21). In this religious trance, surrounded by "dread and great darkness," God reveals to Abram a part of the history of the future of his descendants. Abram learns that his descendants shall be sojourners, part-time dwellers, in a strange land in which they will also be slaves to the oppressors of that land. But God will bring judgment on the nation of oppressors, and Abram's descendants will come out of there with great possessions. As for Abram himself, he will die peacefully, buried at a "good old age." His descendants shall return to this land in "the fourth generation."

These verses have brought about a heated historical argument. The discussion is obviously of the Egyptian sojourn and the subsequent Exodus, but in verse 13 the time of the sojourn is fixed at 400 years, while in verse 16 we read of a return to the land in the fourth generation, a time considerably less than 400 years, no matter how one counts the number of years for a generation. This chronological confusion should warn anyone against rash historical conclusions from material that is not primarily interested in history for its own sake.

To conclude the mysterious covenant ritual, a "smoking fire pot and flaming torch" appear out of the sky and swoop down between the halves of the sacrificial creatures. This action is the seal of the covenant between God and Abram, which God announces as a gift of "this land, from the river of Egypt [a stream that flows from the middle of the Sinai peninsula into the Mediterranean Sea] to the Euphrates." These ideal boundaries of Israel were approximately those of David's later empire (see II Sam. 8:3; I Kings 4:21; 8:65).

Abram and God are thus bound in covenant both by word and by ritual. And we are told that Abram believed God. After the lies of chapter 12, the crisis of the promise seems to have come to an end. But in the story of Abram, one ought never to draw simple conclusions too soon.

Retelling the Story

A dream or a vision I do not know for sure, but God came to me, and I had my question ready. "What can you give me," I asked, "since you have not seen fit to give Sarai a child? Don't you think I know what people say behind my back? God knows that was one reason that I went my own way and let Lot go his. It was worth giving him first choice just to escape the taunts of his herders.

The story says that the herders of Abram and Lot argued, but what did they argue about? The rabbis said that Abram's cattle went about muzzled so they would not eat from anyone else's pastures. Lot's cattle, on the other hand, were not muzzled and grazed wherever they pleased. Abram's herders thought this was unfair and suggested to Lot's herders that it was robbery. Lot's herders laughed, "God promised this land to Abram's descendants, but as it turns out Abram is as barren as a mule. Soon enough Lot, his nephew, will be his heir. These animals are just eating what is theirs." (*Genesis Rabbah* 41.5)

The deal suggested by Abram seems to put him at a disadvantage. The rabbis suggest that the parting of Abram and Lot, with Lot having the first choice of grazing land, might be compared to two people, one who has wheat and one barley. The one says, "If I get the wheat, then you get the barley. Or if you get the barley, then I take the wheat." Are they suggesting, since the outcome is already set between Lot and Abram, that Abram was not really taking a chance by allowing Lot the first choice? (*Genesis Rabbah* 41.6)

"Now my heir will be a slave, Eliezer of Damascus, rather than a child of my own. Is that any way to start a great nation?"

That is when God told me to look up at the sky. "See those stars," God said, "Your descendants will be more numerous than all of them. And they will be yours and Sarai's, not the children of a household slave." That was all very poetic, but God had already promised that my family would be like the dust of the earth; yet, we still could not hear the patter of dusty little feet in our tent. I was beginning to think that the blessing of Melchizedek was more powerful than the blessing of God.

The rabbis say that when God promised to make Abram's descendants like the dust of the earth, it meant more than that they would be numerous. They would be like a road that outlasts those who walk upon it. Thus Israel would outlast the nations that would trod upon it. (*Genesis Rabbah* 41.9)

Then the darkness around me deepened, and I was afraid. I prepared the animals and birds as God instructed, and the dream/trance deepened. I saw my family, Sarai's children down the generations, enslaved by a powerful king who did not recognize their God. I saw the struggles and suffering they would have to endure from the nations to which they were supposed to be a blessing. I tell you the truth, for a moment I was glad that the promise had not come true. What is this land and a large family if suffering is the only legacy I will leave them?

Some say that Abram frequently extended hospitality to strangers. After they had eaten he would ask his guests to say a blessing. The strangers, unused to this custom, would ask, "What shall I say?" Then Abram would teach them this blessing, "Blessed be the God of the universe of whose bounty we have eaten." Seeing this, God would say to Abram, "Before people did not know who I am, but because of you they do. From now on I will look upon you as if you had been with me at the creation." (*Genesis Rabbah* 43.7)

Sarai's Plan

Since the promised child has been so long in coming, Abram and Sarai take into their own hands the matter of getting an heir.

The Story

Abram's wife Sarai had borne him no children. She had, however, an Egyptian slave-girl named Hagar, and Sarai said to Abram, "The LORD has not let me have a child. Take my slave-girl; perhaps through her I shall have a son.' Abram heeded what his wife said; so Sarai brought her slave-girl, Hagar the Egyptian, to her husband and gave her to Abram as a wife. When this happened Abram had been in Canaan for ten years. He lay with Hagar and she conceived; and when she knew that she was pregnant, she looked down on her mistress. Sarai complained to Abram, 'I am being wronged; you must do something about it. It was I who gave my slave-girl into your arms, but since she has known that she is pregnant, she has despised me. May the LORD see justice done between you and me.' Abram replied, 'Your slave-girl is in your hands; deal with her as you please.' So Sarai ill-treated her and she ran away from her mistress.

The angel of the LORD came upon Hagar by a spring in the wilderness, the spring on the road to Shur, and he said, 'Hagar, Sarai's slave-girl, where have you come from and where are you going?' She answered, 'I am running away from Sarai my mistress.' The angel of the LORD said to her, 'Go back to your mistress and submit to ill-treatment at her hands.' He also said, 'I shall make your descendants too many to be counted.' The angel of the LORD went on:

'You are with child and will bear a son.
You are to name him Ishmael,
because the LORD has heard of your ill-treatment.
He will be like the wild ass;
his hand will be against everyone
and everyone's hand against him;
and he will live at odds with all his kin.'

Comments on the Story

In chapter 15 God proclaimed a covenant with Abram, a covenant that promised land and descendants. We were told that Abram believed in God and that God saw that belief as righteousness, and the covenant was sealed by a ritual wherein God affirmed the divine relationship to Abram and Sarai and to the promise that they carry. Yet, in the midst of the glow of that promise, the hard fact remains that "Sarai, Abram's wife, bore him no children" (16:1). And Sarai, like Abram in 15:2-3, is becoming impatient.

But she has a plan to produce an heir that will at long last satisfy this persistent God of an unfulfilled promise. She announces to her husband that for no reason that she can discern, "the Lord has prevented me from bearing children." For them to have descendants at all, she suggests, they will need to use a surrogate wife, and Sarai has just the woman in mind. It is Hagar, an Egyptian maid (perhaps a gift from the pharaoh as a result of the fiasco of chapter 12?). She urges Abram to "go and be with my maid; perhaps I shall be built up through her" (16:2). It has long been known that in many places in the ancient Near East precisely this procedure was used by a childless couple to secure an heir; there is nothing unique, and thereby nothing inherently reprehensible, about this decision. Sarai is a barren woman in a patriarchal world; she must have a child if she is to maintain any standing in that world. The focus of the story is not on the decision itself, but on the results of that decision.

Abram, so talkative in earlier stories, falls silent here. He merely does as he is told, receiving from his wife the Egyptian maid as a kind of co-wife. After a sexual relationship, Hagar indeed conceives. All seems to be working as Sarai had hoped, but almost immediately something goes awry. "When she [Hagar] saw that she was pregnant, her mistress became contemptible to her" (16:4). Hagar's ability to bear children, the key to full acceptance of a woman in such a society and the key to the promise of God, linked irrevocably to the possibility of progeny, has made her see Sarai as a lesser creature than herself. The text itself, with remarkable economy, makes the point clear. Verse 4 reads literally, "Her mistress was contemptible in her eyes." The hierarchy of "mistress" and "maid" is emphasized, but the power of the former has been forever destroyed in the eyes of the latter. Hagar's "eyes" tell her the stark truth; her swelling belly is something that will never happen to her supposed mistress. For Hagar, Sarai has been reduced to a shrunken and empty old woman, incapable of bringing forth life, incapable of fulfilling the command of God.

But Sarai has not yet lost her tongue, but instead of lashing out at Hagar, she unleashes a tirade against Abram. "My oppression be upon you!" The word she uses to describe the wrong done to her is often found in the prophets as a description of the injustice and wanton evils of a society under the judgment of God; it is the word found at Genesis 6.11 to summarize the evil of the pre-flood generation. She continues, "I put my maid [Sarai wants to be certain that the hierarchy remains clear] into your lap [a rather more literal translation than the phrase often receives], but when she saw that she was pregnant, I became contemptible in her eyes! The Lord judge between me and you!" Sarai drops the whole affair right back on Abram. He, after all, as the father of the child, ought to take direct responsibility for the disaster that has occurred.

And finally, Abram is forced to respond. "Look! *Your* maid is in *your* power; do to her whatever is good in *your* eyes." Abram's triple use of the second-person pronoun suggests his wishes in this mess; he wants no part of it at all! The repetition of the phrase "in your eyes" indicates what Abram has in mind more specifically: If you are contemptible in *her* eyes, then do whatever you think right in *your eyes*." Abram simply shuns any responsibility. His response to the pain of Sarai is in effect no response; the portrait of Abram is once again weak, for Sarah is given a free hand by the supposed master of the house. But Hagar, like all lonely fugitives or victims of injustice, is not beyond the care and concern of God. An angel discovers the fleeing Hagar near a spring of water and asks her where she has come from and where she is going. After the truth about her flight, the angel commands her to "return to your superior [the word used here is a much stronger word than *mistress*], and receive affliction under her power." The verb used to describe what Hagar can expect from Sarai is identical to that used to describe what Sarai did to Hagar before she ran away. In effect, the angel promises nothing to Hagar different from what she has already received from the vindictive Sarai.

But the angel does have a promise for her child. In fact, the promise is nearly identical to the one that Abram has been receiving since the initial call of God. Hagar, like Abram, is promised to have "descendants so numerous that they cannot be counted" (see 15:5). The angel goes on to command her to name her unborn child Ishmael ("God hears"), because God has heard your affliction." But the continuation of this promise is more ambiguous. "He shall be a wild donkey of a man, his hand against everyone and everyone's hand against him; he shall encamp over against all of his own kinsmen." In short, Ishmael and his numerous descendants will be proverbial pains in the neck, bullies and brigands and cutthroats. It is at best a double-edged promise, and one might say that the very last thing the world needs is a swelling number of Ishmaels. We are reminded of that terrible fellow Lamech in Genesis 4, who killed for nothing and wished vast death for a world that would dare to kill him.

Hagar's response to the visitation and promise of the heavenly messenger is unfortunately garbled in the Hebrew text. It is obviously an explanatory tale of some kind. Verse 13 says, "She named the Lord who had spoken to her, 'You are a God who sees me' [or "a God of seeing"], because she said, 'Have I really seen God and lived [the Hebrew text must be changed to read this] after God has seen me?' " This appears to make little sense, but anything else is a guess. Then follows an explanation of the well's name where all of this happened: It is called *Beer lahai roi*, or "the well of one who sees and lives."

The story closes with Hagar's return to the oppressions of her overmistress, Sarai, and *Abram's* naming of the child in traditional patriarchal fashion. The angel told Hagar to do the naming, but Hagar has been reduced once again to maid, without status, without power. Hierarchy and oppression are thus preserved.

The upshot of Sarai's plan to provide an heir has been evil for everyone involved. Sarai herself descends to vindictive anger and oppression, Abram in weasel-like fashion has tried to opt out of the whole debacle, and Hagar ends the story in abject submission to the power of Sarai. The human plan has been a miserable failure, but God's promise is still alive. Is there a way for it come to fruition?

Retelling the Story

"Why me?" thought Alicia. "What's wrong with me? I'm the youngest partner in the firm. I work out three times a week. I can still wear the same dress, unaltered, I wore the night Bill and I had our first date, nine years ago. I have the kind of beauty that lasts; lots of people have told me that." But no kids, no little bambinos, no cherubs to mess up the house, Alicia's life, and their pants.

She just could not get pregnant. But it was the twentieth century, not some Old Testament world in which they lived. A couple could have a fulfilled life without children. They had several friends who had vowed never to bring kids into such a world as this.

> While most commentators seem to assume that Abram and Sarai's childlessness was due to Sarai's being unable to conceive, some rabbis [with patriarchal bias] suggest an alternative. They read the verse that said that Sarai bore Abram no children to mean that with another husband she could have conceived. (*Genesis Rabbah* 45.1)

Nevertheless, it gnawed at them. They saw couples and their children, and they were envious. They went by baby stores and turned their faces away. They read the wrong magazines and wept at the diaper ads, for crying out loud! Then one day, Alicia read about surrogate motherhood. It sounded crazy at first, somehow unnatural, but the more she thought the more it looked like a chance to have a child with Bill's participation, at least. And even if hers was not the womb in which the child would grow, she would love that baby even so.

Bill, after initial reluctance, warmed to the idea and began to explore the details. They found a woman willing to be inseminated and to carry the baby. The woman had two very healthy children of her own, and her pregnancies had been a breeze. She was anxious to serve the couple, and the $5,000 would help her struggles with finances immeasurably. It was a contract that seemed good for all.

But the trouble began very soon after Bill's semen had been injected into the woman's body. Oh, she had gotten pregnant almost right away, and in barely two months her belly began to swell. Bill was ecstatic; he visited the woman almost every day to make certain that she was eating right and keeping the baby safe and well. Occasionally, the woman would join Bill and Alicia for dinner, and Bill would go on about the baby and about his future fatherhood. Meanwhile, Alicia grew increasingly quiet, while Bill and the woman laughed and laughed.

Finally, one night after one of these dinners, Alicia exploded at Bill, accusing him of having an affair with the woman, accusing him of ignoring her and acting like an all around jerk. Bill reacted defensively and told Alicia that he still loved her very much. He spent so much time with the woman because she was carrying their baby. Bill told Alicia to grow up; it had been her idea in the first place.

Alicia looked at him coldly and demanded that Bill have the woman abort the baby. She would have nothing to do with the little brat if Bill ever dared to bring it home. Bill was horrified at being forced to choose between his wife and the baby. During this fight the woman had returned to the couple's house because she had accidentally forgotten her purse after dinner. She overheard the entire conversation and immediately went home, called an airline and made a reservation for a distant city. She left a note in the couple's mailbox before she left, but they heard nothing from her until the child was born. It was a boy.

> When Hagar became haughty, Abram was at a loss to respond since her status had changed from servant to surrogate wife (who will bear his child). So he told Sarai that she would have to figure out what to do with Hagar. The rabbis say that Sarai hit her in the face with a shoe and made her carry water and towels for the bath. In essence, she treated her like a slave rather than the mother of Abram's child. (*Genesis Rabbah* 45.6)

Alicia and Bill saw the child from time to time as he grew up, but the woman mothered the boy, adding him to her own family. Alicia and Bill called the child Abraham, but the woman gave him the name Bill, and that was his name until he died. The woman loved young Bill as her own, because, after all, he was.

Another Promise

Abram and all of his male descendants will carry the mark of their covenant with God as a witness to the world that they have been set apart as a blessing to the world.

The Story

When Abram was ninety-nine years old, the LORD appeared to him and said, 'I am God Almighty. Live always in my presence and be blameless, so that I may make my covenant with you and give you many descendants.' Abram bowed low, and God went on, 'This is my covenant with you: You are to be the father of many nations. Your name will no longer be Abram, but Abraham; for I shall make you father of many nations. I shall make you exceedingly fruitful; I shall make nations out of you, and kings shall spring from you. I shall maintain my covenant with you and your descendants after you, generation after generation, an everlasting covenant: I shall be your God, yours and your descendants.' As a possession for all time I shall give you and your descendants after you the land in which you now are aliens, the whole of Canaan, and I shall be their God.

God said to Abraham, 'For your part, you must keep my covenant, you and your descendants after you, generation by generation. This is how you are to keep this covenant between myself and you and your descendants after you: circumcise yourselves, every male among you. You must circumcise the flesh of your foreskin, and it will be the sign of the covenant between us. Every male among you in every generation must be circumcised on the eighth day, both those born in your house and any foreigner, not a member of your family but purchased. Circumcise both those born in your house and those you buy; thus your flesh will be marked with the sign of my everlasting covenant. Every uncircumcised male, everyone who has not had the flesh of his foreskin circumcised, will be cut off from the kin of his father; he has broken my covenant.'

God said to Abraham, 'As for Sarai your wife, you are to call her not Sarai, but Sarah. I shall bless her and give you a son by her. I shall bless her and she will be the mother of nations; from her kings of peoples will spring.' Abraham bowed low, and laughing said to himself, 'Can a son be born to a man who is a hundred years old? Can Sarah bear a child at ninety?' He said to God, 'If only Ishmael might enjoy your special favour!' But God replied, 'No; your wife Sarah will bear you a son, and you are to call him Isaac. With him I shall maintain my covenant as an everlasting covenant for his descendants after him. But I have heard your request about Ishmael; I have blessed him and I shall make him fruitful. I shall give him many descendants; he will be father of twelve princes, and I shall raise a great nation from him. But my covenant I shall fulfill with Isaac, whom Sarah will bear to you at this time next year.' When he had finished talking with Abraham, God left him.

Then Abraham took Ishmael his son, everyone who had been born in his household and everyone he had bought, every male in his household, and that same day he circumcised the flesh of their foreskins as God had commanded him. Abraham was ninety-nine years old when he was circumcised. Ishmael was thirteen years old when he was circumcised. Both Abraham and Ishmael were circumcised on the same day. All the men of Abraham's household, born in the house or bought from foreigners, were circumcised with him.

Comments on the Story

The human attempt to solve the problem of childlessness has been a complete fiasco. The experience brought out the worst in every character: Sarai became vindictive and oppressive, Abram was weak and indecisive, and Hagar was haughty and finally oppressed and subservient, both to Abram and to Sarai. It is clear that a purely human resolution will be impossible, and that is the appropriate context for chapter 17.

Since the rise of the critical study of the Hebrew Bible, it has been recognized that much of this chapter arose in the circle of priestly interests. Scholars noted its deep concern for circumcision, as well as its language, which is so reminiscent of Genesis 1, also said to have a connection to priestly concerns. Granting the truth of that judgment, its placement here in the ongoing story is far more than haphazard. After the disaster of chapter 16, a reiteration of the divine origin of the promise is needed from God's representatives. The mess created by Sarai's plan will not impede the plan of God.

Abram is now ninety-nine years old. With this fact delineated, any sensible reader will automatically rule out any possibility that he may ever have a child of his own with Sarai; it is simply too late. Nevertheless God appears to him and says, "I am El Shaddai; walk before me and be perfect." The original meaning of the divine name *El Shaddai* is less significant than its use in particular contexts. Here it seems to imply a most ancient reality; the one who is appearing to Abram has been God from of old, who is behind the promise all these years. This ancient God commands that Abram "be perfect" (see Job 1:1), and as a result of that perfection God promises to make a covenant with Abram. "I will multiply you tremendously," says God; "You will become the father of a company of nations." The old promise rings in Abram's ears once again. But can a ninety-nine-year-old man be a father of anything at all? Still, at this point in the drama, Abram's response to the reiterated, and increasingly absurd, promise of a child is to "fall on his face" (17:3), an ancient way of expressing complete obedience and trust in a superior. This is a symbol of the kind of trust Abram showed at Genesis 12:1-3, when he left his home at the call of God, and at Genesis 15:6, when he believed God in the face of his lack of an heir.

God's covenant with Abram is here symbolized by a change of name. Instead of Abram (which may mean "mighty father"), the chosen one will henceforth be called Abraham, "because I have made you a father of a company of nations" (17:5). The name *Abraham* is presumably taken to mean something like "father of a multitude." In reality, the two names may mean very much the same, etymologically speaking, but that fact is not really significant. For the author of this story, Abraham's new name means nothing less than he actually *will be* the father of many. The ninety-nine-year-old will be what God wants him to be, and his advanced age will have nothing to do with it.

In the succeeding three verses, God spells out in further detail just what this covenant implies. Abraham will be "fruitful" [the old word of promise; (see 1:28], and "nations" and "kings" shall come from him. The covenant will be both for Abraham and for his descendants after him, and it will be an "everlasting covenant" (*berith 'olam*). Not only that, but the covenant also implies the gift of the land of Canaan as an "everlasting possession" (*'ahuzzath 'olam).* And finally God announces, "I will be their God" (17:8).

As a further symbol of this covenant, God proclaims that all males shall be circumcised in the flesh of their foreskins, whether they be native-born Israelites or males who live in an Israelite household, but were purchased from foreigners. At the tender age of eight days, they shall be circumcised. Those who are not "shall be cut off from his people; he has broken my covenant" (17:14).

Israel was only one of many nations that practiced circumcision. Jeremiah 9:24 tells us that Egyptians, Edomites, Ammonites, and Moabites all practiced this rite, and it is attested in many other places as well. Its significance for Israel, particularly in the later history of the people after their destruction and exile (early sixth century B.C.E.), is made clear in this chapter. It is quite simply a sign of the covenant. After the loss of Temple, land, king, and priesthood, the rite became especially significant as a way of differentiating true believers from the "pagan" Babylonians, who apparently did not practice it.

After the change of name and after the promise of the covenant of progeny and land, the ensuing dialogue is particularly surprising. First, to seal the covenant with the chosen couple, God changes Sarai's name to Sarah. There really is no difference in the meaning of these two names; they are dialectical equivalents, meaning "princess."

But, as in the change of Abram's name, the significance is a symbolic one; it is another sign of the covenant. "I will bless her, and also I will give you a son through her. I *will* bless her; she will become nations; kings of nations shall issue from her." The repetitive quality of this speech of God has a tone of urgent evangelization to it; God is trying to convince the chosen one. This is odd, because we might have assumed that he needed no convincing after falling on his face in obedience in verse 3. And, sure enough, he falls on his face again in response to God's announcement, but this time he does not fall in obedience. Quite the contrary. Abraham is overcome by the absolute absurdity of this promise of a child and falls on his face in helpless laughter! In the midst of his guffawing, he thinks to himself, "Shall a child be born to a man who is a hundred years old? Shall Sarah, who is ninety years old, give birth" (17:7)? Controlling himself, he turns to God and says, "Let Ishmael be in your presence!" The joke is a good one, but it is time to get back to reality. Ishmael will have to do.

But the joke is apparently not a joke at all. God's response is unequivocal. "No! Sarah your wife will bear a son for you, and you shall name him Isaac." *Isaac* in Hebrew means "laughter"; that should remind Abraham that for God nothing is impossible (18:14). And from the human side, what else would you call a child whom you bore at the age of ninety but "laughter"?

This is the child who will receive the "everlasting covenant," as well as his descendants after him. As for Ishmael, he will be blessed to be fruitful and multiply (17:20), but the covenant of God will be reserved for Isaac, the child of laughter, the child whom Sarah will bear "at this time next year" (17:21). The chapter concludes with Abraham performing the sign of the circumcision on all the males of his house, according to the command of God.

Once again, Abraham is revealed to us as not fully convinced that this promise of God will be fulfilled through his and his wife's aging bodies. He accepts the changes of their names as signs of the covenant, and he performs the rite of circumcision as a further sign, but about the actual birth of the actual child, who is to be called Isaac, his most recent response is uncontrolled laughter.

Retelling the Story

Twice he had fallen on his face. The first time it had been the act of a servant paying homage to his master. But the second time he had laughed so hard he bent double and fell. God didn't seem to appreciate that second occasion. Now before you begin feeling smug and saying you would never laugh in God's presence, just listen to what happened.

> The rabbis view Abram as shortsighted here. Of course, they had the advantage of knowing the rest of the story. But they say that Abram was like someone whose boss comes to him and wants to double his pay. Instead, the worker responds by saying, "Look, don't joke with me and hold up false hopes, just don't cut my salary." (*Genesis Rabbah* 47.4)

God told Abram that he (at ninety-nine years of age, mind you) and his wife Sarai (who was ninety) were going to have a child.

Abram had suggested that Ishmael might do, since he was already here. That seemed more reasonable. But no! God insisted that this would be a child born to him and Sarai.

Well, the news was like something you would read in one of those magazines while waiting in the check-out line at the grocery store. You could picture the headlines: NINETY-YEAR-OLD WOMAN TO GIVE BIRTH—THE FATHER'S ALMOST ONE HUNDRED! He had laughed because it was so ridiculous and because it was just a bit embarrassing. He still loved Sarai, and sometimes when he looked at her the old feelings would begin to stir like coals about to burst into flame. He just hadn't been able to express that longing as frequently in recent years. And he didn't appreciate anyone making jokes about it.

God had made two other changes at the same time. First, Abram would not be called by that name anymore. No, now his name was Abraham (father of a multitude). Was that supposed to be a joke or something? And Sarai would be called Sarah. Now the logic behind Sarai's name change was beyond Abram, I mean Abraham, because both names mean "princess." But if that is the way God wanted it, who was he to object?

Now the other change was no laughing matter. Abraham and all his male descendants, including Ishmael, were to be circumcised so they would carry on their flesh the sign that they were followers of God. Now Abraham couldn't understand why God couldn't have settled for a tattoo or something simple like that. After all, this might be called a simple procedure on an eight day old, but Ishmael was entering his teens and Abraham was an old man, and there was no anesthesia, for God's sake. At his age, he looked on this as major surgery.

> The rabbis explain the change of Sarai's name to Sarah this way: Before she had been princess to her own people (Sarai), but now she was princess to all people (Sarah). (*Genesis Rabbah* 47.1)

> When God raised the issue of circumcision Abraham was not so sure it was a good idea, as one might imagine. One objection he raised was that, before, people had followed him and had become followers of God. But would they follow when he told them what they would have to go through to become a follower? After all, circumcision was a lot to ask an adult male to go through just to join a new religion. God answered, "Don't you worry about that. It is enough that I am your God and your patron. It will be enough that I am God and patron for the whole world as well." (*Genesis Rabbah* 64.3)

Abraham was not what you would call vain about his looks, but over the course of ninety-nine years he had grown attached to every line and wrinkle and fold of skin on his body. He had none to spare, as he viewed it. But he wouldn't think about that. God had promised a child and named Abraham "Father of Many." Abraham would do it, then wait and see.

The Laughter of Sarah

Three visitors appear to confirm for Abraham and Sarah that, as incredible as it may seem at their age, they are going to have a child.

The Story

The LORD appeared to Abraham by the terebinths of Mamre, as he was sitting at the opening of his tent in the heat of the day. He looked up and saw three men standing over against him. On seeing them, he hurried from his tent door to meet them. Bowing low he said, 'Sirs, if I have deserved your favour, do not go past your servant without a visit. Let me send for some water so that you may bathe your feet; and rest under this tree, while I fetch a little food so that you may refresh yourselves. Afterwards you may continue the journey which has brought you my way.' They said, 'Very well, do as you say.' So Abraham hurried into the tent to Sarah and said, 'Quick, take three measures of flour, knead it, and make cakes.' He then hastened to the herd, chose a fine, tender calf, and gave it to a servant, who prepared it at once. He took curds and milk and the calf which was now ready, set it all before them, and there under the tree waited on them himself while they ate.

They asked him where Sarah his wife was, and he replied, 'She is in the tent.' One of them said, 'About this time next year I shall come back to you, and your wife Sarah will have a son.' Now Sarah was listening at the opening of the tent close by him. Both Abraham and Sarah were very old, Sarah being well past the age of childbearing. So she laughed to herself and said, 'At my time of life I am past bearing children, and my husband is old.' The LORD said to Abraham, 'Why did Sarah laugh and say, "Can I really bear a child now that I am so old?" Is anything impossible for the LORD? In due season, at this time next year, I shall come back to you, and Sarah will have a son.' Because she was frightened, Sarah lied and denied that she had laughed; but he said, 'Yes, you did laugh.'

Comments on the Story

Abraham, the man of the promise, laughs in the face of that promise in chapter 17; it all seems so absurd! And now it is important to indicate that Sarah's faith in the promise is hardly more than her husband's. The narrator begins this new tale by letting the reader in on a mystery that is about to unfold. We are told in the first verse that "the Lord [that is "Yahweh," God of Israel] appeared to him by the oaks of Mamre" (see 13:18 for an earlier reference to Abram's dwelling place). We now know that the event we will read about is in fact a theophany, an appearance of God. To Abraham, it will appear to be no more than a visit from three desert travelers. Now we know more than Abraham does and are thus afforded the pleasure of watching him act without knowing for whom he is acting. This device is known as dramatic irony; the readers know more than some of the characters of the drama know. Television uses this literary device to great advantage (for example, "Columbo" and "Mission Impossible").

The narrator sets the scene quickly. Abraham is sitting at the door of his tent "in the heat of the day," apparently the searing time when the sun beats unmercifully on the land, sending up false "waves" from the blasted desert floor. Abraham sits at the tent door in whatever minimal shade the tent can provide. In a half-sleep induced by the overpowering heat, Abraham looks up and "behold, three men stood in front of him" (18:2). The narrator's art is subtle here. The word *behold* is an indicator of a shift in the point of view of the narration. By the use of this word, the writer shifts our gaze from the sleepy Abraham to the startling three strangers; they come up as if from nowhere. They are suddenly close enough to Abraham (and to us!) to engage in intimate conversation. Their appearance is decidedly mysterious.

But Abraham moves into rapid and culturally conditioned action. He "runs" to meet them, and he "bows down to the ground," an act of obeisance often reserved for great personages, like royalty. Abraham sees only three weary strangers; yet, still he treats them like regal guests. His first speech to them suggests the perfection of his hospitality: "My lord [the word is the common one used for greeting a guest, often one of superior rank], please! If I have found favor in your [the pronoun is singular] eyes, please do not pass by your [again the pronoun is singular] servant. Let a little water be drawn. Wash your [the pronoun is plural] feet and rest [the command is plural] under the tree" (18:3-4). In this speech, Abraham speaks first to the obvious leader of the group (whom we know already to be the Lord), then turns to include the other two.

While the strangers wash and rest in the shade, Abraham promises to bring "a bit of bread to enable you to refresh yourselves." He then says, "Afterwards you may pass on; why else have you come to your servant?" The text of the last sentence is not quite clear, but the meaning seems to be that Abraham sees this visit as his chance to refresh three travelers; they have come to him, and he must meet their needs. However, the reader can hear more in his words than he intends. "Why else have you come to your servant," he asks, and the reader has a fair notion of why else; the promise is still to be fulfilled.

Abraham swings into even more rapid action. He hurries into the tent to Sarah and blurts out, "Quickly take three measures of finest flour, knead it, and make cakes." Though there is some disagreement about the modern equivalent of a "measure" *(seah),* some scholars suggesting as much as one-third of a bushel, we know that it is a significant amount, far more than a "bit of bread." To add to this generous portion of hot cakes, Abraham "runs" to his herd and selects a "young calf, tender and good," and gives it to his servant, who hurries to prepare it. He then takes curds and milk and the calf, sets them before the strangers, and stands near them under the tree while they eat (18:6-8).

These verses describe in detail the actions of a perfect Middle Eastern host. Experiences in the modern Middle East can parallel this one. The host plays down the worthiness of his gift of a meal and then proceeds to lay on a lavish feast. So Abraham's "bit of bread" turns into a sumptuous luncheon, with the host standing by, waiting to fulfill every need of his guests. Such hospitality stands in sharp contrast to the "hospitality" shown to the strangers who visit the city of Sodom in the next chapter. Any hearer of this story in ancient times would have seen Abraham as the perfect host.

But the strangers from the desert have a surprise of their own. They ask, "Where is Sarah, your wife?" We know that somehow these three strangers represent the Lord, so we are not surprised by their knowledge of Abraham's wife's name. After he tells them that she is in the tent, "the Lord says, 'I will without doubt return to you at the time of life [i.e., the spring] and there will be a son for your wife Sarah" (18:10). It is the promise of a child reiterated one more time. But to keep the huge problems of the tremendous age of the child-less couple before the reader, the narrator reminds us of what we know only too well: "Sarah had ceased to be in the way of women" (i.e., she had stopped menstruating).

Upon hearing God's promise of a child, and remembering all too well her age, Sarah "laughed to herself, 'After I am used up, shall I have pleasure? My lord is old!' " She calls Abraham her "lord," the same word Abraham used to address the leader of the strangers when they first appeared (18:3). The last word of her silent laughter of disbelief is the word *old*; after all, that is the problem. But the Lord hears even the silent laughter of those who do not believe, and, turning to Abraham, says, "Why in the world did Sarah laugh and say, 'Shall I really give birth, now that I am old?' " The saucy old Sarah speaks of no chance for herself; God speaks of giving birth. "Is anything too hard for the Lord?" The answer for this narrative is a decided no. "At the season, I will return to you, at the time of life, and Sarah will have a son." God repeats the promise of 18:10: "But Sarah lied, 'I did not laugh.' She was afraid." At verse 14, Sarah realizes that she has been talking, albeit vicariously through Abraham, with the divinity, who responds to her lie with "No! You did laugh!" The narrator is making it very clear to us that the word *laugh* (*tsachaq*) is the key term for the story. From this verb will come the name *Isaac*, the child born out of the laughter of disbelief.

Thus both Abraham and Sarah deny the promise of God, and in effect deny the power and will of that God. But the aged couple is God's choice, and God will find a way. From all manner of closed wombs can this God bring life!

Retelling the Story

Like ghosts, desert spirits burst from the sand, they were silent, three regal shapes casting short shadows in the blazing heat of the withering mid-afternoon sun. The old man had neither heard nor seen them before they were there, just there, as if they had always been there unnoticed. Well, the heat was unbearable, the senses dulled, eyes clouded, ears clogged, will blunted. Heat beyond imagining, beyond enduring.

But the bony old man, sweat clinging to his filthy cotton cloak, his face caked with centuries of desert dust, somehow roused himself to action born of those same centuries' demand for service. With movement quicker than his feeble frame could sustain, he stood up to greet the strangers from the desert, and ran, yes ran, to meet them, his toes nearly scraping the blasted, hard-packed earth. He may be a pitiable, childless old man, but he knew what custom demanded.

He began the expected litany of the offer of a tiny, inadequate repast—"a little water, a bit of bread"—while his brain was composing the commands he would give for a sumptuous wilderness feast. He knew that the strangers knew this code of behavior well, but that hardly implied that one could go beyond the custom. Never! It was the custom that had kept the old man together while his long life had continued and while that long life had not been blessed with a son. Well, these

> The Talmud states that when the strangers arrived Abraham was talking to God (thus the reference to "my Lord"). But when they came he stopped the conversation and offered them hospitality. This is to show that extending hospitality to the stranger is even more important than our private conversations with God. (Plaut, p. 125)

strangers knew nothing of that and certainly would not care if they did. Just another old man, cursed with a barren wife, doomed to live out his last days with the certain knowledge that with his death would come the death of his name; there would be no memory of this old man even a few years after his ragged corpse began its inexorable return into desert dust.

The strangers answered the coded language with the appropriate coded response, "Do as you have said." The old man increased his remarkable activity, providing large portions of food and drink for the three, then waited while they ate it all. After the prescribed belch of satisfaction, the ultimate act of praise after a superb meal, the strangers politely asked after the old man's wife. This was customary, once again, but the fact that the strangers knew her name was at least curious. "In the tent," was the old man's reply, and he went on to think that was where she belonged, for custom dictated that male guests were never served by women.

One of the strangers assumed a well-nigh divine look about him and announced that he would return next spring and old lady Sarah would have a son. Well, the old man remembered how he had laughed at the claim several times before, but out of politeness to the peculiar stranger, he kept his laughter to himself. And so did Sarah.

Oh, she heard what the stranger had said, but she knew what no stranger could know, although one look at her withered frame would tell all anyone needed to know. She was so far beyond menopause as to have forgotten when and how it had occurred. And old Abraham had been unable to provide her any pleasure for more years than she could count. A son, indeed! The very thought was a cruel mockery of her sagging breasts and empty womb. So she chuckled sneeringly to herself. Sure, she thought, a son for me and old Abe!

"Why did Sarah laugh?" the divine one quietly asked, a bemused smile on his weathered face. "I didn't laugh," the ancient woman lied. "Yes, you did," chuckled the desert stranger, whose amazingly old features suddenly cracked into a broad guffaw as he shouted, "Is anything too wonderful for the Lord?"

> In the Talmud it is suggested that Sarah really said, "How can I have a child with a husband so old?" But when God told Abraham what she had said the last phrase became "since I am so old." The phrase was changed to keep harmony in the family. (Plaut, p. 125)

Hearing such unrestrained laughter, the old man and the old woman could not help themselves; they laughed, too, and the next spring the prune-faced pair had a son. They called him "laughter" (Isaac), what else?

Abraham Reminds God About Justice

God confides in Abraham the rumors going around concerning Sodom and its fate if the rumors are true. Abraham reminds God that one who is just, indeed the author of justice, would not punish the righteous along with the wicked.

The Story

The men set out and looked down towards Sodom, and Abraham went with them to see them on their way. The LORD had thought to himself, 'Shall I conceal from Abraham what I am about to do? He will become a great and powerful nation, and all nations on earth will wish to be blessed as he is blessed. I have singled him out so that he may charge his sons and family after him to conform to the way of the LORD and do what is right and just; thus I shall fulfil for him all that I have promised.' The LORD said, 'How great is the outcry over Sodom and Gomorrah! How grave their sin must be! I shall go down and see whether their deeds warrant the outcry reaching me. I must know the truth.' When the men turned and went off towards Sodom, Abraham remained standing before the LORD. Abraham drew near him and asked, 'Will you really sweep away innocent and wicked together? Suppose there are fifty innocent in the city; will you really sweep it away, and not pardon the place because of the fifty innocent there? Far be it from you to do such a thing— to kill innocent and wicked together; for then the innocent would suffer with the wicked. Far be it from you! Should not the judge of all the earth do what is just? The LORD replied, 'If I find in Sodom fifty innocent, I shall pardon the whole place for their sake.' Abraham said, 'May I make so bold as to speak to the Lord, I who am nothing but dust and ashes: suppose there are five short of fifty innocent? Will you destroy the whole city for the lack of five men?' 'If I find forty-five there,' he replied, 'I shall not destroy it.' Abraham spoke again, 'Suppose forty can be found there?' 'For the sake of the forty I shall not do it,' he replied. Then Abraham said, 'Let not my Lord become angry if I speak again: suppose thirty can be found there?' He answered, 'If I find thirty there, I shall not do it.' Abraham continued, 'May I make so bold as to speak to the Lord: suppose twenty can be found there?' He replied, 'For the sake of the twenty I shall not destroy it.' Abraham said, 'Let not my Lord become angry if I speak just once more: suppose ten can be found there?' 'For the sake of the ten I shall not destroy it,' said the Lord. When the LORD had finished talking to Abraham, he went away, and Abraham returned home.

Comments on the Story

The two sections that conclude chapter 18 are filled with a discussion of justice. In the first section (18:16-21), the Lord proposes to tell Abraham what is to be done to Sodom and charges Abraham with the task of "doing righteousness and justice." In the second section (18:22-33), Abraham appears to do just that by questioning the very justice of God's decision to destroy the cities as long as there remain in them some righteous people. The latter is a favorite story of many rabbinic commentators who see Abraham's argument with the Almighty as a kind of paradigm for the enormous responsibility we humans have in the ongoing maintenance of the universe.

After Sarah laughs in the face of the promise of a child and then lies about her laughter, "the men [all three?] set out from there and looked toward Sodom." Abraham served as guide to direct them toward the place. But suddenly, the Lord becomes self-reflective and wonders, "Shall I hide from Abraham what I am doing, since Abraham will become a great and powerful nation and all the nations of the earth will be blessed by him?" The promise of nationhood and blessing is repeated here in the form of a question and becomes in this context the reason for the communication between Abraham and God in the following section. Abraham is raised to a truly lofty height here, becoming worthy in the sight of God to receive details about the divine plan.

God answers the divine question in the negative; God will not conceal the plan from the chosen one precisely because the very function of his chosenness is "to command his children and his household after him to keep the way of the Lord by doing righteousness and justice in order that the Lord may bring to Abraham what was said to him" (18:19). This call for Abraham to be a teacher and a doer of righteousness and justice reminds us of similar demands in the prophetic literature (see Amos 5:24 and Jer. 22:15, for example) and also certain later concerns of the post-exilic period (see Ps. 33:5 and Prov. 21:3). To do justice and righteousness is to be actively concerned for the rights of the innocent before the law, to be motivated by interest in the rights of the oppressed, rights denied by their oppressors. Abraham has been chosen to be such a seeker after justice and to teach all of his household to be such seekers as well. As a result of Abraham's seeking and teaching, the Lord may then "bring to Abraham what was said to him"—namely, the fulfillment of the promise. Doing justice and righteousness is the definition in this context for keeping the "way of the Lord"; Jeremiah 22:15 provides a similar definition.

Because Abraham is God's chosen one, a doer of justice and righteousness, he must be told about the plan to destroy Sodom. God's plan is unambiguous: "Because the outcry of Sodom and Gomorrah is enormous and their sin very weighty, I will now go down to see whether their actions are precisely what the outcry indicates; if not, I will know" (18:20-21). The word *outcry* may mean the lament of those oppressed in the cities or a demand for revenge for evils done against the people (see Gen. 4:10). The meaning here seems to be a bit more general; the cities are evil, and the cries of both the evil *and* whoever may be good have reached the heavenly throne.

So the men turned from there and moved toward Sodom, but "Abraham remained standing before the Lord." (In the original Hebrew text, that sentence was reversed, reading: "But the Lord remained standing before Abraham." However, certain pious commentators found it objectionable that the Lord should stand before anyone, so they changed the text for religious reasons and "footnoted" their actions. Commentators made similar changes in seventeen other places.) Abraham and God are left alone, and the chosen one, the teacher of justice and righteousness, is about to engage a notable pupil in debate.

"Will you even sweep away righteous with wicked? Suppose there are fifty righteous ones in the city; will you even sweep away and not spare the place for the sake of the fifty righteous who are in it? Far be it from you to do such a thing as this, to destroy righteous with wicked, where the righteous become like the wicked! Far be it from you! Shall the judge of all the earth not do justice?" (18:23-25). Abraham presumes to teach his God the full meaning of justice! And yet it is precisely what God urged on the chosen one above. He *is* to be a teacher of justice, and so he is such right here. And the implication of the lesson is an extremely important one. If the judge of all the earth is *not* a doer of justice, then any human attempts to pursue it are doomed to failure. Without ultimate justice there can be no proximate justice.

Fifty righteous persons can save the evil city. This idea is the reverse of that found in Deuteronomy 21, where the evil must be expunged to save the community. God hears Abraham's cry for justice and agrees not to destroy the city for the sake of fifty righteous, if so many are to be found. But Abraham is not fully satisfied with fifty as saviors of the many; he pursues the question with relentlessness. "I who am dust and ashes have presumed to speak to my lord [he does not use the divine name here, but the common address of a human superior; see 18:3]. Suppose five of the fifty righteous are lacking. Will you destroy the city because of the five?" (Gen. 18:27-28). God says that the city will not be destroyed if forty-five are found. Down and down goes the figure, from forty to thirty to twenty to ten, as Abraham bargains with God over the fate of Sodom. They sound as if they are haggling over a used car!

Yet, the point of the story is not Abraham's failed attempt to save the evil Sodom by his clever use of mercantile bargaining practices. The point of the story is to establish beyond the shadow of a doubt the fact that God is indeed a God of justice and is never in the business of destroying the righteous with the wicked. The implication is clear that even if *one* righteous person were found, God would save the entire place for the sake of that one. (This idea finds remarkable expression in the powerful and terrifying twentieth-century novel *The Last of the Just* by Andre Schwartz-Bart.)

Abraham's bargaining will not save Sodom; it is ticketed for destruction. Yet, we are not yet certain just what the "outcry" of the city is. In the next chapter, more will be explained, and the city will be obliterated.

Retelling the Story

The students were greatly troubled by the story, so they went to their teacher. "Rabbi," they asked, "could it be that Abraham had to remind God to act justly toward Sodom? Would not God know better than even Grandfather Abraham the fate that the people of Sodom deserved?"

The rabbi responded, "Once there was a woman who had a basket of apples in one corner of her storage room. One day she entered the room and smelled the distinct aroma of rotting apples. She decided to look into the basket and throw the apples out if they were indeed rotten.

"Then she said to herself, 'Shall I not tell my daughter what I am about to do?' So she told her daughter that she was considering throwing out the basket of apples. Her daughter replied, 'Will you, who told me never to waste food, throw out the good apples with the rotten? What if half the apples are good?' Was the mother troubled that her daughter had learned so well?

"Abraham was like a rabbi who decides that, because many of his students are not attentive, he will turn them all out and have nothing to do with them. Then one student, a joker who seemed never to listen, said, 'Did you not teach us that each person is precious in God's sight? Then will you not continue to teach us for the sake of those who will gain from your teaching?' Then the rabbi smiled with satisfaction that one who seemed never to pay attention had learned so much."

> Why did Abraham intercede with God for the people of Sodom? With a human judge it is possible to appeal from a lower court to a higher one. But God is the highest court, the court of last resort. So Abraham pleaded for God to act with justice as if it were a final appeal. (*Genesis Rabbah* 49.9)
>
> Why did Abraham choose ten as the least number of righteous persons for whose sake God would save Sodom? Some thought that it was because ten was a *minyan*, the number that must be present for worship to take place. Others said that in the family of Noah eight survived the flood. Perhaps God would spare the city for the sake of only two more. Still others thought that Abraham believed that with Lot's family ten righteous could be found. (*Genesis Rabbah* 49.13)

The Destruction of the Cities

Unfortunately not even ten righteous persons can be found in Sodom, so after a tragic encounter at Lot's house the city is destroyed along with Gomorrah.

The Story

The two angels came to Sodom in the evening while Lot was sitting by the city gate. When he saw them, he rose to meet them and bowing low he said, 'I pray you, sirs, turn aside to your servant's house to spend the night there and bathe your feet. You can continue your journey in the morning.' 'No,' they answered, 'we shall spend the night in the street.' But Lot was so insistent that they accompanied him into his house. He prepared a meal for them, baking unleavened bread for them to eat.

Before they had lain down to sleep, the men of Sodom, both young and old, everyone without exception, surrounded the house. They called to Lot: 'Where are the men who came to you tonight? Bring them out to us so that we may have intercourse with them.' Lot went out into the doorway to them, and, closing the door behind him, said, 'No, my friends, do not do anything so wicked. Look, I have two daughters, virgins both of them; let me bring them out to you, and you can do what you like with them. But do nothing to these men, because they have come under the shelter of my roof.' They said, 'Out of our way! This fellow has come and settled here as an alien, and does he now take it upon himself to judge us? We will treat you worse than them.' They crowded in on Lot and pressed close to break down the door. But the two men inside reached out, pulled Lot into the house, and shut the door. Then they struck those in the doorway, both young and old, with blindness so that they could not find the entrance.

The two men said to Lot, 'Have you anyone here, sons-in-law, sons, or daughters, or anyone else belonging to you in the city? Get them out of this place, because we are going to destroy it. The LORD is aware of the great outcry against its citizens and has sent us to destroy it.' So Lot went out and urged his sons-in-law to get out of the place at once. 'The LORD is about to destroy the city,' he said. But they did not take him seriously.

As soon as it was dawn, the angels urged Lot: 'Quick, take your wife and your two daughters who are here, or you will be destroyed when the city is punished.' When he delayed, they grabbed his hand and the hands of his wife and two daughters, because the LORD had spared him, and they led him to safety outside the city. After they had brought them out, one said,

'Flee for your lives! Do not look back or stop anywhere in the plain. Flee to the hills or you will be destroyed.' Lot replied, 'No, sirs! You have shown your servant favour, and even more by your unfailing care you have saved my life, but I cannot escape to the hills; I shall be overtaken by the disaster, and die. Look, here is a town, only a small place, near enough for me to get to quickly. Let me escape to this small place and save my life.' He said to him, 'I grant your request: I shall not overthrow the town you speak of. But flee there quickly, because I can do nothing until you are there.' That is why the place was called Zoar. The sun had risen over the land as Lot entered Zoar, and the LORD rained down fire and brimstone from the skies on Sodom and Gomorrah. He overthrew those cities and destroyed all the plain, with everyone living there and everything growing in the ground. But Lot's wife looked back, and she turned into a pillar of salt.

Early next morning Abraham went to the place where he had stood in the presence of the LORD. As he looked over Sodom and Gomorrah and all the wide extent of the plain, he saw thick smoke rising from the earth like smoke from a kiln. Thus it was, when God destroyed the cities of the plain, he took thought for Abraham by rescuing Lot from the total destruction of the cities where he had been living.

Comments on the Story

The second section of chapter 18 established that God was a God of justice, one who would on no account destroy the righteous along with wicked. Also, the first section of the chapter indicated that the "outcry" of the cities of the plain had reached this God of justice. Thus the reader may anticipate that the just God will act now on that justice and that a more detailed account of the exact nature of that "outcry" will motivate the action.

While God and Abraham discuss the reality of divine justice (18:22-23), God's two companions, now identified as divine messengers, arrive at Sodom in the evening. The first person they meet is Lot, Abraham's nephew, who reappears in the story after an absence of five chapters (13:11-13). Lot's actions upon meeting these strangers mirror those of his famous uncle: "He rose to meet them and bowed with his face to the earth" (see 18:2 for the actions of Abraham). He immediately invites them into his home, urging them to spend the night with him and to take refreshment with him. Lot, in short, plays the perfect Middle Eastern host, just as Abraham did.

But the messengers refuse quite bluntly and say, "No! We will sleep in the street." Lot, however, "entreats them strongly," and they agree to stay with him for the night. Lot prepares for them a generous feast, which they all enjoy together. But just before they retire for the night, there is a loud commotion in the streets outside. The translation of the next line is very important. "The *people* of the city, the *people* of Sodom, surrounded the house, from the youngest to the oldest, *all the people* to the last one" (v. 4). The first two instances of the

98

word that I have translated "people" come from a Hebrew word that is a synonym for the word *'adam*, that word we read earlier as "human being" or "humanity" (see Gen. 2). The word *'enosh* is *never* used to mean a male. We must then conclude that those who surround the house of Lot and demand to have sex with the messengers are not only the men of Sodom, but the women as well, "from the youngest [under ten years of age] to the oldest, *all* the people." The word translated "people" is the word *am*, meaning "nation," and contains no hint of gender exclusiveness. *All* the Sodomites are depraved, both men and women, of whatever age, and the meaning of the "outcry" to God becomes clearer. We need to remember in this context the story of the great flood and the reasons given for its coming at Genesis 6:5: *"Every* imagination of the thoughts of their hearts was *only* evil *all day long."* Just as people before the flood were described as wholly evil, so also are *all* of the people of Sodom; the reader may now expect some sort of universal cataclysm with the possible rescue of one man and his family.

Yet, it is not merely a question of diseased sexual desires which constitute the evil of Sodom and will bring on the destruction. Verse 8 offers another explanation. Lot goes outside in an attempt to dissuade his neighbors from acting in this wicked way: "Look! I have two daughters who have never known a man; let me bring them out to you in order that you may do to them whatever you want. But as for these men, do nothing to them, for they have come under the shelter of my roof" (19:8). One of the major themes of chapters 18 and 19 is that of appropriate hospitality. Abraham and Lot know about hospitality, while the people of Sodom have no conception of it at all. The rule of hospitality in the ancient community is very strong, and Lot's appalling offer of his own daughters instead of the strangers who have come to stay with him makes the strength of the demand as certain as anything could. Thus both sexual depravity and the perhaps more basic concern of denied hospitality make up the "outcry" about the people of Sodom.

The complete evil of the people makes it impossible for them to hear the entreaties of Lot. They rush toward Lot's house and attempt to break down the door, but the mysterious strangers snatch Lot from their hands and strike all of the people blind. Once safely back in the house, the messengers announce the real reason for their visit to Sodom. The evidence of the evil of the city is overwhelming, so they offer Lot the chance to warn any members of his family—sons-in-law, sons, daughters—to get out of the city, "for we are about to destroy this place" (19:13).

Lot dutifully rushes off to warn his sons-in-law about the coming catastrophe, "but to them it seemed like laughing" (19:14). The implication seems to be that the boys thought that Lot was joking, but the more important point is that the word translated "laughing" is the same word from which the name *Isaac* is formed. The laughter of disobedience, manifested by Abraham and

Sarah, appears again in the incredulity of Lot's relatives. God's actions in the world often call forth the laughter or ridicule of humanity.

The sons-in-law have missed their chance to be saved. Just as the sun comes up, the messengers increase their urgent appeals to Lot. They demand that he take his wife and his daughters and flee, "lest you be consumed with the city's evil" (19:15). But, amazingly, "Lot hesitated, " forcing the messengers to grab him and his wife and his two daughters and physically drag them out of the city. This was done only because "the Lord had compassion (*chamol*) on him." (This word is found at Exod. 2:6, where Pharaoh's daughter took a look at the baby Moses, floating in his little ark, and "had compassion on him," thus saving him from the death sentence of her father. In a similar way, God's compassion will now save Lot.)

But Lot seems less than grateful for his being saved. The messengers demand that they all flee for their lives to the hills, not looking back toward anything in the accursed valley (19:17). But Lot refuses to flee to the hills, demanding instead that he be allowed to go to a nearby *city,* insisting that he will be destroyed if he goes to the hills. He says that the city is just "a little one"; its name is then revealed to us as Zoar, a Hebrew word for "little." Here, then, is an old explanation for the name of that place.

The destruction of God is universal, *"all* the valley and *all* the inhabitants of the city and whatever grew on the ground" (19:25). Lot's unfortunate wife disobeys the express command of the messengers and looks back at the destruction, and she immediately turns into a pillar of salt. By this dramatic action the narrator adds to the several portraits of disobedience in the chapter, from the "laughter" perceived by Lot's sons-in-law to Lot's own hesitation to Lot's wife's looking back at the place of evil. God's plans find human obstacles at nearly every turn, but the plan is fulfilled in any case. And so shall it be with the promise of the child for Abraham and Sarah.

A most peculiar story closes the chapter. Lot is in effect seduced by his own daughters, each in turn. They become pregnant by their father, and each gives birth to a son, one named Ammon and the other named Moab. On the surface this story seems to provide ammunition for hatred of Israel's near neighbors to the south and east, describing their origins in the incestuous relationship of Lot and his daughters. Still, whether the story arose for that reason or came to be understood in that way in the later history of Israel is beyond our knowledge. We can say that this story is in one important way very like the story we have been reading about Abraham. In a desperate situation, where a child must be born to ensure the continuance of family and a tribe and nation (see 19:31), children *will* be born to make a future possible, however astonishing the birth. Incest, a very ancient taboo, brings about a future for Ammon and Moab. In a similar way, an astonishing birth to an aged couple soon will provide a future for the promise of God and thus for the whole world.

Retelling the Story

She had never known anything else. Life was just like that. Her father and mother, her sisters and brothers, uncles, aunts, cousins, all her acquaintances and friends were that way. What else could she do? When you were raised in Sodom, you acted like that.

No, not only like *that*. I know what you are thinking, that all of us spent our days in bed with one another and did not bother to inquire about just who (or what?) our partner was. Well, we won't deny it, there was a lot of that going on. It is just the way we are; we've always done that. That's what life in Sodom is like. It's also that way in Gomorrah, too, as I have heard, but I've never been there, so don't quote me. And it is true that whenever any strangers showed up, we quickly went after them to initiate them into the ways of the city, if you get my drift, and I expect you do.

Oh, we knew all about the old laws of hospitality, how you were supposed to treat the sojourners, the part-time visitors, with special care and concern. But we in Sodom enjoyed thumbing our noses at convention and custom, both of which seemed terribly old-fashioned and stuffy, and certainly had a nasty way of dampening a good time, if you know what I mean, and I think you do. So, it wasn't just our unusual sexual proclivities, often laced with the added excitement of violence, that upset the snooty outsiders; it was our complete refusal to honor any of *their* laws and customs. Why should we? If they don't like it, they can keep their long noses out of our city. We do what we like, and we like what we do!

But back to the girl. Two delicious strangers had come to the city about dusk, and word had gotten around; the

Sodom had very exacting standards for the height of its visitors. If a stranger entered the city, that visitor would be placed on a bed of a certain length. If the visitor was too short, he or she would be stretched to fit; if too tall, the visitor would be mashed and pressed until he or she fit. It must have been very important in Sodom that everyone conform to the people's idea of perfection. (Ginzberg, vol. 1, p. 247.)

The rabbis said that a young woman of Sodom went to the well and there met another young woman. The second young woman was so weak from hunger that she could hardly carry her water jar. When the first asked why, the famished young woman told her that her family had no food. The girl from Sodom filled the other girl's jar with flour and helped her carry it home. When the people of Sodom discovered their young citizen's kindness they burned her at the stake. (*Genesis Rabbah* 44.6)

The tradition says that the citizens of Sodom, though so wealthy that their streets were paved with gold, did not show hospitality to strangers. They would punish anyone who shared food with a stranger and even checked their trees to make sure the birds had not eaten from them. (Plaut, pp. 134-35)

The reason ten righteous persons could not be found was not necessarily that all the citizens came to Lot's house, but those who didn't come never tried to stop those who did or even speak out against them. To condone injustice is just as bad as participating in it. (Plaut, p. 135)

grapevine in Sodom was always efficient. As usual, all of us, I mean *all* of us, hit the streets, and headed for the house of that foreigner, Lot. By the time we got to the house, the crowd was immense, and we were anxious for a good time. We demanded that the fool send those strangers outside so we could get at them. I noticed that the girl was shouting even louder than the rest of us; oh, she wanted some fun all right! Well, stupid Lot tried to calm us down (fat chance!), offering us his two daughters instead of the strangers. *He* took that hospitality stuff awfully seriously, didn't he? We shouted that he had no business telling us what to do, and besides we really wanted to see those strangers.

We pressed closer to the door of the house, the sheer weight of the mass of people driving us to trample those unfortunate enough to be in the front. For some reason, I looked at the girl's eyes at just that moment. And as I looked, they turned completely white! The pupils just disappeared! I remember being quite sorry for her at that moment, as she scrambled blindly to escape the writhing human herd. She was the last thing I ever saw; her falling form, crushed under the mob, is imprinted on my brain forever, because I, too, became blind in a way I still have no way of understanding.

We *all* became blind, so we did not see Lot leave, but we heard him go, dragged away from our city by those two strangers. He took those daughters with him, I suppose. Never to see again! It seems unimaginable, horrible. Still, the things I have seen in my life in Sodom. . . . Well, not many of them were really worth seeing. But . . . what? What is that sound? Heat, great heat, burning, burning. . . .

Abraham Lies Again

This is another version of the story of Abraham's attempting to pass Sarah off as his sister, rather than as his wife.

The Story

Abraham journeyed by stages from there into the Negeb, and settled between Kadesh and Shur, living as an alien in Gerar. He said of Sarah his wife that she was his sister, and King Abimelech of Gerar had her brought to him. But God came to Abimelech in a dream by night and said, 'You shall die because of this woman whom you have taken; she is a married woman.' Abimelech, who had not gone near her, protested, 'Lord, will you destroy people who are innocent? He told me himself that she was his sister, and she also said that he was her brother. It was in good faith and in all innocence that I did this.' 'Yes, I know that you acted in good faith,' God replied in the dream. 'Indeed, it was I who held you back from committing a sin against me. That was why I did not let you touch her. But now send back the man's wife; he is a prophet and will intercede on your behalf, and you will live. But if you do not give her back, I tell you that you are doomed to die, you and all your household.'

Next morning Abimelech rose early and called together all his court officials; when he told them the whole story, the men were terrified. Abimelech then summoned Abraham. 'Why have you treated us like this?' he demanded. 'What harm have I done you that you should bring this great sin on me and my kingdom? You have done to me something you ought never to have done.' And he asked, 'What was your purpose in doing this?' Abraham answered, 'I said to myself, "There is no fear of God in this place, and I shall be killed for the sake of my wife." She is in fact my sister, my father's daughter though not by my mother, and she became my wife. When God set me wandering from my father's house, I said to her, "There is a duty towards me which you must loyally fulfil: wherever we go, you must say I am your brother." ' Then Abimelech took sheep and cattle and male and female slaves and gave them to Abraham. He returned Sarah to him and said, 'My country is at your disposal; settle wherever you please.' To Sarah he said, 'I have given your brother a thousand pieces of silver to compensate you for all that has befallen you; you are completely cleared.' Then Abraham interceded with God, and he healed Abimelech, his wife, and his slave-girls, so that they could have children; for the LORD had made every woman in Abimelech's household barren on account of Sarah, Abraham's wife.

Comments on the Story

The story now returns to Abraham. His stature has increased in the eyes of the reader after his demonstration of wonderful hospitality to the three strangers in the desert and after his lesson to God about the necessity of divine justice in the world. It may then be surprising to some to find at this point another story of the bold-faced lie about Sarah, which is somehow related to the earlier story in chapter 12. Why is this story told to us now? As we examine it in more detail, we will want to keep that concern uppermost in our minds.

This account of the lie is set in the southern region of the land of Israel near the territory of the Negeb. The structuring of this story is quite different from the one found in chapter 12. The narrator this time begins with the lie without explanation: Abraham said of Sarah, his wife, 'She is my sister' " (20:2). As a result of the lie, Abimelech, king of Gerar, takes Sarah into his harem. In the earlier story, Abraham gives us an explicit and precise reason for having lied; he does it to save his own skin. Here, the reader is given the fact of the lie, but is not told what is at stake in the lie. This time the story has an inductive shape; that is, we have the facts, but are led to discover the reason for those facts. This technique is the very opposite of the one called dramatic irony, an example of which may be found in chapter 18.

Immediately, the story departs radically from the earlier one. "God came to Abimelech in a dream by night and said, 'You are dead because of the woman whom you have taken; she is married!' " The narrator assures us quickly that "Abimelech had not approached her," a problem that may have concerned more than a few readers. Yet, Abimelech's first statement to God is rather different from what we might have expected. "Lord [he uses the common address to superiors, but not the divine name], would you even kill an innocent people?" (20:4). Abimelech is combative about the injustice of the situation, rather than fearful in the face of divine power. We are thus returned to the dialogue of chapter 18, where Abraham teaches God about justice. Now even a foreign king is made to lecture the divine one. Clearly, this question of divine justice is central for the narrators of Genesis and especially for the cycle of the Abraham stories. Abimelech proceeds to state his very strong case against punishment: "Did he not himself say, 'She is my sister?' And she, yes she herself, said, 'He is my brother.' With upright heart and innocent hands I have done this thing" (20:5). Thus a second question of the story of chapter 12 is raised: The foreign king really did nothing wrong. Hence, why should he be punished? The answer is that he will not be punished (unlike the plagues sent on Pharaoh in 12:17), because God knew all of this beforehand. "Yes, I know that you did this with upright heart which is why I stopped you from sinning against me. That is why I did not let you touch her" (20:6). Sarah is untouched after all, thanks to the hidden protection of God, and Abimelech will apparently receive no punishment for his completely innocent actions, though members of his household are barren for a time.

Then God demands that Abimelech restore Sarah to Abraham, because "he is a prophet and will pray for you so that you will live." Refusal to restore her will result in the death of Abimelech and of all that he has. Not only is Sarah a man's wife, but also she is the wife of a prophet, a man of real power, the power of life and death in this case.

So Abimelech, in the face of this less than subtle divine threat, "rose early in the morning," and advises his servants that death could be their lot very soon. The servants are properly afraid, but Abimelech, who is a very feisty man indeed, still has some choice words for Abraham. "What have you done to us? What have I done to you that you have brought upon me and my kingdom a great sin? You have done to me things that ought not be done!" And he adds, "What were you thinking of that you did this thing?" These are rightfully angry words to a man who has lied to a king. In the chapter 12 story, Pharaoh asks similar angry questions of Abraham but receives no answer at all. Here, Abraham has an answer: Abraham said, "I thought that there really was no fear of God in this place; they will kill me because of my wife." Abraham suggests that Abimelech is an ungodly man, ruling over an ungodly kingdom, and as a result of that fact, his life would be taken so others might take his wife. Hence, he lied. Once again, this telling of the story picks up a problem of the earlier one. Abraham was not merely concerned for himself (compare 12:13); he found the theology of the people of Gerar to be somewhat lacking. And there is one more thing: "Besides she *is* my sister, the daughter of my father, but not my mother. She became my wife. And when God caused me to wander from the house of my father, I said to her, 'This is the kindness you will do for me. Every place to which we come say, "He is my brother." ' "

And so a fourth problem from the earlier story is addressed: Sarah really is Abraham's sister. Thus the sting is extracted from his lie; it was not completely bold-faced, even if still deceptive. Or is it? In reality, this story provides a picture of Abraham that is not very different from the one we saw in chapter 12. In fact, in some senses, this account is *worse*. It hardly cleans the lie up to announce, well *after* the fact and after "the Lord had closed all of the wombs of the house of Abimelech" (20:18), that Sarah really is his half-sister. Nor is it fully satisfactory to provide explanations so much after the fact about Abraham's theological concerns. In short, I do not think that the primary concern of this chapter is to "clean up" chapter 12.

Abimelech certainly never forgives him, and the money he gives Abraham is very specifically designated as "vindication for Sarah in the eyes of the public." It is to symbolize that she is spotless; nothing amiss occurred between Abimelech and her.

And so we return to the question: What is this story doing here? I think it is placed here to remind us of something we must never forget about God's chosen ones and about ourselves. No matter how impressive we may be at times in our lives, the fact remains that our deceptions and weaknesses are never far below the surface. Abraham may be able to call the Holy One to account for divine justice, but we must never think that his boldness somehow makes of him a divine person. He is human, all too human, as are we all. The child to be born comes from fully human stock; there is no place else from which he *could* come. Chapter 20 is a warning: Abraham is a mighty character, but he remains human through and through.

Retelling the Story

That foreigner lied to me! Then he accused me and my people of being ungodly. He's a good one to judge. As long as we are assessing each other, I would say that this Abraham is a coward as well as a liar.

He told me that Sarah was his sister, and she went along. Understand me now, I am not blaming her. She is obviously a woman of intelligence as well as beauty. In fact, I never touched her—I mean not that way. We talked. That's right, believe it or not, I would rather talk to her than share any other intimacy with any other woman in my harem.

The woman is a princess and deserves better than that wandering liar of a prophet. I told her I could make her a queen, give her anything she wanted. But she is not one whose affections can be bought.

Then one night after the most delightful conversation with Sarah I came to my bed, only to be troubled by dreams. In one dream the God of this so-called prophet and this princess appeared to set me straight. In truth, I liked Abraham's God far better than I liked Abraham—at least this God is no liar. Besides in the dream I was told

> The rabbis say that Abimelech was angry with Abraham for treating Sarah as if she were property to be traded. "You went to Egypt and treated her like merchandise and then came here and tried to trade her like cargo. Do not treat her so again. I will give you what your God requires, but for Sarah's sake. She should be robed in royal garments and her beauty veiled as such a noble woman deserves." (*Genesis Rabbah* 52.12)

> Some tell that God sent an angel to protect Sarah from Abimelech's advances and that the angel had a whip to keep him away from her. Some also say that Sarah was the first to tell the king the truth that she was Abraham's wife. (*Genesis Rabbah* 52.13)

that it was Sarah's God who had protected her honor (by creating in her such a wise and witty companion, I presume) and kept me from meeting an even worse fate.

The only problem is that I had to allow Sarah to return to that nomad and get him to intercede for me. That really galled me at first. But by this time I would have done almost anything for Sarah.

So I gave them cattle, sheep, slaves, and money and told Sarah she could settle anywhere she wanted in my country. But I made sure she understood that it was for her sake, not for that husband—brother or whatever he is.

Now they are gone, and there will be the shouts and laughter of children in my palace again. But there will never be another like her, whose words still shine like a lamp in the chambers of my memory, bringing with them light and warmth.

A Son Is Born; a Son Is Driven Out

Finally, a son is born to Abraham and Sarah. The beginning of the promise is named Isaac, meaning laughter.

The Story

The LORD showed favour to Sarah as he had promised, and made good what he had said about her. She conceived and at the time foretold by God she bore a son to Abraham in his old age. The son whom Sarah bore to him Abraham named Isaac, and when Isaac was eight days old Abraham circumcised him, as decreed by God. Abraham was a hundred years old when his son Isaac was born. Sarah said, 'God has given me good reason to laugh, and everyone who hears will laugh with me.' She added, 'Whoever would have told Abraham that Sarah would suckle children? Yet I have borne him a son in his old age.' The boy grew and was weaned, and on the day of his weaning Abraham gave a great feast.

Sarah saw the son whom Hagar the Egyptian had borne to Abraham playing with Isaac, and she said to Abraham, 'Drive out this slave-girl and her son! I will not have this slave's son sharing the inheritance with my son Isaac.' Abraham was very upset at this because of Ishmael, but God said to him, 'Do not be upset for the boy and your slave-girl. Do as Sarah says, because it is through Isaac's line that your name will be perpetuated. I shall make a nation of the slave-girl's son, because he also is your child.'

Early next morning Abraham took some food and a full water-skin and gave them to Hagar. He set the child on her shoulder and sent her away, and she wandered about in the wilderness of Beersheba. When the water in the skin was finished, she thrust the child under a bush, then went and sat down some way off, about a bowshot distant. 'How can I watch the child die?' she said, and sat there, weeping bitterly. God heard the child crying, and the angel of God called from heaven to Hagar, 'What is the matter, Hagar? Do not be afraid: God has heard the child crying where you laid him. Go, lift the child and hold him in your arms, because I shall make of him a great nation.' Then God opened her eyes and she saw a well full of water; she went to it, filled the water-skin, and gave the child a drink. God was with the child as he grew up. He lived in the wilderness of Paran and became an archer; and his mother got him a wife from Egypt.

About that time Abimelech, with Phicol the commander of his army, said to Abraham: 'God is with you in all that you do. Here and now swear to me in the name of God, that you will not break faith with me or with my children and my descendants. As I have kept faith with you, so must you

108

keep faith with me and with the country where you are living.' Abraham said, 'I swear it.'

It happened that Abraham had a complaint to make to Abimelech about a well which Abimelech's men had seized. Abimelech said, "I do not know who did this. Up to this moment you never mentioned it, nor did I hear of it from anyone else.' Then Abraham took sheep and cattle and gave them to Abimelech, and the two of them made a pact. Abraham set seven ewe lambs apart, and when Abimelech asked him why he had

done so, he said, 'Accept these seven lambs from me as a testimony on my behalf that I dug this well.' This is why that place was called Beersheba, because there the two of them swore an oath. When they had made the pact at Beersheba, Abimelech departed with Phicol the commander of his army and returned to the country of the Philistines. Abraham planted a tamarisk tree at Beersheba, and there he invoked the LORD, the Everlasting God, by name. He lived as an alien in the country of the Philistines for many years.

Comments on the Story

There are three separate concerns in this chapter, but they are all significant for the ongoing story we are reading. At long last, after waiting for many chapters through doubt and difficulty, the child of the promise is born. "The Lord visited Sarah just as the Lord said. The Lord did to Sarah just what the Lord said" (21:1). The obvious repetition here, and the emphasis on the fulfillment of "just what the Lord said," announces to the reader that the promise of God is about to be consummated. Sarah gives birth to a son in Abraham's old age (not to mention her own!) "at the time when God had told him." Abraham quickly names the son Isaac ("laughter") and circumcises him "just as God had commanded him" (21:4).

Then, to fix the child's name in the ear of the reader, the narrator gives to Sarah a lovely speech: "God has made laughter for me. All who hear it will laugh [with joy] because of me. Who would have thought that Sarah would suckle children! But I have borne him a son in his old age" (21:6-7). The laughter of doubt and derision has become the glad laughter of the aged couple and all of their friends. But the narrator is not quite finished with the word *laughter*.

Isaac grows up and is weaned from his mother. On the day of the weaning, Abraham has a great feast to celebrate his beloved son's first step toward manhood. But Sarah's eyes are not on her son, but on the son of her Egyptian maid, Hagar: "Sarah saw the son of Hagar the Egyptian, whom she had born to Abraham, laughing." That is a nearly literal reading of the Hebrew text. The Greek translation of the text, the Septuagint, adds the phrase "with her son Isaac." As is often the case, the spare quality of the Hebrew strikes with greater power. Sarah sees that the older boy, Ishmael, is laughing—that is, enjoying himself at the feast given in honor of her son. His laughter (it *is* the same root from which Isaac is named) seems to mock her joy, perhaps bringing back her own doubting laughter and reminding her that there remains an older child of her husband's who could still cause problems for her darling Isaac.

In a fury, she demands that Abraham "throw out this slave woman and her son, because the son of this slave woman shall not be heir with my son, with Isaac" (21:10). Sarah refuses to name Hagar but twice she separates herself from her by use of the demonstrative pronoun and by calling her "slave woman," a demeaning term. Note, too, that Isaac is *her* child, not Abraham's and not *ours*.

Verse 11 is deliciously ambiguous: "The idea was very evil to Abraham because of his son." Abraham says nothing to the demand of Sarah; he silently considers the idea of throwing out Hagar and Ishmael to be evil, "because of his son." Which son does he have in mind? The obvious answer is Ishmael, but his concern must also be for Isaac, who must witness the family turmoil and suffer the loss of his half-brother. As in chapter 16, Abraham takes no initiative when confronted by the angry demands of Sarah and acts only after God reveals to him that all of this is somehow the divine will (21:12-13). God reminds him that because Ishmael is his child, he, too, will become a "nation," but that Abraham's descendants will arise through Isaac.

Thus reassured, Abraham sends Hagar and Ishmael out into the blasted wilderness of Beersheba, provisioned only with "bread and a skin of water." Abraham by this action attempts to satisfy the angry command of his jealous wife, but gives something of a chance for survival in the desert to Hagar and Ishmael. But the inadequacy of Abraham's meager gifts becomes clear all too soon, as the water runs out quickly. In terrible desperation and pain, Hagar puts her child under a bush to give him what comfort she can from the merciless sun, and then she goes away about the distance of a bowshot, because she cannot bear to watch her child die of exposure.

The Hebrew text then says that "she lifted up her voice and wept." The fact that the next line (21:17) says that "God heard the voice of the child" caused the Greek translators to read the previous line "he lifted up his voice and wept," referring to the cries of the child. That change is a rational one, but an incorrect one. The emphasis of the story is on the pain of Hagar, on her foul treatment at the hands of Sarah and Abraham. She is at this point of the story thoroughly innocent and completely undeserving of this oppression. Her tragedy is all the more powerful if we see her weep over the cruel fate of her child, born from her body only at the direct request of Sarah and the eager involvement of Abraham.

In any case, "God hears [the literal meaning of "Ishmael"] the voice of the lad" (21:17), and tells Hagar not to be afraid. God's messenger tells her: "Arise, lift up the child, hold him tight by the hand, because I will make him a

110

great nation." Suddenly, God reveals to Hagar a nearby well, from which she fills the skin and gives a life-giving drink to Ishmael.

In quick strokes, the narrator describes the growth of Ishmael, how he lives in the wilderness, becoming especially adept with the bow. Eventually, Hagar gets a wife for him from her home country, Egypt. In all of this, "God was with the lad" (21:20).

What effect will all of this have on our telling this story? Just because the child of the promise is finally in the world is no certain guarantee that the blessing of God will be with all people. Quite the contrary! The immediate result of the miraculous birth is anger, jealousy, rejection, banishment, and near death. Because human beings are the carriers of the promise, one must always be ready for obstacles to appear. Also, God's promise to end activity in the world is hardly restricted to Israel alone; God "makes great nations" outside of Israel. At an early point in the compilation and editing of the Bible, the universality of this God is being urged upon all readers and tellers of these stories.

The third section of this complex chapter returns us to the relationship with Abimelech, king of Gerar (see Gen. 20). Abimelech sees the great prosperity of Abraham and concludes that "God is with you in all that you do" (21:22). But before the wary king can agree to make a contract with Abraham, he must "swear to me here by God that you will not deal falsely with me as I have dealt loyally with you" (21:23). Abraham so swears, and when a dispute about a well arises between the two, Abraham and Abimelech make a covenant with each other, Abraham offering to the king seven ewe lambs. When Abimelech asks the meaning of the seven lambs, Abraham says they are a living symbol that he dug the disputed well. As a result of that symbol, the well is known as Beersheba, or "well of the seven." However, another possible explanation of the name is "well of the oath," as verse 31 suggests.

Again we find a storied explanation of an existing condition, but there is more here than just that. In this brief account, the blessing of God through Abraham is in fact active and working.

King Abimelech makes covenant with the blessed man and receives the reward of that blessing. But the wariness of the king due to the lies of the blessed one remind us never to elevate Abraham beyond the level of humankind. We need to remember that as we prepare to read the next astonishing story. Just when we thought that the promise was now fulfilled for all time, the greatest threat to it of all comes, and the source this time is not a human one.

Retelling the Story

If only I could find some water! This terrible desert is no place to be without water! That miserable Abraham! His attempt to assuage his conscience with that tiny skin of water and a little bit of bread is scant comfort to me and Ishmael now. Both are long gone. How could he treat his own firstborn like this? How could he treat me, the mother of the boy, like this? Why has he sent us into the desert to our certain deaths? What has gotten into him, anyway?

Well, of course, I know precisely what has gotten into him; it is the insane jealousy of his shrewish wife, Sarah. I was as astonished as anyone when she managed to get pregnant at her age. I still suspect that there was some magic in it; surely ninety-year-old women do not get pregnant! It was still not too bad as long as the miracle child was a baby, but the day the boy was weaned, the day of the feast, my Ishmael was doing nothing more than having a good time. He was laughing with pleasure at all the fun, when from nowhere Sarah exploded, telling Abraham that he must throw me and my son (*his* son, too) out into the wilderness. She saw us as some sort of a threat to the exclusive rights of her Isaac. I *never* said or even implied that Isaac was not a unique child, who had the clear claim, as child of the woman of the promise, to be Abraham's heir. But Sarah was, I guess, taking no chances. She wanted us banished from her tents and her life forever.

> The rabbis, who were not too fond of Ishmael, said that his making sport was mocking those who celebrated at Isaac's birth. He told them that they had nothing to celebrate, since he was the firstborn and would receive all the benefits of that station. This is what angered Sarah. (*Genesis Rabbah* 53.12)

I expected better from my husband. He had fathered my child; what else would you call him but husband? Surely, he would defend me, his wife, and if not me, his firstborn son. I was astounded and enraged when he said nothing at all! He looked displeased, but I could not tell if he was displeased because of Sarah's cruel request or because of the threat to our Ishmael or because he found himself in the terribly awkward position of having to choose between his children. He often was a maddeningly indecisive man!

After silently hearing Sarah's demands for our death, Abraham left us alone. I later learned that he was convinced that God had told him that somehow our Ishmael was going to be the forebear of a great nation. That, he felt, gave him the right to make his choice, in effect washing his hands of the whole affair!

So he threw us out with that pathetic water-skin and that tiny piece of old bread. I hope he is satisfied! I hope he can sleep at night, having the deaths of his loving spouse and his eldest son on his conscience. What did I ever do to deserve this from him? I received his amorous advances and delivered the child, thus fulfilling my assigned function. It was, after all, insane Sarah's decision to do all this; Abraham seemed only too willing to fulfill the wishes of his wife in that case, too. Earlier he had been eager to embrace a young and vital woman after years of emptiness with that old hag. But what do I get in return? A blazing sun, a dying son, and a desert grave. Ah, God! At least hide from my eyes the death of my child, and let my death be swift after his. But, God, do not forget my death, though all the world seems ready to forget. I die innocent, as does Ishmael. Do not forget, O God! And do not forget, O world! My son, my son! Would that we could both live!

There is a way to tell the true seed of God in the world, according to the rabbis. Those who look for and see God's wisdom and justice in this world, even when the evil prosper and the righteous suffer, are "true seed." Those who do not see God's wisdom and justice beyond the appearance of the world are not. (*Genesis Rabbah* 53.12)

The Binding of Isaac

Abraham faces the possibility of losing the son he loves and the promise of a great and numerous family when he follows God's command to sacrifice the boy. But don't be alarmed; everything turns out well in the end.

The Story

Some time later God put Abraham to the test. 'Abraham!' he called to him, and Abraham replied, 'Here I am!' God said, 'Take your son, your one and only son Isaac whom you love, and go to the land of Moriah. There you shall offer him as a sacrifice on one of the heights which I shall show you.' Early in the morning Abraham saddled his donkey, and took with him two of his men and his son Isaac; and having split firewood for the sacrifice, he set out for the place of which God had spoken. On the third day Abraham looked up and saw the shrine in the distance. He said to his men, 'Stay here with the donkey while I and the boy go on ahead. We shall worship there, and then come back to you.'

Abraham took the wood for the sacrifice and put it on his son Isaac's shoulder, while he himself carried the fire and the knife. As the two of them went on together, Isaac spoke. 'Father!' he said. Abraham answered, 'What is it, my son?' Isaac said, 'Here are the fire and the wood, but where is the sheep for a sacrifice?' Abraham answered, 'God will provide himself with a sheep for a sacrifice, my son.'

The two of them went on together until they came to the place of which God had spoken. There Abraham built an altar and arranged the wood. He bound his son Isaac and laid him on the altar on top of the wood. He reached out for the knife to slay his son, but the angel of the LORD called to him from heaven, 'Abraham! Abraham!' He answered, 'Here I am!' The angel said, 'Do not raise your hand against the boy; do not touch him. Now I know that you are a godfearing man. You have not withheld from me your son, your only son.' Abraham looked round, and there in a thicket he saw a ram caught by its horns. He went, seized the ram, and offered it as a sacrifice instead of his son. Abraham named that shrine 'The LORD will provide'; and to this day the saying is: 'In the mountain of the LORD it was provided.'

Then the angel of the LORD called from heaven a second time to Abraham and said, 'This is the word of the LORD: By my own self I swear that because you have done this and have not withheld your son, your only son, I shall bless you abundantly and make your descendants as numerous as the stars in the sky or the grains of sand on the seashore.

Your descendants will possess the cities of their enemies. All nations on earth will wish to be blessed as your descendants are blessed, because you have been obedient to me.'

Abraham then went back to his men, and together they returned to Beersheba; and there Abraham remained.

After this Abraham was told, 'Milcah has borne sons to your brother Nahor: Uz his firstborn, then his brother Buz, and Kemuel father of Aram, and Kesed, Hazo, Pildash, Jidlaph, and Bethuel; and a daughter, Rebecca, has been born to Bethuel.' These eight Milcah bore to Abraham's brother Nahor. His concubine, whose name was Reumah, also bore him sons: Tebah, Gaham, Tahash, and Maacah.

Comments on the Story

This story can only come as a tremendous shock to any reader who has been carefully following the stories of Abraham. After waiting long years for the child of promise, years characterized by lying, confusion, and profound longing for the fulfillment of the ridiculous promise of God, the birth of the child gave us the freedom to sigh in relief. At last! God has indeed worked the miracle that brought birth out of the nearly dead couple. Still, we should have been rather less confident about the future of the child when we read of the fury and jealousy of Sarah with respect to the older child, Ishmael (21:8-14). Perhaps even the apparent fulfillment of the promise will not allow us to rest easy. Yet, in our wildest nightmares, we could hardly have imagined that God would demand death for the promise made by God.

The narrator begins with a very direct and very spare statement: "It happened after these things that God tested Abraham." The phrase "after these things" (see 15:1) is intended to be a reference to all of the events that have preceded this one. The deceptions and unbelief and vain human attempts to coerce the fulfillment of the promise flood back into our minds as we listen to this "test." In the Hebrew Bible the word suggests the possibility of failure. Abraham could *fail* this test. The fact that it is then a *real* test indicates that God is interested in finding out something about the chosen one, something God is apparently not absolutely certain about, even after the birth of the child.

Abraham responds readily to God's call, and then comes God's test: "Take your son, your only one, whom you love, Isaac, and go to the land of Moriah. Sacrifice him there as a sacrifice on one of the mountains of which I will tell you" (22:2). An old rabbinic reading of this story suggests what was in Abraham's mind as he heard this request: "Take your son (which one), your only son (both are only sons, one of Hagar and one of Sarah), the one you love (I love them both!), Isaac (oh, the child of promise)." This piece of speculation points to the delay in the announcement of the child to be sacrificed, thereby increasing the tension of a narrative that will be characterized by tension.

The long-awaited child is to be killed on a distant mountain! God demands the child as sacrifice, but the human effect of the demand is nothing less than murder. It is customary at this point in the story to inject natural human reactions to this bizarre request, the reaction of Abraham to the command is to go to sleep! That is the force of the verb that begins verse 3; it indicates a period of sleep. This fact is eloquent witness to Abraham's willingness to perform the deed. He "rises early in the morning, saddles his ass, takes two lads with him, and his son Isaac, cuts the wood for the burnt offering, and arises and goes to the place of which God told him." The actions are performed in silence and with obvious resolution. There is no remonstrance, no argument, no complaint. We have seen time and again in earlier stories about this man that he has not been reluctant to complain and to argue. His silence in the face of this command is literally deafening.

The little group arrives at the place after a quick three-day journey. Upon arriving, Abraham tells the two lads, "Stay here with the ass; I and the lad will go up there, we will worship, and we will come again to you" (22:5). All verbs are plural; we should not conclude, however, that Abraham is somehow convinced that he and his son will in fact return together from the mountain. He appears to be assuaging the fears of the two servants, and he seems intent on performing the command of his God.

Abraham takes the wood for the sacrifice and puts it on Isaac's shoulder, while he takes in his own hands the flint for the fire and the knife. The text then says, "So they went both of them together." The reader must be touched at this point; their togetherness is soon to end. The narrator is merely tugging at our heart-strings. "Here are fire and wood" (he does not mention the knife), says Isaac, "But where is the lamb for a burnt offering?" Abraham responds, "God will provide a lamb for a burnt offering, my son." The full irony of Abraham's reply can be felt if a long pause is taken after the comma; when the son *is* the sacrifice, the irony is rich indeed. And the narrator repeats the earlier phrase, "So they went both of them together."

Abraham builds an altar on the appointed spot, lays the wood in order, "binds" (the Hebrew word *akedah,* the traditional Jewish title of this story) Isaac, and lays him upon the altar on the wood. He then grabs the knife to kill his son, following to the letter the strict command of God. But from heaven comes the welcome voice of God's messenger, urging Abraham to stop, because "now I know that you are in awe of God in that you have not withheld your son, your only one from me." Abraham looks behind him and sees a ram stuck in a bush. He rushes over to the ram and offers it instead of his son Isaac. He then names the place where all of these events have occurred "the Lord will provide" or, in another possible translation, "the Lord will see." The place and

116

the event have even given rise to a proverb still well known in the time of the writer, "On the mount of the Lord it will be provided" (or "it will be seen").

The story continues, however, as the messenger comes to Abraham a second time and reiterates the patriarchal blessing, joining together for the first time in the entire story the two metaphors of "stars of the sky" and "sand on the shore" as indications of the descendants Abraham may anticipate. It is fully appropriate that the promise of blessing should be spoken here; Abraham has passed the test of God and is fully worthy of the great charge to which he has been called.

To indicate that the blessing is operative, the chapter closes with a short genealogy wherein Abraham's relatives are having children too numerous to count. The blessing of Abraham is working!

In one crucial respect, this chapter is the climax of the story of Abraham. The chosen one of God has lied and laughed, but now has triumphed. The promised child, the very symbol of the presence and power of God, has become for Abraham *not* the necessity for his belief in that presence that the story has urged almost from its beginning. Abraham has moved beyond the need to see any tangible evidence of the presence and certainty of God's promise. Though the child were to die, the promise would still be alive, although in ways that Abraham cannot even imagine. Little wonder that the author of the letter to Hebrews defined faith as "the assurance of things hoped for, the conviction of things not seen" (Heb. 11:1), and turned to Abraham's actions at the mountain as confirmation of the definition (Heb. 11:17-19). After this story, Abraham's name becomes for all time synonymous with the risk and triumph of faith.

Retelling the Story

The children came to their teacher with a question that clearly troubled them. "We have heard stories that other people in other countries kill their children to please their gods. Is that true?"

The teacher heard fear buoying up the children's words, but answered honestly, "That's very true. In fact in our own city, Jerusalem, there is a valley that belonged to the sons of Hinnom where people sacrificed children before our people came to live here. Now we use that name for a place of torment, Gehenna."

"Did our people ever do anything so horrible?" asked one small voice almost too soft to hear.

"Of course not!" "We're not barbarians!" "Never!" came the voices of the other children, washing over the questioner like a tidal wave.

"Don't be so sure," the teacher interrupted, "It did happen—almost—only once."

"When?" The children's mouths were open with disbelief, and their eyes were wide and round as birds' eyes.

"Once God decided to test Grandfather Abraham," the teacher began, "and told him that he was to sacrifice his son."

"Which one," a child asked, "Ishmael or Isaac?"

"The son he loved," the teacher continued, pleased that someone remembered so much of their lessons.

"Surely he loved them both as our parents love us and our sisters and brothers." The children were being drawn into the suspense already.

"His only son," the teacher teased them with the mystery.

"But there were two," the students shouted in annoyed chorus.

"Isaac." The answer was spoken in a whisper. "After he slept, Abraham prepared to leave. With Isaac and two servants he traveled to the mountain God showed him. Abraham told the servants to wait while he and Isaac worshiped and that they would return. The father and son climbed the mountain, and Abraham made an altar ready for the sacrifice. 'I see the fire and wood for a sacrifice, but where is the lamb to be sacrificed?' Isaac asked. The old man answered his son without really answering him: 'God will provide the lamb,' was all he said. The answer came as Abraham began binding Isaac to the wood for the sacrifice. Just as he lifted the knife. . . . "

> Some say that Isaac was a willing participant in this drama. As he lay bound to the altar, he called on his father to tighten the bonds. He was afraid that Abraham's hand might tremble with grief or that he (Isaac) might move suddenly, causing the knife to scar him, making a blemish and, therefore, making him unfit for a sacrifice. (*Genesis Rabbah* 56.8)

"Don't do it! Stop! Wait" The children's shouts were a wild uproar filling the room.

"That's just what the angel said to Abraham. And when Abraham looked he found a ram caught by its horns in a thicket. So he sacrificed the ram instead of his son. Now you rough and rowdy angels may hear of other people sacrificing their children, but never among our people. You see, so we wouldn't forget that it almost happened once, our ancestors built the Temple on the very spot where Abraham almost sacrificed Isaac."

> The rabbis say that Abraham was so grieved by what he was about to do that his tears fell into Isaac's eyes, but he was willing to do even such a gruesome thing if God required it. Yet, at that moment, the angels cried out on behalf of Isaac. (*Genesis Rabbah* 56.8)

After his ordeal, Isaac was taken up to paradise for three years by the angels who had pleaded for his life. While Abraham and Isaac were gone, Satan had come to tell Sarah that her husband had taken their son to sacrifice him. When Sarah saw Abraham returning alone she assumed that he had killed Isaac, and she fell down dead. (Ginzberg vol 1, p. 286)

This linking the binding of Isaac with Sarah's death led some rabbis to speculate that Isaac was not a child but was 37 years old when he was almost sacrificed—since Sarah was 90 when he was born and 127 when she died. (*Genesis Rabbah* 56.8)

Isaac and Rebekah

Abraham sends to find a wife for his son Isaac so that the promise of God that his descendants will be a great nation will be realized. As a result Rebekah joins the family.

The Story

Abraham was by now a very old man, and the LORD had blessed him in all that he did. Abraham said to the servant who had been longest in his service and was in charge of all he owned, 'Give me your solemn oath: I want you to swear by the LORD, the God of heaven and earth, that you will not take a wife for my son from the women of the Canaanites among whom I am living. You must go to my own country and to my own kindred to find a wife for my son Isaac.' 'What if the woman is unwilling to come with me to this country?' the servant asked. 'Must I take your son back to the land you came from?' Abraham said to him, 'On no account are you to take my son back there. The LORD the God of heaven who took me from my father's house and the land of my birth, the LORD who swore to me that he would give this land to my descendants—he will send his angel before you, and you will take a wife from there for my son. If the woman is unwilling to come with you, then you will be released from your oath to me; only you must not take my son back there.' The servant then put his hand under his master Abraham's thigh and swore that oath.

The servant chose ten camels from his master's herds and, with all kinds of gifts from his master, he went to Aram-naharaim, to the town where Nahor lived. Towards evening, the time when the women go out to draw water, he made the camels kneel down by the well outside the town. 'LORD God of my master Abraham,' he said, 'give me good fortune this day; keep faith with my master Abraham. Here I am by the spring, as the women of the town come out to draw water. I shall say to a girl, "Please lower your jar so that I may drink"; and if she answers, "Drink, and I shall water your camels also," let that be the girl whom you intend for your servant Isaac. In this way I shall know that you have kept faith with my master.'

Before he had finished praying, he saw Rebecca coming out with her waterjar on her shoulder. She was the daughter of Bethuel son of Milcah, the wife of Abraham's brother Nahor. The girl was very beautiful and a virgin guiltless of intercourse with any man. She went down to the spring, filled her jar, and came up again. Abraham's servant hurried to meet her and said, 'Will you give me a little water from your jar?' 'Please drink, sir,' she answered, and at once lowered her jar on to her hand to let him drink. When she had finished giving him a drink, she said, 'I shall draw water for your camels also until they have had enough.' She quickly emptied her jar into the water trough, and then hurrying again to the well she drew water and watered all the camels.

The man was watching quietly to see whether or not the LORD had made his journey successful, and when the camels had finished drinking, he took a gold nose-ring weighing half a shekel, and two bracelets for her wrists weighing ten shekels, also of gold. 'Tell me, please, whose daughter you are,' he said. 'Is there room in your father's house for us to spend the night?' She answered, 'I am the daughter of Bethuel son of Nahor and Milcah; we have plenty of straw and fodder and also room for you to spend the night.' So the man bowed down and prostrated himself before the LORD and said, 'Blessed be the LORD the God of my master Abraham. His faithfulness to my master has been constant and unfailing, for he has guided me to the house of my master's kinsman.'

The girl ran to her mother's house and told them what had happened. Rebecca had a brother named Laban, and, when he saw the nose-ring, and also the bracelets on his sister's wrists, and heard his sister Rebecca's account of what the man had said to her, he hurried out to the spring. When he got there he found the man still standing by the camels. 'Come in,' he said, 'you whom the LORD has blessed. Why are you staying out here? I have prepared the house and there is a place for the camels.' The man went into the house, while the camels were unloaded and provided with straw and fodder, and water was brought for him and his men to bathe their feet. But when food was set before him, he protested, 'I will not eat until I have delivered my message.' Laban said, 'Let us hear it.'

'I am Abraham's servant,' he answered. 'The LORD has greatly blessed my master, and he has become a wealthy man: the LORD has given him flocks and herds, silver and gold, male and female slaves, camels and donkeys. My master's wife Sarah in her old age bore him a son, to whom he has assigned all that he has. My master made me swear an oath, saying, "You must not take a wife for my son from the women of the Canaanites in whose land I am living; but go to my father's home, to my family, to get a wife for him.' I asked, "What if the woman will not come with me?" He answered, "The LORD, in whose presence I have lived, will send his angel with you and make your journey successful. You are to take a wife for my son from my family and from my father's house; then you will be released from the charge I have laid upon you. But if, when you come to my family, they refuse to give her to you, you will likewise be released from the charge."

'Today when I came to the spring, I prayed, "LORD God of my master Abraham, if you will make my journey successful, let it turn out in this way: here I am by the spring; when a young woman comes out to draw water, I shall say to her, 'Give me a little water from your jar to drink.' If she answers, 'Yes do drink, and I shall draw water for your camels as well,' she is the woman whom the LORD intends for my master's son." Before I had finished praying, I saw Rebecca coming out with her water-jar on her shoulder. She went down to the spring and drew water, and I said to her, "Will you please give me a drink?" At once she lowered her jar from her shoulder and said, "Drink; and I shall also water your camels." So I drank, and she also gave the camels water. I asked her whose daughter she was, and she said, "I am the daughter of Bethuel son of Nahor and Milcah." Then I put the ring in her nose and the bracelets on her wrists, and I bowed low in worship before the LORD. I blessed the LORD, the God of my master Abraham, who had led me by the right road to take my master's niece for his son. Now tell me if you mean to deal loyally and faithfully with my master. If not, say so, and I shall turn elsewhere.'

Laban and Bethuel replied, 'Since this is from the LORD, we can say nothing for or against it. Here is Rebecca; take her and go. She shall be the wife of your master's son, as the LORD has decreed.' When Abraham's servant heard what they said, he prostrated himself on the ground before the LORD. Then he brought out silver and gold ornaments, and articles of clothing, and gave them to Rebecca, and he gave costly gifts to her brother and her mother. He and his men then ate and drank and spent the night there.

When they rose in the morning, Abraham's servant said, 'Give me leave to go back to my master.' Rebecca's brother and her mother replied, 'Let the girl stay with us for a few days, say ten days, and then she can go.' But he said to them, 'Do not detain me, for it is the LORD who has granted me success. Give me leave to go back to my master.' They said, 'Let us call the girl and see what she says. They called Rebecca and asked her if she would go with the man, and she answered, 'Yes, I will go.' So they let their sister Rebecca and her maid go with Abraham's servant and his men. They blessed Rebecca and said to her:

'You are our sister, may you be the mother of many children;
may your sons possess the cities of their enemies.'

Rebecca and her companions mounted their camels to follow the man. So the servant took Rebecca and set out.

Isaac meanwhile had moved on as far as Beer-lahai-roi and was living in the Negeb. One evening when he had gone out into the open country hoping to meet them, he looked and saw camels approaching. When Rebecca saw Isaac, she dismounted from her camel, saying to the servant, 'Who is that man walking across the open country towards us?' When the servant answered, 'It is my master,' she took her veil and covered herself. The servant related to Isaac all that had happened. Isaac conducted her into the tent and took her as his wife. So she became his wife, and he loved her and was consoled for the death of his mother.

Comments on the Story

This longest story in the patriarchal tradition serves as a kind of interlude in the ongoing rough and tumble stories that make up Genesis. Unlike the Abraham stories that precede it and the Jacob stories to follow, this story seems strangely peaceful, almost idyllic in tone. A very old Abraham sends his faithful servant back to the land of the clan's roots, to Mesopotamia and the city of Nahor (see 11:31), to find a suitable wife for his son Isaac. The servant does all that his master commands, and his faithful actions are rewarded with success; the beautiful Rebekah is secured as wife for Isaac.

The story is written in classic Hebrew narrative style. Abraham bids his servant go to Haran after he has made him swear an ancient oath that he will not give a Canaanite woman to Isaac for his wife. The servant is commanded to "put your hand under my thigh," a clear reference to the genitals, the source of power and life. At Genesis 47:29, the dying Jacob commands his son, Joseph, to put his hand under his thigh and swear that he will not allow Jacob to remain buried in Egypt. Similarly, Abraham is near death, and his greatest wish is that his son marry a woman of the clan rather than one of the local Canaanite women.

The servant is at first reluctant to swear such an oath, fearing that any woman he might find in the "old country" may not be willing to return with him. He is further afraid that he would then be forced to take Isaac back to Mesopotamia, thus requiring a second long and dangerous journey (24:5). But Abraham frees the anxious servant from such a requirement, telling him that the God who "took me from my father's house" and swore to him the promise of the land, will "send an angel before you, and you will take a wife for my son from there" (24:7). He continues by saying that "if the woman will not come," then the servant will be free of the oath. In other words, the servant is responsible merely to identify a suitable marriage partner in Haran; if she will not return with him to Israel, the servant will not be held responsible. He will not be forced to make a second journey no matter the outcome of the first. With those stipulations clear, the servant "put his hand under the thigh of Abraham his master, and swore to him concerning this thing" (24:9).

The servant departs on his trip, taking with him ten camels, a significant number, and "all sorts of choice gifts," the substance of which will play an important role in the story. Upon arriving in Nahor, he goes right to the well of the city, the place where one may expect to find the women, since it was commonly their task to draw water for their respective households (see Gen. 29 and Exod. 2 for similar stories). The servant prays to "the Lord, God of my master Abraham" for success in his venture. He asks that God "show steadfast love (*chesed*) to my master." If the covenant God has made with Abraham, the line of the promise of blessing to the nations, is to continue, an appropriate bride must be found for the heir of the promise, Isaac.

Like Gideon and his fleece (Judg. 6:36-40), the servant sets a series of criteria by which he may know whether God is showing steadfast love by providing a woman for Isaac. He will say to her, "Please let down your water jug that I may drink," to which she will say, "Drink and I will water your camels" (24:14).

"Before he had finished speaking, Rebekah, daughter of Bethuel, son of Milcah" (Gen. 22:23) came to the well. The narrator quickly adds that she was both "very beautiful to look at" and "a virgin, unknown by any man." The servant begins his overture, and Rebekah responds precisely as his prayer had required. But the prayer has not been fully answered yet, for the servant does not know what we know, that Rebekah *is* indeed of the appropriate family.

In his joy at the fulfillment of the first part of his prayer, he gives her costly jewelry, a gold nose ring and two bracelets, and only then asks her the crucial question: "Tell me whose daughter you are!" Upon hearing who she is, the servant "bows his head and worships the Lord," thanking the God who has not "abandoned steadfast love and faithfulness toward my master" (24:26-27).

Rebekah runs quickly to her brother, Laban, who rushes out to the man. Now comes the only place in this narrative where the narrator slyly offers us a keen insight into one of the characters, Laban, about whom we will hear much more: "When he [Laban] saw the ring, and the bracelets on his sister's arms, *and* when he heard the words of Rebekah, his sister, he went to the man" (24:30). We are asked to see that the *first* thing that attracted his attention was the fine quality of the jewelry the servant had given to his sister. Laban stands before us revealed for what he will later prove to be, a man very interested in money and fine things.

Laban readily invites the servant in for a meal, but the servant insists on telling of his errand *in full* before he eats, and this he proceeds to do in complete detail (24:24-49). Still, at the end of his long discourse the servant issues a challenge to those who have listened to his story of God's providence: "Now then, if you will deal with steadfast love (*chesed*) and faithfulness [see v. 27 above] with my master, tell me; but if not, tell me, that I may turn to the right or to the left" (24:49). In other words, if you are not clever enough to see the hand of an all-powerful divinity in these affairs, I will be happy to take my commission (including my jewels!) from my master elsewhere to those who can see the hand of God.

But Laban and Bethuel are wise enough to see God's action here, and they urge the servant to take Rebekah back with him. When the servant realizes that he is free to return with Rebekah, if she consents, he gives her many more fine gifts and gives to Laban and the mother "many costly ornaments." After a night's sleep, the servant is anxious to complete his mission. At first, Laban and his mother try to delay the return trip (24:55). It will not be the last time that Laban will attempt to delay a return trip to Israel, as the story of Jacob will make clear. But the servant insists on immediate departure, and so they begin the journey to Israel without further delay.

Isaac and Rebekah first meet while he is meditating in the field. He looks up and sees the camels coming home. Rebekah catches sight of the man and asks the servant who he is. When she finds out that it is Isaac, her husband-to-be, she quickly veils her face in the proper Middle Eastern way. Isaac brings her to his tent, and she becomes his wife. "And he loved her," the narrator adds with a lovely touch. Thus we know that the match of Isaac and Rebekah was one truly "made in heaven," or perhaps more accurately, one made by the guiding hand of God on earth. However, in the next cycle of stories about the patriarch Jacob, the guiding hand of God may not be quite so easy to discern

Retelling the Story

Time to go to the well again. Another trip to the well, just like yesterday, and the day before that, and the day before that! The well, as important as it was for all of their lives, had become the very symbol of sameness to Rebekah. Nothing ever seemed to change in this hot and dusty place. She lived in her parents' tent and had to share a part of it with her greedy brother Laban. Being a woman was no easy thing in this culture. She had few choices, and the ones she did have meant very little in the long run. She walked every day to the well, and she waited. Most of all, she waited—for a man to notice her, to take interest in her. It was hardly fair! She had laid her eyes on several of the young men of the tribe, but she could do little until they made the first move. She had been told that she was beautiful, and she had been trained in the good manners of her people, so what was the problem? These thoughts made her very unhappy as she moved toward the well one more time.

Standing close to the well today was a man she had never seen before. He was obviously a stranger, and by the look of his filthy clothes and his less than pleasant smell, he had traveled to the well from a great distance. As she dipped her jar into the well to fill it, the stranger moved quickly toward her. He was a small man, and he appeared to be kind, so she was not afraid. He asked her very politely for a drink, and she immediately gave him one. It was custom and common courtesy that she do so. Her eyes glanced behind the stranger while he thirstily drank from the cool water, and she noticed a small herd of fine camels, which apparently belonged to him.

Without a second thought, she began to water the camels. She noticed an odd smile on the face of the stranger as she completed the watering of the beasts. He, rather too eagerly she thought, asked her about her family. She told him, and his face exploded into a huge guffaw, while he danced around praising the name of his God. In a flash, he brought out lovely presents to give to her, gold rings and bracelets, such beautiful things beyond her wildest imaginings.

Rebekah ran with breathless haste and eager longing to tell her father and her brother about this wonderfully romantic meeting at the well. She did not know at all what to make of it, but at least it was a marvelous change from the dull days of her boring life. Before her father could say a word, her brother

> The rabbis play with the name of Laban (meaning white) to say that in addition to being a scoundrel he was very white—we can presume light-skinned. He was so because he had been refined or shined by his evil ways. (*Genesis Rabbah* 60.7)
>
> While Sarah was alive strangers were welcomed at her tent, and the divine presence dwelt there. After she died these ceased until Isaac brought Rebekah to his mother's tent. Then God's presence and the hospitality of the past were both returned. (*Genesis Rabbah* 60.16)

Laban cast his eyes on the gold and demanded to know where the man was. He made great noise about proper hospitality, but Rebekah knew what he was really after.

She ran to get the stranger, who came into the tent, but even before he would eat a thing he told his entire story to the family, including her greedy brother Laban. Rebekah listened as carefully as she could while she worked at the meal, and with growing excitement learned that there was a man in a far away country who was anxious for a bride, a man from their own larger family. Rebekah was thrilled with the romance and mystery of it all. It seemed that the ways in which she had treated the stranger and his beasts at the well had made all of this possible. She wanted to go right now to meet her prospective husband.

How disappointed she was to hear her family say that they should wait ten day before setting out on the journey! But the stranger was as anxious as she was to go, so they agreed to ask *her* what she wanted to do. She could hardly believe that they were asking her opinion! There was no hesitation at all in her voice; she was ready to go today. So she rode out with the stranger, heading west, away from the familiar, away from her family, away from the well of her imprisonment. She was not certain of what to expect, but it was adventure, it was romance, and it was mystery. Rebekah had made *her* choice, and for the first time in her life she felt truly alive.

The Birth of Esau and Jacob

Twins, named Jacob and Esau, are born to Isaac and Rebekah. We learn that these twin sons are as different as night and day, and their differences become evident even from the womb.

The Story

This is an account of the descendants of Abraham's son Isaac. Isaac's father was Abraham. When Isaac was forty years old he married Rebecca daughter of Bethuel, the Aramaean from Paddan-aram and sister of Laban the Aramaean. Isaac appealed to the LORD on behalf of his wife because she was childless; the LORD gave heed to his entreaty, and Rebecca conceived. The children pressed on each other in her womb, and she said, 'If all is well, why am I like this?' She went to seek guidance of the LORD, who said to her:

'Two nations are in your womb,
two peoples going their own ways
    from birth.
One will be stronger than the other;
the elder will be servant to the
    younger.'

When her time had come, there were indeed twins in her womb. The first to come out was reddish and covered with hairs like a cloak, and they named him Esau. Immediately afterwards his brother was born with his hand grasping Esau's heel, and he was given the name Jacob. Isaac was sixty years old when they were born. As the boys grew up, Esau became a skilful hunter, an outdoor man, while Jacob lived quietly among the tents. Isaac favoured Esau because he kept him supplied with game, but Rebecca favoured Jacob. One day Jacob was preparing broth when Esau came in from the country, exhausted. He said to Jacob, 'I am exhausted; give me a helping of that red broth.' This is why he was called Edom. Jacob retorted, 'Not till you sell me your rights as the firstborn.' Esau replied, 'Here I am at death's door; what use is a birthright to me?' Jacob said, 'First give me your oath!' So he gave him his oath and sold his birthright to Jacob. Then Jacob gave Esau bread and some lentil broth, and he ate and drank and went his way. Esau showed by this how little he valued his birthright.

Comments on the Story

After the interlude of the search for a bride for Isaac, the collectors of the cycle of Abraham stories insert a genealogy at the beginning of chapter 25 for

127

two reasons. First, the death of Abraham must be reported: "Abraham exhaled and died at a good age, an old man full of years, and was gathered to his fathers" (25:8). In a nice touch, the narrator tells us that both Isaac and Ishmael bury him in a cave at Machpelah, a place purchased for the purpose by Abraham himself (see Gen. 23). In death at least, the two sons, whose births brought on so much bitterness from their respective mothers, find a measure of unity.

The second reason for this section is found within the long list of the descendants of Ishmael (25:12-18). The story here affirms that the promise to Ishmael, given by God to his mother, Hagar (16:10), is being fulfilled. Also, the list of descendants ties the ancestry of many non-Israelite people directly to Abraham, especially the Arabian tribes (see also 25:2-4 as another attempt to illustrate the unity of Israelites and non-Israelites by the common ancestor, Abraham, this time through another wife, Keturah). Whatever strife occurs later in history between these groups (and conflict will almost never be absent!), originally they were related by blood. The fact that all three major religions arising from this region of the world—Judaism, Christianity, and Islam—trace their origins in one way or another to Abraham suggests that human and family ties run deeper than any subsequent political divisions.

But the main stream of the story is, of course, the family of Isaac, and the narrative returns to that stream in verse 19. Immediately, the story presents a familiar theme: "Isaac prayed to the Lord fervently for his wife, because she was barren" (25:21). The tension of the story increases as, once again, the line of the promise is threatened by an infertile couple. But unlike the long barrenness of Sarah, *the* problem that drove the stories of the cycle of Abraham, Isaac's prayer is answered very quickly, and Rebekah conceives. But there is something extraordinary about her pregnancy. "The children were crushing each other in her womb, so she said, 'If it is like this, why in the world am I alive?' " The verb translated "crushing (*ratsats*) is a violent word, appearing in contexts of social oppression and physical abuse (see, for example, Deut. 28:33; I Sam. 12:3; Isa. 42:4; Judg. 9:53). The Greek translation of the Hebrew Bible, the Septuagint, translates this word *skirtao*; the word appears later in the Gospel of Luke 1:41-44 as a description of the action of Elizabeth's baby in her womb at the greeting of Mary. "The babe leaped for joy," Luke says, but the crushing struggle in Rebekah's womb is no sign of joy. The subsequent struggle between these twin boys has already begun before their birth. And Rebekah's resulting cry of despair, which suggests that she would rather be dead than have to endure the struggle of her unborn children, also warns the reader that the story to follow will have more than its share of confusion and heartache.

To address her pain, Rebekah goes "to inquire of the Lord" (25:22). This means that she seeks an oracle from the divine realm to help her in her distress.

The Lord speaks to her in poetic address: "Two nations are in your womb/two peoples are dividing themselves even in your body. One is stronger than the other/but the elder will serve the younger" (25:23). This is a very important oracle for Rebekah and will give meaning to her actions later in the story; she is now convinced that the younger of the two children fighting in her womb is the one who will rule, not the elder as custom would have it.

She gives birth to twins. The name *Esau* has no grammatical relationship to the explanation of reddish hair all over the boy's body. It has some oral relationship to the word for "hairy"; the two words are *Esau* and *Se'ar*. In any case, this hairy son is the eldest, and Rebekah is certain that his destiny is to serve his younger brother.

The name *Jacob* in Hebrew is related to the word *heel*, which Jacob grabbed. Later in the cycle of Jacob stories (27:36), in an eighth-century prophetic book (Hos. 12:4), and in a seventh-century prophetic book (Jer. 9:3; 9:4 in English), the name comes to mean "deception" or "supplanting." As the story unfolds, Jacob is something of a "heel," but "deceiver" or "supplanter" is clearly the meaning intended here.

The narrative wastes no time. "The lads grew. Esau became a skillful hunter, a man of the open fields, while Jacob was a quiet man, living in tents" (25:27). The word translated "quiet" is often used in the sense of moral integrity and uprightness (see especially Job 1:1, 8; 8:20; 9:20-22). It can hardly carry that meaning here, since integrity and uprightness hardly characterize Jacob's behavior. "Quiet" is used to differentiate the kind of man Jacob is (of the tents) from the kind of man Esau is (of the fields). "Isaac loved Esau, because the hunt was in his nostrils, while Rebekah loved Jacob" (25:28). Isaac's love for Esau seems to be based on their common love of the hunt and the savory food that comes from hunting. We already know why Rebekah loves Jacob; he is to her the chosen one of God. This theme of favorite children will recur in later stories.

We now learn something of the character of these boys. As always in Hebrew narrative, the narrator does not explain to us; rather, the narrator *shows* us what we need to know. "Once, when Jacob was cooking soup, Esau came in from the field, and he was exhausted." The two boys are doing what we already have been told that they are prone to do: Jacob is the domestic, while Esau is the man of the field. "Esau said to Jacob, 'Let me swallow some of the red stuff, this red stuff, because I am exhausted.' That is why they call him Edom ["red"]." What the narrator tells us is "soup" (or "lentils"), Esau crudely calls "red stuff." He offers no greeting to his brother; he merely demands the "stuff." The portrait of Esau is less than flattering. (The narrator also connects the crude manners with the name *Edom*, whose ancestor Esau becomes.)

"But Jacob said, 'Sell me now your right as firstborn.' " Just as Esau reveals himself as crude, so also Jacob reveals himself as clever, always ready to take advantage of the situation. As we might imagine, the crude Esau says to that amazing request, "Well, I am about to die (of hunger?); what good is the right of firstborn to me?" Esau, in an incredibly shortsighted act of stupidity, says that he will give up his right as eldest, his right of inheritance of property and blessing, all for some red stuff. But the clever Jacob is careful to make the ridiculous bargain legal and binding. "Swear to me now," he demands, and Esau swears, thus selling his birthright to his brother.

"So Jacob gave Esau a bowl of lentils; he ate, drank, rose, and left." The picture of crudity continues as the famished and exhausted man of the field eats the food like some sort of animal, devouring it in hurried silence and rushing out without a word to his brother. The narrator concludes quite rightly, "Thus he disdained his right as firstborn."

Surely Rebekah is not wrong to have chosen Jacob as the promised one; Esau's folly and stupidity are evident. Yet, Jacob's trickery and shady business practices are not themselves admirable. Once again, the narrator has thrown us into a complex world. What is to be said for the choices of God? How can the promise be worked out through these sorts of folk? There are still some surprises in store as we read on in the story of Jacob the deceiver.

According to the rabbis Jacob was not the only tricky brother. Esau is described by them as a trapper as well as a hunter. He would trap people with leading questions. "So you are not a thief. Who did you say helped you steal that?" Or, "When did you stop abusing your animals." So that any answer would ensnare the answerer. (Genesis Rabbah 63.10)

It was rumored that Esau had inherited a special garment from Adam that allowed him an advantage in the field. Whenever he would put it on, the birds and animals would flock around him. For this reason, Nimrod, another hunter, sought to kill Esau. So when he tells his brother, Jacob, that he is near death, it is not necessarily from hunger. (*Genesis Rabbah* 63.13)

Retelling the Story

She knew that a mother should love her children equally. All the parents' magazines said so. And she had tried; she really had. She just couldn't seem to be as genuine in her affection for both her boys.

To start with, the twins were as different as any two children could be. Esau, the first of the twins to be born, was his father's son—all boy, as men like to say. He loved to be outside hunting and fishing. He was good at every sport he took up. She hardly saw him all day. After dark he would come home smelling of sweat and the out-of-doors and bolt his food as if he hadn't had a bite in weeks. Besides, she hated that nickname, Red.

Jack was just the opposite. Anyone could tell in a minute that he was her son. He stayed around the house and helped her. He was a quiet child who loved to read and think. He even learned to cook and was good at it.

Jack wasn't perfect, mind you. He had a sly way about him, like those conniving characters on her television programs. This made him even more likable in a strange way. Jack always had the most delightful twinkle in his eye just before he was about to put something over on someone.

She had known trouble was coming even before they were born. Even before her doctor did the ultrasound to know for sure that she was carrying twins she had known something was wrong. It felt like World War III was going on inside her. Her doctor told her that the babies were just active. She said that they would have to be careful that one twin didn't steal from the other. *Steal* was the word she had used.

The labor was hard, but when the time came the two boys were born quickly. Jack came right on the heels of Esau. They were clearly not identical twins. You could see that as soon as they arrived. Esau was red and wrinkled and had lots of hair. Jack, on the other hand, looked like one of those babies on television. His skin was smooth, and his coloring was almost that of a month-old child rather than a newborn.

Now Jack was going away. Oh, it was his own doing. He played upon Esau's weaknesses to trick his brother out of his expected inheritance. All their neighbors would be on Esau's side; after all, he was the elder. But she couldn't help thinking that Jack was chosen for some greater task, that God had set him apart and could even use his trickery. That's why she had arranged for him to live with her brother, Laban. He would find a home there. Besides, Laban was such a trickster himself that he might just appreciate Jack.

The truth was, though, she hated to see him go. She would miss him; she would miss him terribly.

When Rebekah was carrying the twins, Jacob would become very active whenever she would pass by a house of study (of Torah). On the other hand, Esau would act up whenever she walked by a place where idols were worshiped. It may be important to note that for the rabbis who told these stories Esau was identified with Rome and its emperors, while Jacob was Israel, of course. (*Genesis Rabbah* 53.6)

131

GENESIS 27:1-45

Rebekah and Jacob Deceive Isaac

Jacob conspires with his mother to trick his blind father into thinking he is Esau so he will receive his father's blessing, intended for his brother.

The Story

When Isaac grew old and his eyes had become so dim that he could not see, he called for his elder son Esau. 'My son!' he said. Esau answered, 'Here I am.' Isaac said, 'Listen now: I am old and I do not know when I may die. Take your hunting gear, your quiver and bow, and go out into the country and get me some game. Then make me a savoury dish, the kind I like, and bring it for me to eat so that I may give you my blessing before I die.'

Now Rebecca had been listening as Isaac talked to his son Esau. When Esau went off into the country to hunt game for his father, she said to her son Jacob, 'I have just overheard your father say to your brother Esau, "Bring me some game and make a savoury dish for me to eat so that I may bless you in the presence of the LORD before I die." Listen now to me, my son, and do what I tell you. Go to the flock and pick me out two fine young kids, and I shall make them into a savoury dish for your father, the kind he likes. Then take it in to your father to eat so that he may bless you before he dies.' 'But my brother Esau is a hairy man,' Jacob said to his mother Rebecca, 'and my skin is smooth. Suppose my father touches me; he will know that I am

playing a trick on him and I shall bring a curse instead of a blessing on myself.' His mother answered, 'Let any curse for you fall on me, my son. Do as I say; go and fetch me the kids.' So Jacob went and got them and brought them to his mother, who made them into a savoury dish such as his father liked. Rebecca then took her elder son's clothes, Esau's best clothes which she had by her in the house, and put them on Jacob her younger son. She put the goatskins on his hands and on the smooth nape of his neck. Then she handed to her son Jacob the savoury dish and the bread she had made.

He went in to his father and said, 'Father!' Isaac answered, 'Yes, my son; which are you?' Jacob answered, 'I am Esau, your elder son. I have done as you told me. Come, sit up and eat some of the game I have for you and then give me your blessing." Isaac said, 'How did you find it so quickly, my son?' Jacob answered, 'Because the LORD your God put it in my way.' Isaac then said to Jacob, 'Come close and let me touch you, my son, to make sure that you are my son Esau.' When Jacob came close to his father, Isaac felt him and said, 'The voice is Jacob's voice, but the hands are the hands of

Esau.' He did not recognize him because his hands were hairy like Esau's, and so he blessed him.

He asked, 'Are you really my son Esau?' and when he answered, 'Yes, I am,' Isaac said, 'Bring me some of the game to eat, my son, so that I may give you my blessing.' Jacob brought it to him, and he ate; he brought him wine also, and he drank it. Then his father said to him, 'Come near, my son, and kiss me.' So he went near and kissed him, and when Isaac smelt the smell of his clothes, he blessed him and said, 'The smell of my son is like the smell of open country blessed by the LORD.

> 'God give you dew from heaven
> and the richness of the earth,
> corn and new wine in plenty!
> May peoples serve you
> and nations bow down to you.
> May you be lord over your brothers,
> and may your mother's sons bow
>   down to you.
> A curse on those who curse you,
> but a blessing on those who bless
>   you!'

Isaac finished blessing Jacob, who had scarcely left his father's presence when his brother Esau came in from hunting. He too prepared a savoury dish and brought it to his father. He said, 'Come, father, eat some of the game I have for you, and then give me your blessing.' 'Who are you?' his father Isaac asked him. 'I am Esau, your elder son,' he replied. Then Isaac, greatly agitated, said, 'Then who was it that hunted game and brought it to me? I ate it just before you came in, and I blessed him, and the blessing will stand.' When Esau heard this, he lamented loudly and bitterly. 'Father, bless me too,' he begged. But Isaac said, 'Your brother came full of deceit and took your blessing.' 'He is not called Jacob for nothing,' said Esau. 'This is the second time he has supplanted me. He took away my right as the firstborn, and now he has taken away my blessing. Have you kept back any blessing for me?' Isaac answered, 'I have made him lord over you and set all his brothers under him. I have bestowed upon him grain and new wine for his sustenance. What is there left that I can do for you, my son?' Esau asked, 'Had you then only one blessing, father? Bless me, too, my father.' Esau wept bitterly, and his father Isaac answered;

> 'Your dwelling will be far from the
>   richness of the earth,
> far from the dew of heaven above.
> By your sword you will live,
> and you will serve your brother.
> But the time will come when you
>   grow restive
> and break his yoke from your neck.'

Esau harboured a grudge against Jacob because of the blessing which his father had given him, and he said to himself, 'The time of mourning for my father will soon be here; then I am going to kill my brother Jacob.' When Rebecca was told what her elder son Esau was planning, she called Jacob, her younger son, and said to him, 'Your brother Esau is threatening to kill you. Now, my son, listen to me. Be off at once to my brother Laban in Harran, and stay with him for a while until your brother's anger cools. When it has died down and he has forgotten what you did to him, I will send and fetch you back. Why should I lose you both in one day?'

133

Comments on the Story

Jacob has bartered for the rights of the firstborn with his stupid and uncouth brother. Legally, he now can claim to be the heir of his father, Isaac, and can expect the promise of the patriarch to fall upon him. But there remains the problem of the bestowing of the father's blessing. Unless Isaac in fact offers his blessing to Jacob, there can be no thought of Jacob's inheritance; Genesis 27 addresses that problem.

In between Genesis 25 and 27 there is still another story of the wife of a patriarch passed off as his sister (see Genesis 12 and 20). This time it is Isaac's turn to tell the lie, and Abimelech of Gerar is on the receiving end. As before, the patriarch and his wife end up far richer than they were before the lie, but this time they live with the foreign king and help him prosper, too. After a dispute about water rights (26:17-33), Isaac and Abimelech make a covenant with one another and agree to live in peace in separate places. The repetition of the story of the lie serves to tie Isaac in to the line of his father and to remind the reader that he, too, is all too human.

Two other ideas in chapter 26 are important. First, the blessing of God is expressly given to Isaac (26:4, 24); he is clearly the heir of his father. Second, in two concluding verses, Esau "makes life bitter" for his parents by marrying two Hittite women. It seems that poor Esau can do little right! These ideas will come up again.

But now the time for the transferral of the patriarchal blessing has arrived. Isaac is old and blind; he "does not know the day of [his] death." He charges his eldest and favorite son, Esau, to go on a hunt and to prepare the "savory food" that Isaac so loves (25:28). After this last meal, he says that he "will bless you [Esau] before I die."

But Rebekah, ever watchful on behalf of her favorite, Jacob, whom she is convinced is the rightful heir because of the oracle of God (25:23), overhears the conversation. As soon as she sees Esau leave on his hunt, she turns to Jacob and tells him that Isaac is about to pass the blessing on to Esau. She cannot let that happen, and she has a plan to see that it does not. "Now, my son," she says, "hear my voice and do exactly as I command you" (27:8). The plan is for Jacob to go to the flock, get two choice kids, and bring them to his mother, who will prepare them in the "savory" way that Isaac loves. Jacob is then to take the food to his father and receive the blessing. It is, of course, an overt deception of a blind, old, dying man.

Jacob's response is instructive. He does not suggest to his mother that what she has asked is deceitful or morally problematic. His problem is that he might get caught! "Look! Esau my brother is a hairy man, while I am a smooth (*cheleq*) man." The literal meaning of the word translated "smooth" is indeed the opposite of "hairy"; Jacob protests that his lack of Esau's coarse covering of hair will surely give him away the minute his blind father touches him. But the word more often has the metaphorical meaning of "insinuating" or "double-faced"(see Prov. 5:3; 26:28; Ezek. 12:24). Jacob *is* smooth in every way that we normally understand the word. Jacob continues his whining fears: "Perhaps my father will see me, and it will be a mockery to him; I will bring curse on myself, not blessing" (27:12).

But Rebekah will not be deterred. "Upon me be the curse, my son. Obey my voice and go get it!" It is a fearful thing in the ancient world to call down a curse on oneself as Rebekah has just done; it indicates the astonishing lengths to which she will go to ensure that Jacob receives the blessing. Jacob, now reassured that if he is discovered he will not have to accept the full consequences of the deed, rushes out to do as Rebekah asks. When he returns with the kids, Rebekah cooks them in Isaac's favorite way and then dresses Jacob in Esau's best clothes, covering his arm and neck with the skins of the kids to give the feel of hair. Thus clothed in his brother's garment, draped with goat skins and carrying the savory food, Jacob presents to the reader a portrait of a clown, disguised for mockery, wrapped in deception. A detailed dialogue ensues.

"My father," Jacob announces. The old man responds in the traditional way, "Here I am," but instead of adding the expected "my son" he says, "Who are you?" The blind one seems immediately on his guard. Jacob answers, "I am Esau, your firstborn. I have done just as you told me. Sit up and eat of my game in order that you may bless me by your life" (27:19). But Isaac's suspicions apparently deepen: "How in the world did you find [game] so quickly, my son?" Jacob answers with a most terrible blasphemy: "The Lord your God gave me success." In truth, it was Rebekah, your wife!

Isaac seems to be far from convinced. "Please come near so that I may feel you and see whether you are my son Esau or not" (27:21). Jacob comes close to his father, who feels him and says, "The voice is Jacob's voice, but the hands are Esau's." The narrator then intrudes on the scene to say, "He did not recognize him, because his hands were hairy like Esau's, and he blessed him." We must see this first blessing as a rather perfunctory one, a kind of traditional "bless you" given from elder to younger. It cannot yet be the patriarchal blessing that is still to come.

Indeed, Isaac appears still quite uncertain about just which son is with him. "Are you really my son Esau?" The answer is a definite "I am." Isaac now asks for the food, which he proceeds to eat. He then calls his son to kiss him, and upon smelling the garments of Esau, who is a man of the fields, Isaac pronounces the blessing: "May God give you of the dew of heaven/and of the fatness of the earth/and plenty of grain and wine." Most notable and surprising about this blessing is that it is a blessing for a farmer, not for a hunter, a "man of the field." Why would Isaac give his hunter son the blessing of a farmer?

Who is in fact being tricked here? Is it possible that Isaac is as convinced as Rebekah that Jacob must receive the blessing, that it must be denied to Esau? Is it possible that the blind man himself goes through an elaborate charade in order to deny the blessing to its rightful recipient, his elder son? I find the story rich with ambiguity and am not willing to close the door on either reading.

When Esau returns, the old man is convincing in his claims to have been deceived by Jacob, at least convincing enough for Esau. The blessing has been given to Jacob, and it cannot be taken away. Once spoken, the blessing is as binding as any modern legal contract. Esau tells us what he thinks of Jacob: "Is he not well named, this Jacob? He tricked me twice; he has taken my firstborn rights and now my blessing" (27:36). He cries out for a blessing, too, but the only one he gets is a kind of mirror image of the one for Jacob: "Away from the fatness of the earth shall your home be/away from the dew of heaven on high." Esau must live by his sword and serve his brother, but he will in future "break the yoke" of that brother (27:39-40).

Esau now resolves to kill his brother just as soon as a proper period of mourning is observed for his father, who is now nearly dead. But the ever-vigilant Rebekah again discovers the plan and demands that Jacob flee from his murderous brother and go back to the home country of Mesopotamia, "to Laban my brother in Haran. Stay with him for a while, until your brother's fury turns away, and he forgets what you have done to him" (27:43-45). There seems little likelihood that even an apparent ignoramus like Esau will ever forget the trickery that has robbed him of his future. But we have come to expect surprises from these stories, so we ought to rule nothing out of the realm of possibility.

As Jacob heeds the advice of his mother and goes to Haran, he takes with him the promise and blessing of God, however deceitfully he gained them. We can only marvel that once again God's choices have proved so peculiar! How will Jacob, the tricky one, deal with this most sacred gift of God? We are anxious to read on!

Retelling the Story

They think I don't know! They think I am monumentally stupid! They think that my brain is as constricted as my eyes! How wrong they are! Do they really think that I could pass the blessing of God on to that dolt, Esau? All he does all day long is hunt and carouse with those appalling Hittite tarts. He even had the temerity to marry two of those sluts last week. I tell you that made me bitter to think of one of my sons in bed with Hittites, breeding little half-Hittite brats!

Of course, I had also heard (I'm not deaf, you know!) how the fool had given away the rights of the firstborn, which he happens to be, by sheer coincidence, to his far more clever brother, Jacob, for the absurd price of a bowl of soup! Well, it is just like that idiot to do such a thing. Believe me, he deserves everything he is going to get, which is not much, I assure you.

Now don't get me wrong; I really am not all that fond of Jacob either. He is a little weaseling momma's boy who never did a good day's work in his life. He hangs around the tents too much for my taste. But make no mistake; the little twerp is smart. There is no doubt in my mind who should be my heir, the one to carry the great promise of God into the next generation. But we do have this problem; the firstborn *is* supposed to get the promise. But I think I've got that all figured out. Listen:

> The rabbis say that when Isaac spoke, "The voice is Jacob's, but the hands are Esau's," he meant that the voice was wise, but the hands were those of one who plunders the dead. So in later years, when children's voices are heard praising God in the synagogue, the hands of the violent cannot harm them. (*Genesis Rabbah* 65.20)

I have sent that boob, Esau, out on one of his famous hunts and told him that my death is imminent. I got a little catch in my voice as I said I don't want to meet my maker until I had once more tasted some of his delicious food. He rushed right out. He never misses a chance to go hunting. I am certain that Rebekah heard me. I love that woman, but she is a conniver, and she does dote most unhealthily on Jacob. I have no doubt that she will cook up some sort of plan to convince me that Jacob is in fact Esau, so that stupid old blind me will pass the patriarchal blessing on to him. Little do she and that son of hers know that this charade is precisely what I have in mind myself! I cannot be quite certain just how my clever wife will manage the deception, but she will think of something. She has told me often enough of the oracle she received in the temple when the twins were wrestling in her womb, an oracle that convinced her that Jacob was the child of promise no matter what the order of birth was. Besides, she was even more bitter than I was about Esau's disgusting Hittite marriages.

She won't wait too long to act, I'm sure. She has to get Jacob in to see me before Esau gets back. Let's see. I'll settle myself here in a sort of half-dead way so that I can get into the part. Ah, someone has just entered the tent. I'll bet it's Jacob; it won't take me long to find out. Yes, it's Jacob. How could he

> When Isaac heard his son mention the name of God, he knew immediately that it was Jacob, not Esau. In addition, God got into the act. When Isaac told Jacob (pretending to be Esau) to come closer, Jacob began to sweat, and his knees went weak. So God sent an angel for each arm to hold him up as he approached his father. (*Genesis Rabbah* 65.19)

possibly expect me not to recognize his voice after hearing it all of these years? Well, here goes. I've got to convince him that I'm being duped so that I can give him the blessing and promise without anyone getting too suspicious. It won't be hard; they think I am such a simpleton anyway! Deception, huh? Well, two can play at that game!

Jacob's Dream

Jacob is sent to live with Rebekah's brother, Laban, and on the way he has a dream in which he senses the presence of God.

The Story

Rebecca said to Isaac, 'I am weary to death of Hittite women! If Jacob marries a Hittite woman like those who live here, my life will not be worth living.'

So Isaac called Jacob, and after blessing him, gave him these instructions: 'You are not to marry a Canaanite woman. Go now to the home of Bethuel, your mother's father, in Paddan-aram, and there find a wife, one of the daughters of Laban, your mother's brother. May God Almighty bless you; may he make you fruitful and increase your descendants until they become a community of nations. May he bestow on you and your offspring the blessing given to Abraham, that you may possess the land where you are now living, and which God assigned to Abraham!' Then Isaac sent Jacob away, and he went to Paddan-aram, to Laban, son of Bethuel the Aramaean and brother of Rebecca, the mother of Jacob and Esau.

Esau learnt that Isaac had given Jacob his blessing and had sent him away to Paddan-aram to find a wife there, that when he blessed him he had forbidden him to marry a Canaanite woman, and that Jacob had obeyed his father and mother and gone to Paddan-aram. Seeing that his father disliked Canaanite women, Esau went to Ishmael, and, in addition to his other wives, married Mahalath sister of Nebaioth and daughter of Abraham's son Ishmael.

Jacob set out from Beersheba and journeyed towards Harran. He came to a certain shrine and, because the sun had gone down, he stopped for the night. He took one of the stones there and, using it as a pillow under his head, he lay down to sleep. In a dream he saw a ladder, which rested on the ground with its top reaching to heaven, and angels of God were going up and down on it. The LORD was standing beside him saying, 'I am the LORD, the God of your father Abraham and the God of Isaac. This land on which you are lying I shall give to you and your descendants. They will be countless as the specks of dust on the ground, and you will spread far and wide, to west and east, to north and south. All the families of the earth will wish to be blessed as you and your descendants are blessed. I shall be with you to protect you wherever you go, and I shall bring you back to this land. I shall not leave you until I have done what I have promised you.'

When Jacob woke from his sleep he said, 'Truly the LORD is in this place, and I did not know it.' He was awestruck and said, 'How awesome is this place! This is none other than the house of God; it is the gateway to heaven.' Early in the morning, when Jacob awoke, he took the stone on which his head had rested, and set it up as a sacred pillar, pouring oil over it.

He named that place Beth-el; but the earlier name of the town was Luz.

Jacob made this vow: 'If God will be with me, if he will protect me on my journey and give me food to eat and clothes to wear, so that I come back safely to my father's house, then the LORD shall be my God, and this stone which I have set up as a sacred pillar shall be a house of God. And of all that you give me, I shall allot a tenth part to you.'

Comments on the Story

As we ended the previous story of the deception of Isaac, Esau was planning to murder his brother, Jacob. Rebekah had caught wind of the plot and had demanded that Jacob go to Haran to escape the fury of his brother. However, rather than have him simply flee away secretly, Rebekah devises still another ruse to get him safely out of the country. Rebekah expresses her extreme distaste for Hittite women and says to her husband that if Jacob should marry one of these women, "What good will my life be to me?" (27:46). Isaac takes this strong hint and urges Jacob not to marry one of the local Hittites. Instead, he insists that Jacob go to Haran and find a wife among the daughters of Laban, Rebekah's brother; this, of course, is precisely what Rebekah had in mind (27:43). Once again, either Isaac has been duped by his scheming wife or he is fully aware that Jacob should receive the family blessing, and thus he merely appears to be deceived. That the latter may be the answer is suggested by Isaac's public gift of that blessing in 28:3-4: "May El Shaddai bless you, make you fruitful, and increase your number in order that you become a company of peoples. And may God give the blessing of Abraham to you and to your descendants with you, that you may take possession of the land of your sojournings, which God gave to Abraham." After this, there is no doubt that Isaac has transferred the promise to his younger son, Jacob.

When poor Esau witnesses again the gift of the blessing to Jacob, a blessing rightfully his, and that the blessing follows a strong command against marriage with foreign women, Esau, having already married two Hittites (26:34), rushes out to marry an Israelite (28:8-9). It is a pathetic attempt to earn his way back into the favor of his parents, who have invested their hopes almost exclusively in the life of their younger, rascally son. It is surely a bitter pill for Esau to swallow!

Meanwhile, Jacob travels to the east, leaving Beer-sheba and heading toward Haran. "He encountered a certain place, and stayed there, for the sun had set." I translate the first verb "encounter" because the word suggests a meeting, a planned rendezvous. The implication is that Jacob has in some sense been led to this place. "And he took one of the stones of that certain place, put it under his head, and slept in that particular place" (28:11). Three times in this verse the word for "a certain place" (*hamaqom*) is used. This repetition emphasizes the particularity of the place and suggests that something extraordinary is about to happen in that certain spot. In the third use of the word, the narrator adds the demonstrative pronoun *that* to heighten the emphasis. Hebrew narration often uses exact repetition to emphasize an idea, or sometimes, as here, a small word is added to a repetition to highlight the idea even more.

Jacob begins to dream, and it soon becomes clear that his stony pillow is not the cause of this dream. "He dreamed. Look! A stone stairway set up on the earth, its top stretching for the sky. Look! Messengers of God ascending and descending on it!" The word translated "stone stairway" is used only here in the Hebrew Bible, but appears to refer to the Babylonian building ziggurat. The ziggurat was a stepped pyramid, not smooth-faced like those of the Egyptians. The word *messengers* is often translated "angels," but the modern connotation of angels seems rather clouded in many minds, so I choose to translate the word as "messengers," which is the true function of these beings, whoever or whatever they are thought to be in their persons.

"Look! The Lord was standing on it, and said, 'I am the Lord, the God of Abraham, your father, and God of Isaac. The land which you are lying on I give to you and to your descendants' " (28:13). The context of this reiteration of the gift of the land to Jacob is all-important. One could have anticipated that God would react rather differently to the little cheat, sleeping peacefully on his rocky pillow. These hallowed words are uttered to a hollow cheat who has just played part in a ruse against his brother and perhaps against his father, himself the possessor of the divine blessing. We might have expected a divine rebuke of such behavior, a taste of divine wrath against the errant one. Instead, Jacob receives the promise of the gift of the land from his God.

But that is not all. The familiar patriarchal blessing quickly follows. "Your descendants will be like the dust of the earth. You will scatter to the west and to the east, to the north and to the south. Through you and your descendants all the tribes of the earth will be blessed" (28:14). Yes, it is no one other than Jacob the deceiver who now carries the hope of the whole world, the hope of the blessing of God. Though other recountings of the gift of this blessing stop after the promise of the mission of blessing to "all the tribes of the earth," God is still not finished talking to Jacob: "Look! I am with you, and I will guard you wherever you go. I will bring you back to this land. Yes, I will not abandon you until I have done what I told you" (28:15). It is the most comprehensive announcement of the promise of God we have heard: land, blessing for both Jacob and his heirs, and the presence of God with him until *all* is accomplished.

Our attention now shifts to Jacob. How will he respond to this astonishing gift? "Jacob awoke from his sleep and said, 'Certainly the Lord is in this particular place and I did not know.' He was afraid: 'How awesome is this particular place! Why, it is none other than the house of God, the gateway to the sky!' " (28:17). His first reaction is not to the announcement of God but to the awesome mystery of this place, a place charged with the somewhat spooky presence of God. But about the promise that God made to him he says nothing.

He gets up early in the morning and sets up his stone pillow as a standing pillar, a sacred monument to the sacred place. To consecrate the stone, Jacob pours oil on its top. He then names the place Bethel ("house of God"); the narrator tells us that it used to be called Luz. Thus the story is in part the explanation of the name of the sacred spot, Bethel, an important sanctuary throughout most of the history of Israel.

Still, Jacob has yet to respond to the incredible gift of God, but finally he does. "Then Jacob vowed a vow, 'If God will be with me, and will guard me on the way I am going, and will give me food to eat and clothes to wear, and will bring me back safely to the house of my father, then the Lord will be my God' " (28:20-21). Jacob concludes his vow by offering God one tenth of what God will give him. One can only imagine God listening to that and saying, "Well, thank you very much!" God freely gives the promise of land, blessing, and divine presence to this deceiver, and his response is a bargain. If God really will do those things for Jacob, along with a few other things he might add, then God can be Jacob's God. If not, of course, perhaps he will wait for another.

This is Jacob after all. What else may we expect from him? His name is connected with deceit and cleverness; why should he treat his God any differently from the way he treated his brother? With this amazing response to the free gift of God to the undeserving one, the narrator brings us more completely into the world of Jacob, a world in which cleverness is paramount and trickery rules.

Hence, we must not expect from this cycle of tales simple lessons in morality. We must watch as God works the divine will through a motley collection of human beings, and while we may relish for a time the triumph of deceit, we must never take our eyes off of the One who is the true ruler of all.

> Certain of the rabbis tell that on the day God appeared to Jacob night came early. They compared God's visit to a king who wanted to speak with a close friend who came to visit from time to time. The king would order the lamps be extinguished so the two could hold their conversation in privacy. Thus God caused the sun to go down early. (*Genesis Rabbah* 68.10)

Retelling the Story

Jacob was groggy when he awoke from a very strange dream. What could he expect, camping out like this?

Sleeping under the sky with a stone for a pillow was more Esau's style than his. But he was on the run to Uncle Laban's house and daughters and away from Esau's furious scowl and strong arm.

An image from the dream was vivid in Jacob's memory. There was a stone stairway with messengers of God going up and down the stairs. As he had experienced before in dreams, he didn't know how he knew these were God's messengers. He just knew it with the intuitive assurance that comes only in dreams.

In the dream God had offered him "The Promise." It was the same promise in the same words he had heard his father and grandfather repeat again and again, and it used to aggravate him when he was young. It seemed that it was all they wanted to talk about.

When he awoke he said to himself, "What an awesome dream. God was in this place, and I didn't even know it. This must be the gate to God." So he found a stone and poured oil over it to mark the place, which he named Bethel, or God's House.

Then Jacob said to God, "I tell you what I'm going to do. If you will do all that you said plus throw in food, clothing, and protection until I get back home, you can be my God. In fact I'll return 10 percent of everything you give me."

God accepted Jacob's offer. Of course, only God could come out ahead when bargaining with a wheeler-dealer like Jacob.

While Jacob put one stone under his head for a pillow he placed the rest so that they formed a wall around him, since he was afraid of wild beasts. (*Genesis Rabbah* 68.11) This fits the description of Jacob as a "quiet" person used to staying indoors. We can only imagine that Esau would be more comfortable sleeping outside.

The messengers going up the steps were singing the praises of Jacob, while those who were coming down were leaping and dancing and saying terrible things about him, said some rabbis. Some said that these were just two places from which to view the sleeping Jacob, one close by and the other far away. Others said that in God's realm those who praise Israel (Jacob's new name, given later) are "lifted up," while those who speak against Israel are "brought low." On earth, unfortunately, just the opposite is true. (*Genesis Rabbah* 68.12)

Just as a knife is sharpened by rubbing the blade against the edge of another knife (or a whetstone), so also, the rabbis said, are a scholar's skill and wit sharpened by "rubbing up against" another scholar. Here Jacob has no less a colleague than the Creator of the universe against whom to sharpen his abilities. (*Genesis Rabbah* 69.2)

Jacob Marries Two Sisters

Jacob meets Rachel, falls in love, and is tricked by her father, Laban, into marrying her older sister, Leah, before he can marry the woman of his dreams.

The Story

Jacob, continuing his journey, came to the land of the eastern tribes. There he saw a well in the open country with three flocks of sheep lying beside it, because flocks were watered from that well. Over its mouth was a huge stone, and all the herdsmen used to gather there and roll it off the mouth of the well and water the flocks; then they would replace the stone over the well. Jacob said to them, 'Where are you from, my friends?' 'We are from Harran,' they replied. He asked them if they knew Laban the grandson of Nahor. They answered, 'Yes, we do.' 'Is he well?' Jacob asked; and they answered, 'Yes, he is well, and there is his daughter Rachel coming with the flock.' Jacob said, 'It is still broad daylight, and not yet time for penning the sheep. Water the flocks and then go and let them graze.' But they replied, 'We cannot, until all the herdsmen have assembled and the stone has been rolled away from the mouth of the well; then we can water our flocks.' While he was talking to them, Rachel arrived with her father's flock, for she was a shepherdess. Immediately Jacob saw Rachel, the daughter of Laban his mother's brother, with Laban's flock, he went forward, rolled the stone off the mouth of the well and watered Laban's sheep. He kissed Rachel, and was moved to tears. When he told her that he was her father's kinsman, Rebecca's son, she ran and told her father. No sooner had Laban heard the news of his sister's son Jacob, than he hurried to meet him, embraced and kissed him, and welcomed him to his home. Jacob told Laban all that had happened, and Laban said, 'Yes you are my own flesh and blood.'

After Jacob had stayed with him for a whole month, Laban said to him, 'Why should you work for me for nothing simply because you are my kinsman? Tell me what wage you would settle for.' Now Laban had two daughters: the elder was called Leah, and the younger Rachel. Leah was dull-eyed, but Rachel was beautiful in both face and figure, and Jacob had fallen in love with her. He said, 'For your younger daughter Rachel I would work seven years.' Laban replied, 'It is better that I should give her to you than to anyone else; stay with me.'

When Jacob had worked seven years for Rachel, and they seemed like a few days because he loved her, he said to Laban, 'I have served my time. Give me my wife that I may lie with

144

her.' Laban brought all the people of the place together and held a wedding feast. In the evening he took his daughter Leah and brought her to Jacob, and he lay with her. At the same time Laban gave his slave-girl Zilpah to his daughter Leah. But when morning came, there was Leah! Jacob said to Laban, 'What is this you have done to me? It was for Rachel I worked. Why have you played this trick on me?' Laban answered, 'It is against the custom of our country to marry off the younger sister before the elder. Go through with the seven days' feast for the elder, and the younger shall be given you in return for a further seven years' work.' Jacob agreed, and completed the seven days for Leah.

Then Laban gave Jacob his daughter Rachel to be his wife; and to serve Rachel he gave his slave-girl Bilhah. Jacob lay with Rachel also; he loved her rather than Leah, and he worked for Laban for a further seven years.

Comments on the Story

God has freely given to the rascally Jacob the gift of the land, the promise of blessing, and the assurance of God's presence until the fulfillment of both gift and promise. Jacob, in response, bargained with God rather than offering God gift or promise in return. Nonetheless, we know him to be the heir of the promise of Abraham, and so we follow his journey with the greatest anticipation.

"Jacob lifted his feet [says the literal text] and went toward the land of the easterners" (29:1). As often happens in Genesis, he comes first to a well, always the scene of community activity in an ancient desert world. A typical picture of that world is quickly painted. He noticed "three flocks of sheep crouching beside" the well, and we wonder why they are not being watered right now. One could imagine that the users of the well have made the stone so large that it takes *all* of them to move it off the well-head. In that way, they can be sure that no one user gets more than a fair share of the precious water. It is rather like the multiple key system on the vaults of modern banks; no one person may open the vault, an arrangement that ensures the safety of the money.

Jacob engages the shepherds in conversation and discovers that they are from Haran. He has arrived at his destination. Also, they know Laban, and they tell Jacob that he is well. Not only has Jacob arrived, but also the shepherds notice that Rachel, Jacob's first cousin and the daughter of Laban, is coming now to water her father's flock. When Jacob hears that Rachel is there, it seems that Jacob would like to be alone with Rachel, and he attempts to get the shepherds away from the well as quickly as he can. But the shepherds are having none of it. "We cannot until all the flocks are gathered together and the stone is rolled from the mouth of the well to water the sheep" (29:8). This long tradition of waiting until all come to the well cannot be changed, certainly not for a stranger just arrived from the west.

When Jacob sees Rachel, it is love at first sight. However, it is also true that his initial look was not confined to the beautiful Rachel; his eyes also took in

145

the fine flock she was tending. Thus the combination of Rachel and the flock proves irresistible to Jacob, and he rushes over, throws the huge stone off of the mouth of the well, and waters Rachel's fine flock of sheep. Is this a burst of adrenaline that charges Jacob with the extraordinary strength needed to remove the stone, or is it just impatience to get on with it, not being willing to wait for the traditional communal removal of the stone? In either case, Jacob may be showing off for the lovely Rachel, when tossing aside the huge stone by flexing young muscles.

After Jacob and Laban meet, a month passes. Laban says, "Just because you are my relative, does that mean that you should work for me for nothing? Tell me what your wages should be" (29:15)? Laban, in apparent magnanimity, allows Jacob to name some payment for the work he is doing for his uncle. However, the narrator warns us that Laban's motives may be less than magnanimous by telling us about Laban's daughters right after his suggestion about wages. "Now Laban had two daughters [the first time we have heard of a sister for Rachel]. The name of the elder was Leah; the name of the younger was Rachel" (29:16). Immediately, the reader is reminded of the younger-elder dilemma that was central to the story just read. Is the same confusion to arise here? Will the younger somehow get the upper hand again? Will trickery again be involved? Our suspicions should be high.

The problem is compounded by the description of the two women: "The eyes of Leah were weak, but Rachel was beautiful and graceful" (29:17). Precisely what is meant by the phrase "weak eyes" is difficult to determine. The name *Leah* arises from an Akkadian word meaning "cow"; a related meaning is "strong." Thus her name, "Strong," is belied by her eyes which are "weak." The stark contrast between the two women is what is important whether or not we can fully grasp the exact nature of the contrast.

Who more than Jacob should be wary of a younger-elder confusion? But he asks no questions and receives what he thinks is affirmation from the clever Laban: "It is better that I give her to you than to any other man. Stay with me. So Jacob worked for Rachel for seven years, but they seemed to him only a few days because of the love he had for her" (29:19-20). This is a justly famous line and is often viewed as the very epitome of romance. We should know better by now that Jacob's motivations are never simple and that his own interests are always close to the surface.

The seven years pass, and Jacob demands that Rachel be given to him as wife. So Laban prepares a huge marriage feast, gathering everyone to the party. The culmination of the feast is always the procession of the bride as she is taken to the tent of the anxious groom. There have been long bouts of eating and drinking, and the night is dark. "So it happened in the evening that Laban brought his daughter Leah to Jacob, and he had sex with her. And in the morning, oh my, it was Leah! Jacob said to Laban, 'What in the world have you

done to me! Did I not work for you for Rachel? Why have you deceived me?' "
(29:23, 25). Jacob's whining about being tricked has an especially hollow ring
as we remember that his entire life has been one long practice of deception; the
worm has turned, and the shoe is on the other foot. I cannot deny feeling a certain satisfaction as I stand with Laban and his cronies to watch Jacob emerge
from his marriage tent!

Laban has a ready response to Jacob's wounded cry: "It is not done in our
place to give the younger before the firstborn" (29:26). Laban reverts to words
used to describe Esau and Jacob in the preceding stories; up to now Leah and
Rachel have been called literally "big daughter and little daughter." By
reminding us of the other story, the narrator makes us more aware that Jacob is
getting his just desserts, and the bargaining Jacob is now driven a hard bargain
by the equally hard Laban. "Complete the work for this one [Leah] and we will
also give you this one [Rachel]." But one week will hardly complete the deal:
"The work you will do for me will be another seven years" (29:26-27). A hard
bargain indeed! And it is not said that these additional seven years were "as a
few days to Jacob."

But Rachel is given to Jacob, and they have sex, too, but "he loved Rachel
more than Leah." Once again, favorites are played in a story, and the result can
only be confusion and pain.

The name of God does not appear in this story. It is a tale of a trickster
tricked, a deceiver deceived. But we may never forget that this red-faced trickster is still the chosen one of God, and, as such, we must watch him, for in him
lies the future blessing of the world. The Apostle Paul's words were never
more true: "We have this treasure in earthen vessels, to show that the transcen-
dent power belongs to God and not to us" (II Cor. 4:7).

Retelling the Story

"At last, the well! I thought I would never see water again! It must be a good
one; just look at the three flocks lying near it, waiting for their drink. I wonder
who these shepherds are? Ah, they are from Nahor, the ancestral home of my
family. My uncle, Laban, is here and doing well they say. There comes his
daughter Rachel. My, my, such a beauty
she is, not to mention the grand flock of
sheep following close behind her. Uncle
Laban is richer than I dared imagine.

" 'It's too early in the day for a gathering of all of the animals of the neigh-
borhood; why don't you folk who have
come first go ahead and water your
flocks and take them back to pasture?' I
must get rid of them so I can be alone

> Why would Jacob presume to
> tell these shepherds when to
> water their flocks, being a for-
> eigner to that place? This shows
> us that just because we are in a
> strange place, we are not
> relieved from speaking out
> against injustice. (Plaut, p. 207)

with this enchanting, rich woman. Oh, no! They have this treaty that the stone that covers the mouth of the well is never to be removed until all those who use it have arrived. This prevents any one of them from getting more than a fair share of the life-giving water. Well, the stone is not *that* big, and I can't wait all day for these traditionalists to decide when to start their watering. I'll just head over there, push the stone off the well, and water lovely Rachel's lovely flock. That should get their attention!"

• • •

"Who is this upstart foreigner, anyway? How dare he suggest that we water our flocks before all have arrived! Does he not know the long-held grudges we have against those who decided to water their flocks independently from all the rest of us? We have had more than a few wars over such problems. We finally have a system whereby we don't kill one another over the water.

> Even though she was a beautiful woman and all alone, the shepherds did not harm Rachel. Some rabbis say that this is because God sent an angel along to protect her. Others say that such decent behavior is no surprise among those who worship God. (*Genesis Rabbah* 70.11)

"Just look at the shameful way he is leering at the daughter of Laban. Of course, his eyes fell on Laban's fine flock of sheep as well. I don't think this stranger is so much in love that he misses a potentially grand dowry. Why, he just rushed over, moved the stone, and is watering Rachel's flock! This is not going to end here; already I see several of my compatriots fingering their knives and short swords. This rash fool has upset the balance of our lives, a balance we spent many hard years achieving."

• • •

"You could have knocked me over with a bit of bread! I went to water my father's flock, and a stranger was standing near the well. He certainly gave me the once over! I am woman enough to know when a man has designs beyond 'brotherly love.' Nor did I miss those same piercing eyes gazing eagerly at my father's flock. It was instantly clear to me that this stranger was a person who did not miss very much, nor was he one to be tricked easily either.

"To my surprise, instead of waiting for the gathering of all the flocks before the watering could begin, he rushed right over to the well, tossed the stone aside, and began to water my flock. I suppose it was an arrogant act, perhaps designed to impress me, and it did, but not in the way the stranger intended, I think. I was just glad to see something different happen in this hide-bound traditional world in which I live. Could this stranger be the one to get me out of here? I think I will run and tell my father of all this. Who can guess what might happen?"

The Trickster Tricks the Trickster

Jacob has done rather well during his stay with Laban and now takes his household and wealth, along with something of Laban's, and starts for home.

The Story

Jacob learnt that Laban's sons were saying, 'Jacob has taken everything that our father had, and all his wealth has come from our father's property.' He noticed also that Laban was not so well disposed to him as he had once been. The LORD said to Jacob, 'Go back to the land of your fathers and to your kindred; I shall be with you,' and Jacob sent word to Rachel and Leah to come out to where his flocks were in the country. He said to them, 'I have been noticing that your father is not so friendly to me as once he was. But the God of my father has been with me. You yourselves know I have served your father to the best of my ability, yet he has cheated me and changed my wages ten times over. But God did not let him do me any harm. If your father said, "The spotted ones are to be your wages," then all the flock bore spotted young; and if he said, "The striped ones are to be your wages," then all the flock bore striped young. It is God who has taken away your father's livestock and given them to me. In the season when the flocks were in heat, I had a dream in which I saw that the he-goats which were mating were striped and spotted and dappled. The angel of God called to me in the dream, "Jacob!" and I replied, "Here I am!" He said, "See what is happening: all the he-goats mating are striped and spotted and dappled, for I have seen all that Laban has been doing to you. I am the God of Bethel where you anointed a sacred pillar and made a vow to me. Now leave this country at once and return to your native land." ' Rachel and Leah answered him, 'We no longer have any share in our father's house. Does he not look on us as strangers, now that he has sold us and used the money paid for us? All the wealth which God has saved from our father's clutches is surely ours and our children's. Now do whatever God has told you to do.' At once Jacob put his sons and his wives on camels, and he drove off all the cattle and other livestock which he had acquired in Paddan-aram, to go to his father Isaac in Canaan.

When Laban had gone to shear his sheep, Rachel stole the household gods belonging to her father. Jacob hoodwinked Laban the Aramaean and kept his departure secret; he fled with all that he possessed, and soon was over the Euphrates and on the way to the hill-country of Gilead. Three days later, when Laban heard that Jacob had fled, he took his kinsmen with him and pursued Jacob for seven days until he caught up with him in the hill country of Gilead. But God came to Laban the Aramaean in a dream by night and said to him, 'Be careful to say nothing to Jacob, not a word.'

When Laban caught up with him, Jacob had pitched his tent in the hill-country of Gilead, and Laban encamped with his kinsmen in the same hill-country. Laban said to Jacob, 'What have you done? You have deceived me and carried off my daughters as though they were captives taken in war. Why did you slip away secretly without telling me? I would have set you on your way with songs and the music of tambourines and harps. You did not even let me kiss my daughters and their children. In this you behaved foolishly. I have it in my power to harm all of you, but last night the God of your father spoke to me; he told me to be careful to say nothing to you, not one word. I expect that really you went away because you were homesick and pining for your father's house; but why did you steal my gods?'

Jacob answered, 'I was afraid; I thought you would take your daughters from me by force. Whoever is found in possession of your gods shall die for it. In the presence of our kinsmen as witnesses, identify anything I have that is yours, and take it back.' Jacob did not know that Rachel had stolen the gods. Laban went into Jacob's tent and Leah's tent and that of the two slave-girls, but he found nothing. After coming from Leah's tent he went into Rachel's. In the mean time Rachel had taken the household gods and put them in the camel-bag and was sitting on them. Laban went through the whole tent but found nothing. Rachel said, 'Do not take it amiss, father, that I cannot rise in your presence: the common lot of woman is upon me.' So for all his searching, Laban did not find the household gods.

Jacob heatedly took Laban to task. 'What have I done wrong?' he exclaimed. 'What is my offence, that you have come after me in hot pursuit and have gone through all my belongings? Have you found a single article belonging to your household? If so, set it here in front of my kinsmen and yours, and let them decide between the two of us. In all the twenty years I have been with you, your ewes and she-goats have never miscarried. I have never eaten rams from your flocks. I have never brought to you the carcass of any animal mangled by wild beasts, but I bore the loss myself. You demanded that I should pay compensation for anything stolen by day or by night. This was the way of it: the heat wore me down by day and the frost by night; I got no sleep. For twenty years I have been in your household. I worked fourteen years for you to win your two daughters and six years for your flocks, and you changed my wages ten times over. If the God of my father, the God of Abraham and the Fear of Isaac, had not been with me, you would now have sent me away empty-handed. But God saw my labour and my hardships, and last night he delivered his verdict.'

Laban answered Jacob, 'The daughters are my daughters, the children are my children, the flocks are my flocks; all you see is mine. But what am I to do now about my daughters and the children they have borne? Come, let us make a pact, you and I, and let there be a witness between us.' So Jacob chose a great stone and set it up as a sacred pillar. Then he told his kinsmen to gather stones, and they took them and built a cairn, and there beside the cairn they ate together. Laban called it Jegar-sahadutha, and Jacob called it Gal-ed. 'This cairn', said Laban, 'is a witness today between you and me. That was why it was named Gal-ed; it was also named Mizpah, for Laban said, 'May the LORD watch between you and me when we are absent from one another. If you ill-treat my daughters or take other wives besides them, then though no one is there as a witness, God will be the witness between us.'

Laban said to Jacob, "Here is this cairn, and here the pillar which I have set up between us.' Both cairn and pillar are witnesses that I am not to pass beyond this cairn to your side with evil intent, and you must not pass beyond this cairn and this pillar to my side with evil intent. May the God of Abraham and the God of Nahor judge between us.' Jacob swore this oath in the name of the Fear of Isaac, the God of his father. He slaughtered an animal for sacrifice there in the hill-country, and summoned his kinsmen to the feast. They ate together and spent the night there.

Laban rose early in the morning, kissed his daughters and their children, gave them his blessing, and then returned to his home.

Comments on the Story

The chapters just before our passage tell of the astonishing way in which the children of Jacob, the fabled "twelve tribes of Israel," are born. Leah and her maid Zilpah and Rachel and her maid Bilhah engage in a birthing war to determine who can have the most children. This war is fought over the affections of Jacob. Leah, the unloved wife, attempts to win the heart of her uncaring husband by bearing him children, four sons in quick succession (29:31-35). Each of their names has something to do with Leah's search for Jacob's love. Reuben ("See, a son") is firstborn, and Leah hopes "now my husband will love me." In those words echo the hopes of many people down through the years who have attempted to create relationships by means of children.

The birth of Simeon (from the verb meaning "hears") suggests to Leah that "the Lord has heard I am hated" and has given her this son to lessen that hate. Levi's birth tells her that "now my husband will be joined (*lawah* in Hebrew, the root of the name Levi) to me." "This time I will praise (*hodah*) the Lord," she says, and names her fourth son Judah, from the root "to praise." Only these remarkable writers would tell us that the births of their most noble ancestors came about as the result of a domestic squabble.

With the birth of Joseph ("he adds"), Rachel, once barren, now hopes God will add to her another son (30:24), the birth war stops, and Jacob determines that it is time for him to return to his home in Israel. Now the two tricksters, Jacob and Laban, will attempt to get the upper hand in this game of deception. To Jacob's request to be allowed to leave with his wives and children, Laban claims that he has "learned by divination that the Lord has blessed me because of you. Name your wages; I will give it" (30:27). Laban has no intention of letting Jacob go so easily; since Jacob's coming, Laban has become rich and hardly wants the meal ticket to leave.

Jacob agrees that he is the cause of Laban's newfound wealth, stating that "you had little before I came" and "the Lord has blessed you wherever I turned" (30:30). Then Jacob accepts Laban's offer, but his plan is a devious one. He claims first not to want anything at all, but asks Laban to allow him to select from Laban's flock "every speckled and spotted sheep, every black lamb, and every speckled and spotted goat" (30:32). Jacob adds, "My righteousness [or honesty] will answer for me; if any are found in my flocks not speckled, spotted, or black, they should be counted stolen" (30:33). Whenever Jacob starts talking about honesty, we should be especially cautious!

Laban agrees, but immediately removes all goats and lambs from his flock that resemble the descriptions given by Jacob, and gives them to his sons, who drive them three day's journey away from Jacob. Thus Jacob is left with no animals to select (30:34-36). Laban appears to have bested him again.

But Jacob is not finished yet. By means of sympathetic magic, Jacob is able to create speckled, spotted, and striped livestock by laying peeled almond rods in the places where the animals breed. They see the rods and always give birth to offspring that resemble the peeled wooden rods. Of course, Jacob performs this trick only when the very strongest of the animals come to breed. In time, Jacob creates a huge and powerful flock, while Laban is left with a few, much weaker, animals.

This is where our passage picks up the story. After bilking Laban in this way, Jacob then turns to Rachel and Leah, daughters of Laban, and in a rousing speech convinces them that their father is little better than a rascal and that they must leave him immediately and without remorse to return to Israel with their husband (31:1-16). They are convinced, and the whole family with all their many possessions leave to return to Israel, while Laban is out shearing sheep (31:19). Rachel, however, adds insult to injury by "stealing her father's household gods (*teraphim*)." These are small divine images, common to all ancient cultures, that were thought to confer blessing and protection to a house.

Laban sets off in hot pursuit of the fleeing Jacob and his considerable retinue. He easily overtakes them due to the slow pace of the large company. In a hilarious bit of lying, Laban claims that if he had been told of Jacob's departure, he would have sent him off "with mirth and songs, with tambourine and harp." *No one,* neither Jacob nor we, could believe that for one moment; Laban would rather die than lose his ticket to prosperity. Nor could he be pleased that Jacob's trickery had divested him of the best of his flock!

Nevertheless, he admits that Jacob's desire to return home is a strong one (31:30), but he concludes his lengthy speech by accusing Jacob of stealing his teraphim. Now it is Jacob's turn to grow self-righteous, since he does not know that Rachel, his favorite, has indeed stolen the gods, so the tension increases. But we are soon to discover that deception in this story is not confined to the men.

Laban begins his search for the missing gods. He first enters the tents of the concubines, and then Leah's tent, but comes up empty. He then goes into Rachel's tent, where we know the gods are to be found. It is an outrageous scene with Rachel sitting on the sacred gods, but the best is yet to come. During Laban's frantic search, Rachel apologizes to her father for not rising to greet him. "It is my time of the month," lies Rachel, and no male of the ancient community would dare get close to that mystery. Thus the gods are not found, and Rachel is shown to be her father's child and her husband's wife.

Then Jacob becomes very righteously indignant, and he uses the occasion to assault Laban for nearly twenty years of foul treatment, changed wages, miserable working conditions, and no real recognition of Jacob's incredible worth as the creator of Laban's wealth (31:36-42). Finally, in apparent resignation to the inevitable, Laban wearily looks at Jacob's goods and family and says, "The daughters are my daughters, the children are my children, the flocks are my flocks, and all that you see is mine" (31:43). He is, of course, quite right; Jacob has become rich and satisfied with him, which is memorialized by a stone pillar, not unlike the pillar Jacob set up long ago at Bethel.

In this case, they build a pile of stones "and ate [a covenant meal] there by the pile" (31:46). Laban calls the pile in Aramaic what Jacob calls it in Hebrew—namely, "heap of witness." Laban then pronounces the so-called Mizpah blessing: "May the Lord watch between you and me while we are out of each other's sight" (31:49). Laban goes on to warn Jacob not to mistreat his daughters or to take other wives, "because God is witness between you and me." The implication of this so-called blessing is that Laban does not trust Jacob as far as he can throw one of the stones of the pile! In that, he is a smart man; Jacob is hardly a man to be trusted. After that contract is made, Jacob sets his face westward again. But now he must face a much more dangerous adversary, his furious brother, the brute Esau. It is a confrontation he would readily avoid.

Retelling the Story

Laban and Jacob stood nose to nose. Neither would back down. "You took my daughters and grandchildren and herds and flocks, but you didn't have to take my household gods," shouted Laban.

The rabbis gave a gruesome description of how these gods were made. Someone's head was cut off, the hair shaved off, and the head preserved. Then the name of God (or one of their gods, there is disagreement on this) was placed under the tongue. When asked questions, the head was supposed to answer by the power of the name of God (or the gods). (Ginzberg, vol. 1, p. 371)

The rabbis said that Rachel had a good reason to take the household gods with her when she left. She asked herself, "Can I leave my father here to continue to be an idol worshiper?" So she took the idols from the house to protect Laban. (*Genesis Rabbah* 74.5)

"What would I, who worship the one true God, want with your trinkets of clay?" Jacob retorted.

"That doesn't answer my question," Laban had Jacob's eyes fixed by his own stare. "Where are the household gods?"

Jacob answered, "Search me."

And Laban responded, "That's exactly what I intend to do."

So Laban searched the tents of Jacob, Leah, and the servants. Then he went to Rachel's tent. Now Rachel had hidden them in the camel pack and was sitting on them.

"I'm looking for my household gods," her father told her.

"Fine, look wherever you want. Just excuse me if I don't get up. You see, it's my time of the month." Rachel could hardly keep a smirk from betraying her secret.

After a brief look around the tent, Laban left. Outside he confronted Jacob again, "All right, take my daughters and my grandchildren and my flocks and herds and go home. And here's a blessing you can take along with you: If you ever mistreat any of my family or attempt to marry another wife, just remember that God is watching between you and me when I can't be there to check up on you."

And so they parted, Laban to his now godless home and Jacob to meet the wrath of his brother, Esau.

Jacob and the Wrestler

Jacob, on his way home, sends a message to his brother, Esau, to try to avoid confronting his brother's hatred.

The Story

As Jacob continued his journey he was met by angels of God. When he saw them, Jacob exclaimed, "This is the company of God,' and he called that place Mahanaim.

Jacob sent messengers ahead of him to his brother Esau to the district of Seir in Edomite territory, instructing them to say to Esau, 'My lord, your servant Jacob sends this message: I have been living with Laban and have stayed there till now. I have acquired oxen, donkeys, and sheep, as well as male and female slaves, and I am sending to tell you this, my lord, so that I may win your favour.' The messengers returned to Jacob and said, 'We went to your brother Esau and he is already on the way to meet you with four hundred men.' Jacob, much afraid and distressed, divided the people with him, as well as the sheep, cattle, and camels, into two companies. He reasoned that, if Esau should come upon one company and destroy it, the other might still survive.

Jacob prayed, 'God of my father Abraham, God of my father Isaac, LORD at whose bidding I came back to my own country and to my kindred, and who promised me prosperity, I am not worthy of all the true and steadfast love which you have shown to me your servant. The last time I crossed the Jordan, I owned nothing but the staff in my hand; now I have two camps. Save me, I pray, from my brother Esau, for I am afraid that he may come and destroy me; he will spare neither mother nor child. But you said, "I shall make you prosper and your descendants will be like the sand of the sea, beyond all counting." '

After spending the night there Jacob chose a gift for his brother Esau from the herds he had with him: two hundred she goats, twenty he-goats, two hundred ewes and twenty rams, thirty milch-camels with their young, forty cows and ten young bulls, twenty she-donkeys and ten donkeys. He put each drove into the charge of a servant and said, 'Go on ahead of me, and leave gaps between one drove and the next.' To the first servant he gave these instructions: 'When my brother Esau meets you and asks who your master is and where you are going and who owns these animals you are driving, you are to say, "They belong to your servant Jacob, who sends them as a gift to my lord Esau; he himself is coming behind us." ' He gave the same instructions to the second, to the third, and to all the drovers, telling each to say the same thing to Esau when they met him. And they were to add, 'Your servant Jacob is coming behind us.' Jacob thought, 'I shall appease him with the gift that I have sent on ahead, and afterwards, when we come face to face, perhaps he will receive me kindly.' So Jacob's gift went on ahead of him, while he himself stayed that night at Mahaneh.

During the night Jacob rose, and taking his two wives, his two slave-girls, and his eleven sons, he crossed the ford of Jabbok. After he had sent them across the wadi with all that he had, Jacob was left alone, and a man wrestled with him there till daybreak. When the man saw that he could not get the better of Jacob, he struck him in the hollow of his thigh, so that Jacob's hip was dislocated as they wrestled. The man said, 'Let me go, for day is breaking,' but Jacob replied, 'I will not let you go unless you bless me.' The man asked, 'What is your name?' 'Jacob, ' he answered. The man said, 'Your name shall no longer be Jacob but Israel, because you have striven with God and with mortals, and have prevailed.' Jacob said, 'Tell me your name, I pray.' He replied, 'Why do you ask my name?' but he gave him his blessing there. Jacob called the place Peniel, 'because', he said, 'I have seen God face to face yet my life is spared'. The sun rose as Jacob passed through Penuel, limping because of his hip. That is why to this day the Israelites do not eat the sinew that is on the hollow of the thigh, because the man had struck Jacob on that sinew.

Jacob looked up and there was Esau coming with four hundred men. He divided the children between Leah and Rachel and the two slave-girls. He put the slave-girls and their children in front, Leah with her children next, and Rachel and Joseph in

the rear. He himself went on ahead of them, bowing low to the ground seven times as he approached his brother. Esau ran to meet him and embraced him; he threw his arms round him and kissed him, and they both wept. When Esau caught sight of the women and children, he asked, 'Who are these with you?' Jacob replied, 'The children whom God has graciously given to your servant.' The slave-girls came near, each with her children, and they bowed low; then Leah with her children came near and bowed low, and lastly Joseph and Rachel came and bowed low also. Esau asked, 'What was all that company of yours that I met?' 'It was meant to win favour with you, my lord,' was the answer. Esau said, 'I have more than enough. Keep what you have, my brother.' But Jacob replied, 'No, please! If I have won your favor, then accept, I pray, this gift from me; for, as you see, I come into your presence as into that of a god, and yet you receive me favourably. Accept this gift which I bring you; for God has been gracious to me, and I have all I want.' Thus urged, Esau accepted it.

Esau said, 'Let us set out, and I shall go at your pace.' But Jacob answered him, 'You must know, my lord, that the children are small; the flocks and herds are suckling their young and I am concerned for them, and if they are overdriven for a single day, my beasts will all die. I beg you, my lord, to go on ahead, and I shall move by easy stages at the pace of the livestock I am driving and the pace of the children, until I come to my lord in Seir.' Esau said, 'Let me detail some of my men to escort you,' but he replied, 'There is no reason why my lord should be so kind.' That day Esau turned back towards Seir, while Jacob set out for Succoth; there he built himself a house and made shelters for his cattle. Therefore he named that place Succoth.

Comments on the Story

Jacob crosses the Euphrates river and is bound for home. The narrator signals that extraordinary events are about to occur by telling us that the first beings to meet Jacob as he takes his final steps toward home are messengers of God. Jacob exclaims, "This is the army of God," and calls the place "Mahanaim," a word meaning "two armies" (32:1-2). This tiny scene sets the stage for the drama to follow in several ways. First, the fact that Jacob sees the messengers as an army tells us that he is convinced that his confrontation with his brother, Esau, will result in battle. Second, he sees two armies; he will soon divide his own company into two parts, hoping to save at least one from the enraged Esau. Third, this will not be his last meeting with mysterious visitors whom he believes are sent from God.

But he must first deal with Esau, who in Jacob's mind can only be bent on revenge. After all, when Jacob was tricked and plundered by Laban, his reaction was to get even, which he did by tricking and plundering Laban in return. If Jacob was in the place of Esau, he certainly would be anxious for revenge. In that spirit, he instructs messengers to go to Esau and say: "Thus says your servant Jacob, 'With Laban I have sojourned and remained until now. I have oxen, asses, flocks, menservants and maidservants, and I have sent to tell my lord in order to find favor in your eyes" (32:4-5). We would expect Jacob to speak just like that! A simple statement of fact about where he has been these twenty years is followed by an enumeration of all the things he now owns, things with which he intends to impress Esau and buy his good favor. Jacob knows but two ways to get what he wants, deception or bargaining.

But this time the bargain appears to have failed, because the messengers return to Jacob and report that Esau is indeed coming to meet his brother, "and four hundred men are with him" (32:6). Jacob is convinced that Esau is bent on bloody revenge and divides his large retinue into two companies, hoping to save one while Esau destroys the other.

And then he prays to God. He is facing death, and this prayer, the longest single prayer in Genesis, appears to be appropriate. But it is Jacob the trickster who prays, so we should read it carefully. He reminds God in verse 9 that God promised to "do you good." He says he is "not worthy of the least of all the steadfast love and faithfulness you have shown to your servant," but he concludes that thought by saying he has in fact become two companies, a bigshot worthy of God's careful consideration. He announces he is very much afraid of the murderous Esau, but concludes the prayer in the same way he began: "But you did say, 'I will certainly do good with you, and will make your descendants as the sand of the sea, which cannot be numbered for multitude' " (32:12). The repetition of the phrase "do good to you" in verses 9 and 12 highlights the central concern of this prayer: Jacob reminds God of divine promises and suggests that those promises can hardly be kept if God allows Esau to destroy Jacob and his company. Jacob, in effect, tells God that he expects God to hold up the divine end of a bargain. Who more than Jacob knows about bargains?

Still, Jacob does not abandon the hope that even a furious Esau has his price. So he offers him extraordinary presents from his considerable holdings, "two hundred she-goats, two hundred ewes and twenty rams, thirty milk camels and their colts, forty cows and ten bulls, twenty she-asses and ten he-asses" (32:14). He instructs his servants to send these presents one at a time, leaving space in between each drove; perhaps if he does not like the goats, then the camels will please him? Jacob thought, "I may cover his face with this present which precedes my face; afterwards I will see his face, and perhaps he will lift my face" (32:20). The remarkable series of puns on the word *face* in this verse indicates how Jacob hopes that his present will make Esau forget his anger, being dazzled by the wealth of his brother. Jacob can imagine no other way that Esau could want to "lift [Jacob's] face."

With the bribe sent to Esau, and with all of his company now across the ford of the Jabbok river, Jacob finds himself alone. Suddenly, he experiences another mysterious encounter. "A man wrestled with him until the breaking of the day," but when this man saw that he could not defeat Jacob, he "touched the hollow of his thigh so that it was thrown out of joint." But the tenacious Jacob still refuses to let go of the man, who cries out, "Let me go, for the day is breaking." Apparently this man is only able to operate safely at night. But Jacob retorts, "I will not let you go unless you bless me." The desperate man asks Jacob's name, and upon hearing it changes his name to "Israel" and says, "You have struggled with God and human beings and have prevailed." The name *Israel* may mean "one who struggles with God" or "God struggles."

Jacob then asks the name of the man, but the man deflects the question by asking Jacob why he wants to know. "And there he blessed him" (32:29). Jacob has wrestled a blessing out of the man. Of course, he has already done the same thing earlier in his life; he wrestled the blessing from his dying, blind father. Even when God gave it to him as a gift, he still insisted on bargaining for its certainty (28:20-22). Whether Jacob is "heel grabber" or "wrestler with God," he remains essentially the same person; only deception or bargaining or wrestling can secure blessings in this world.

After the match ends and the man withdraws, Jacob names the place "Peniel" ("face of God"), saying, "I have seen God face to face, yet my life has been delivered." Of course, it is only Jacob who interprets his nocturnal wrestling as a bout with God; the narrator refuses to call Jacob's opponent anything but a "man." And what is the result of the fight? Jacob is now "Israel," but he is so named because he has wrestled with all comers and has prevailed. To be sure, he limps away from the match at Peniel, but the text leaves us in no doubt that he limps away the winner. The peculiar connection of this fight with a later food taboo against eating a certain part of the thigh of an animal (Gen. 32:32) indicates the great imagination with which later interpreters investigated and applied these ancient texts.

But is Jacob the winner? He still has the much more dangerous fight with Esau to face; the Jabbok river confrontation has not changed that fact at all. He finally catches sight of Esau, and he indeed is accompanied by four hundred men! In a panic, Jacob arranges his family with the concubines and their children in front, followed by Leah and her children, with Rachel and Joseph last of all. Jacob, in abject supplication, goes in front of them all, "bowing himself to the ground seven times until he came close to his brother" (33:3). Jacob can see only one course now: to throw himself on the mercy of Esau.

And now comes the great surprise of the story: "But Esau ran to meet him, embraced him, fell on his neck and kissed him, and wept" (33:4). Nothing in the story prepares the reader for this astonishing scene. We have been seeing Esau only through the lens of the earlier story of Jacob's trickery and lately through the eyes of a terrified Jacob. But the wonder of Esau is that he has completely forgiven his wretched brother. After meeting Jacob's family, Esau asks Jacob why he sent all those goods to him (33:8). Jacob says that he was trying "to find favor in the eyes of my lord." But Esau cares nothing for the material goods: "I have enough, my brother." It is only Esau who uses the familiar term "my brother" in the scene; Jacob continually calls Esau "lord" (vv. 8, 13, 14, 15).

But Jacob urges Esau to accept his present, because, he says, "surely to see your face is like seeing the face of God" (32:10). Here Jacob says far more than he knows. He thought that he had seen the face of God at the Jabbok river in the person of his wrestling partner. He had thought to appease the face of Esau by buying his favor, hoping that Esau would want to "lift his face" in acceptance. But Jacob has been wrong all along about where one sees the face of God. In the open-hearted forgiveness of the old brutish Esau, one can certainly and plainly see the face of God. Whoever would have thought that God would be revealed in *Esau?* But so it is in this wonderful story.

Unfortunately, Jacob has still one more lie in him, even in the face of this revelation through his brother. Esau asks him to accompany him to his home in Seir, and Jacob says that he will, but that he must move slowly due to the size of the company. He tells Esau to go ahead, and he will follow. But he does not. He travels to Succoth, away from his brother; Esau never appears in the story again (33:12-17). However, the reader can never forget the shock of Esau's forgiveness, can never forget that in that forgiveness we really can see the face of God. Once again we learn that God is moving in mysterious ways, and through unlikely folk, divine wonders to perform.

> When God's people encounter situations in which they are afraid, they need not be ashamed of that reasonable fear. After all, Jacob was afraid as he went to meet his brother, Esau. (*Genesis Rabbah* 76.1)

Retelling the Story

Everybody hated him! He was big and fat. He smoked like a chimney, ate like an elephant, and had a complexion to match. He was thoroughly distasteful in every way. Added to his disgusting physical appearance were the manners of a swine with the gout. In class, he blurted out answers to all the questions without raising his hand, and his answers were invariably so wrong as to be laughable. So, we all laughed. At lunch, we jostled one another to avoid the horror of having to sit at the same table with him, let alone the nightmare of actually sitting *next* to him. He ate so much, so fast, that his beady eyes would soon fix themselves on your lunch, and it was all you could do to stop yourself from heaving up the little you had managed to get down, caught as you were in that ravenous, piggish stare.

Then there was recess. Every day it was the same. We chose up sides for the game, and he was always chosen last. We all did a quick count, figuring that if our numbers that day were even, and if we got first choice, he would not be on our team. Most days it worked, this numbering. But some awful days, someone would come late, and he would lumber over to our side, smelling of cigarettes and onions, which he ate like potato chips. If it was baseball, he couldn't hit or run; if football, he couldn't throw or catch; if basketball, he couldn't shoot— but he did anyway, always costing us the win, always laughing when he missed.

The scene never changed. Grade school, high school, he even followed many of us up to State. Some kids when they grew thinned out, their faces cleared up, and their dispositions mellowed along with their hormones. Not this one. He just became bigger, fatter, smellier, and more repulsive. Some of us had the recurring nightmare that on our wedding night he would pop up from under the bridal bed, breathe smoke in our faces, and offer us an onion!

Thank God, he didn't show up at any of our weddings, nor on our wedding nights. Of course, none of us invited him. Who would? I finally lost track of him as my family and I moved out of town. Oh, I knew he was out there some-where, but I didn't care where and doubted that anyone else did either.

Years passed, how many I forget. My marriage began to fall apart for no reason I can put my finger on; we just didn't have that old spark. She took the kids; I moved out. I get to see them on big holidays every other year. Anyway, my apartment is small, and there is not much for them to do when they are here with me. They became less interested in coming, especially after she married that man. Actually he is very nice. I was forty-five and alone.

Then the card came in the mail one day. It was from him. He said that he had often thought of me, but had lost track. He'd been married, he said (that surprised me!), but it hadn't worked out. He said his life had been pretty hard, he'd usually been an outcast, laughed at by most people. He knew he was not easy to like, but all that laughter had hurt. His wife had taken some of the pain away, but when she left he really felt alone.

One rabbi compared the wrestler's match with Jacob to a king who had a ferocious dog and a tame lion. The king would take his son out to wrestle with the lion, and he allowed the dog to watch. Then if the dog ever had thoughts of attacking the boy, the king would say, "A lion couldn't harm him; how do you think you can?" So God tells the nations about Israel, "My angel could not harm him, why do you waste your time?" (*Genesis Rabbah* 77.3)

Then he said he had thought of me. He told me of a time when on the playground, in fifth grade it was, I had asked him how he was doing. I'd meant it, he said. That had meant a lot to him, to be asked how he was doing. I'd forgotten that completely; I still can't recall it. But that big slob had been touched by me, and now he was touching me. I cried. Hearing that memory was like hearing from God.

The Rape of Dinah

*Leah's daughter, Dinah, is attacked by Shechem, and this sets off a plot
of revenge by her brothers on all the men of the city of Shechem.*

The Story

Dinah, the daughter whom Leah had borne to Jacob, went out to visit women of the district, and Shechem, son of Hamor the Hivite, the local prince, saw her. He took her, lay with her, and violated her. But Shechem was deeply attached to Jacob's daughter Dinah; he loved the girl and sought to win her affection. Shechem said to Hamor his father, 'You must get me this girl as my wife.' When Jacob learnt that his daughter Dinah had been dishonoured, his sons were with the herds in the open country, so he held his peace until they came home. Meanwhile Shechem's father Hamor came out to Jacob to talk the matter over with him. When they heard the news Jacob's sons came home from the country; they were distressed and very angry, because in lying with Jacob's daughter Shechem had done what the Israelites hold to be an intolerable outrage. Hamor appealed to them: 'My son Shechem is in love with this girl; I beg you to let him have her as his wife. Let us ally ourselves in marriage; you give us your daughters, and you take ours. If you settle among us, the country is open before you; make your home in it, move about freely, and acquire land of your own.' Shechem said to the girl's father and brothers, 'I am eager to win your favour and I shall give whatever you ask, Fix the bride-price and the gift as high as you like, and I shall give whatever you ask; only, give me the girl in marriage.'

Jacob's sons replied to Shechem and his father Hamor deceitfully, because Shechem had violated their sister Dinah: 'We cannot do this,' they said; 'we cannot give our sister to a man who is uncircumcised, for we look on that as a disgrace. Only on one condition can we give our consent: if you follow our example and have every male among you circumcised, we shall give you our daughters and take yours for ourselves. We will then live among you, and become one people with you. But if you refuse to listen to us and be circumcised, we shall take the girl and go.' Their proposal appeared satisfactory to Hamor and his son Shechem; and the young man, who was held in respect above anyone in his father's house, did not hesitate to do what they had said, because his heart had been captured by Jacob's daughter.

Hamor and Shechem went to the gate of their town and addressed their fellow-townsmen: 'These men are friendly towards us,' they said; 'let them live in our country and move freely in it. The land has room enough for them. Let us marry their daughters

162

and give them ours. But on this condition only will these men agree to live with us as one people: every male among us must be circumcised as they are. Their herds, their livestock, and all their chattels will then be ours. We need only agree to their condition, and then they are free to live with us.' All the able-bodied men agreed with Hamor and his son Shechem, and every able-bodied male among them was circumcised. Then two days later, while they were still in pain, two of Jacob's sons, Simeon and Levi, full brothers to Dinah, after arming themselves with swords, boldly entered the town and killed every male. They cut down Hamor and his son Shechem and took Dinah from Shechem's house and went off. Jacob's other sons came in over the dead bodies and plundered the town which had brought dishonour on their sister. They seized flocks, cattle, donkeys, whatever was inside the town and outside in the open country; they carried off all the wealth, the women, and the children, and looted everything in the houses.

Jacob said to Simeon and Levi, 'You have brought trouble on me; you have brought my name into bad odour among the people of the country, the Canaanites and the Perizzites. My numbers are few; if they combine against me and attack, I shall be destroyed, I and my household with me.' They answered, 'Is our sister to be treated as a common whore?'

Comments on the Story

This tightly written, grim story is set in the context of Jacob's initial settling in the land of Israel after his return from Haran and his separation from Esau, who lived in the land of Edom, to the south and east of Israel. Jacob arrives in the city of Shechem in the land of Canaan (33:18). He buys from the sons of Hamor, Shechem's father (both the city and its favorite son bear the same name), a piece of land that eventually becomes the burial place of the patriarch (see Gen. 23 for a similar story about Abraham). The sons of Hamor are described in Judges 9:28 as the ruling clan of the city of Shechem. Thus Jacob and his family, as foreigners in the land, settle near the city, buying property, which gives them a legitimate right to dwell in the land. But a terrible incident brings great trouble between the inhabitants of the land and the Israelite newcomers.

Dinah, of whom we have been told nothing beyond the fact of her birth (30:21) decides to pay a call on some of the Shechemite women. But her innocent visit turns to tragedy, because a ruling prince in the land rapes and humiliates her. The last verb is found in other places of female sexual abuse in the Hebrew Bible (Judg. 19:24, 20:5; II Sam. 13:12, 14, 22, 32). But something remarkable happens after this cruel rape of the maiden: "But his life was tied to Dinah, daughter of Jacob; he loved the maiden and spoke tenderly to her:" (34:3). The verb I translated "tied to" is the same verb found at Genesis 2:24, where it is used to describe the close relationship between the man and the woman as they try to recreate the initial unity of the creation in marriage. The verb is also found at Ruth 1:14, used there to describe the intensely close relationship that Ruth felt she had with Naomi.

This story becomes the mirror image of the later story of the rape of Tamar by her half-brother Amnon (II Sam. 13). In that story, Amnon is convinced that he is madly in love with Tamar, but after his assault upon her he feels nothing but disgust for her. In this case, Shechem's assault on Dinah is unprovoked rape, a pure act of violence. But afterwards he is drawn to her; the narrator emphasizes his complete change of behavior from raw violence to "speaking tenderly" (literally "to the heart"), "love," naming her "maiden," a term of endearment and intimacy. For whatever reason, Shechem now loves Dinah, and he urges his father, Hamor, to get the maiden for him for his wife.

"But when Jacob heard that he [Shechem] had desecrated his daughter, his sons were with his cattle in the field; Jacob was silent until they came." From Jacob's point of view, the rape was nothing less than "desecration" or "defilement," a cultic abuse, rendering the perpetrator and the victim ritually unclean. With these dark thoughts in his mind, Jacob prepares to meet Hamor, who is coming to speak with the patriarch about the possible marriage of his son to Dinah. At the very same time, Dinah's brothers come in from the field, hear about the rape, and are "indignant, thoroughly enraged, because he [Shechem] had done foolishness in Israel by sleeping with Jacob's daughter. Thus it should not be done!" (34:7). The brothers do not name the act a cultic transgression, but rather a transgression of the customs of their people, "foolishness in Israel."

Hamor's plea on behalf of his son is uttered in the midst of a thoroughly hostile crowd. Hamor claims that his son really does love Dinah and that their marriage can be the beginning of many such intermarriages between the two peoples. Such intimate relationships can only lead to prosperity and peace for all people. Then Shechem adds that he will give literally *anything* as a marriage present and gift if only Dinah can become his wife.

Usually in the narratives of the Hebrews, the author does not give the game away quite so overtly as happens here. In verse 13, the reader is told that the words of the sons of Jacob about to be spoken are words filled with "deceit," precisely because "he had desecrated their sister, Dinah." The word *deceit* occurs much earlier in the story of Jacob. In chapter 27, after Jacob has apparently tricked Isaac out of the patriarchal blessing, Isaac tells a despondent Esau that "your brother came with deceit and stole your blessing" (27:35). Thus like father, like son. Unfortunately, it will not be the last time that these boys prove to be masters of deceit.

Their despicable plan is to say that they can certainly not give their sister to any uncircumcised person, because that would be a disgrace. Therefore, the condition for marriage to Dinah is that *all* the Shechemite males must be circumcised. When that happens, "we will give our daughters to you, and we will take your daughters to ourselves; we will dwell with you and become one people" (34:15-16). No circumcision, no marriage.

164

Both Shechem and Hamor are pleased with the request, and immediately go back to their city to urge the males to begin the circumcision. Shechem was "the most honored in his family" (34:19), so his words carry a special weight. Their persuasion is effective. First, the men are friendly. Second, the land is certainly big enough for both of us. Third, we will marry their daughters, and they will marry ours, thus creating one stronger people. Fourth, "will not their cattle, their property, and all their beasts be ours? (34:23). They, of course, did not say this to Jacob and his sons. Still, it does not seem to indicate a dark plot on the part of Shechem, but is designed to make the act of circumcision more economically attractive. The arguments are persuasive, because all of the males are circumcised.

Now the terrible plot of Jacob's children comes to its grisly conclusion. While the men of Shechem were deep in pain from their circumcision and less able to fight, Dinah's brothers killed every male, including Hamor and Shechem and took Dinah out of Shechem's house and left. This is the first word we have heard of Dinah since the rape itself; she has apparently been staying with Shechem, most likely against her will, all this time.

Murder was not enough for these vengeful sons. Simeon, Levi, and the rest of Jacob's boys now plunder the city, because, we are told again, "their sister had been desecrated." They completely sack the city, taking anything of value, from herds to children to wives, all were captured. Jacob is aghast at his sons' behavior, not because he finds it morally reprehensible, but because his tiny family is now vulnerable to the much larger and more established residents of the land of Canaan. But his sons defiantly respond, "Should he treat our sister like a prostitute? (34:31).

The story ends very abruptly with the murderous sons rejecting the fears of their father as being outweighed by the terrible indignity done to their sister. What might all this mean in the context of the story of Genesis? Something quite terrible is suggested by this trickery. Pharaoh, Abimelech of Gerar, Laban the Aramean have all in turn been victims of the tricky Israelite patriarchs. However, murder was never the goal of that trickery. They are rascals, but not bloody ones. The trickery has here become treachery, and clever hijinks have turned deadly.

In this story we encounter an awful analogy to the primeval history of Genesis. The evil of the garden was the eating of fruit, which led first to fratricide and then to wholesale slaughter. Is the same downward spiral of humanity occurring again? Later laws against intermarriage arise from stories like this one about Dinah. One can imagine the lawmaker saying, "We are pure and undefiled. *They* defiled us. They must die." In response to such attitudes there came forth prophets in Israel who described a day of the Lord in which war had disappeared, in which peace and harmony among *all* people would have no end.

The rabbis are very suspect of the motives of Shechem and his father. They suggest that when they say that all Jacob and his family owned would be theirs they meant it. They intended to kill Jacob's household and take everything. (*Genesis Rabbah* 80.8)

Legend has it that when she returned to her home, Dinah was going to have a baby. When the child was born her brothers wanted it dead, thinking that the Canaanite people might say terrible things about Dinah and the little girl. But Jacob put his granddaughter under a bush with a medallion around her neck that said "Holy to God." Then an angel, Michael, took the child to Egypt, where she was raised as the daughter of a priest and his wife, who had no children.

Others say Dinah went to Egypt when Joseph brought the rest of the family. Still others say she was the second wife of Job, after his fortunes were restored. (Graves and Patai, p. 237)

Retelling the Story

Officer: Tell me about what happened.

Dinah: First, he raped me, then he told me he loved me and took me to his house.

Officer: You're not from this country, are you?

Dinah: No. Does that make any difference?

Officer: Well, no. I just heard your accent.

Dinah: This man attacked me, and I want him arrested!

Officer: You say you were on your way to visit some women friends, is that right?

Dinah: That's right.

Officer: What were you wearing?

Dinah: Just clothes—what we wear where I come from.

Officer: Is that particular style of dress what you would call revealing, very short or low cut?

Dinah: No!

Officer: I have to ask. You know, a pretty girl like you with that complexion and those eyes. . . .

Dinah: Are you trying to say this was my fault, that I did something to encourage him?

Officer: I'm not saying anything. It's just not every day that the son of the governor is accused of being a common criminal. I just have to get all of the information. Had you been intimate with a young man prior to this encounter?

Dinah: No!

Officer: No young men at this place where you were going?

Dinah: I said they were women friends. Look, if you don't at least arrest this man, I'm afraid my brothers will do something terrible when they find out.

Officer: Well, I hope for their sake that you can persuade them not to. We can't have everybody just taking the law into his or her own hands.

Joseph the Dreamer

Joseph is the favorite child of Jacob. As a result, he grows up spoiled and cultivates the hatred of his brothers.

The Story

Jacob settled in Canaan, the country in which his father had made his home, and this is an account of Jacob's descendants.

When Joseph was a youth of seventeen, he used to accompany his brothers, the sons of Bilhah and Zilpah, his father's wives, when they were in charge of the flock, and he told tales about them to their father. Because Joseph was a child of his old age, Israel loved him best of all his sons, and he made him a long robe with sleeves. When his brothers saw that their father loved him best, it aroused their hatred and they had nothing but harsh words for him.

Joseph had a dream, and when he told it to his brothers, their hatred of him became still greater. He said to them, 'Listen to this dream I had. We were out in the field binding sheaves, when all at once my sheaf rose and stood upright, and your sheaves gathered round and bowed in homage before my sheaf.' His brothers retorted, 'Do you think that you will indeed be king over us and rule us?' and they hated him still more because of his dreams and what he had said. Then he had another dream, which he related to his father and his brothers. 'Listen!' he said. 'I have had another dream, and in it the sun, the moon, and eleven stars were bowing down to me.' When he told his father and his brothers, his father took him to task: 'What do you mean by this dream of yours?' he asked. 'Are we to come and bow to the ground before you, I and your mother and your brothers?' His brothers were jealous of him, but his father did not forget the incident.

Joseph's brothers had gone to herd their father's flocks at Shechem. Israel said to him, 'Your brothers are herding the flocks at Shechem; I am going to send you to them,' Joseph answered, 'I am ready to go.' Israel told him to go and see if all was well with his brothers and the flocks, and to bring back word to him. So Joseph was sent off from the vale of Hebron and came to Shechem, where a man met him wandering in the open country and asked him what he was looking for. 'I am looking for my brothers,' he replied. 'Can you tell me where they are herding the flocks?' The man said, 'They have moved from here; I heard them speak of going to Dothan.' Joseph went after his brothers and came up with them at Dothan. They saw him in the distance, and before he reached them, they plotted to kill him. 'Here comes that dreamer,' they said to one another. 'Now is our chance; let us kill him and throw him into one of these cisterns; we can say that a wild beast has devoured him. Then we shall see what becomes of his dreams.' When Reuben heard, he came to his rescue, urging them not to take his life. 'Let us have no bloodshed,' he said. 'Throw him into this cistern in the wilderness, but do him no injury.' Reuben meant to rescue him from their clutches in order to restore him to his father. When Joseph reached his brothers, they stripped him of the long robe with sleeves which he was wearing, picked him up, and threw him into the cistern. It was empty, with no water in it.

They had sat down to eat when, looking up, they saw an Ishmaelite caravan coming from Gilead on the way down to Egypt, with camels carrying gum tragacanth and balm and myrrh. Judah said to his brothers, 'What do we gain by killing our brother and concealing his death? Why not sell him to these Ishmaelites? Let us do him no harm, for after all, he is our brother, our own flesh and blood'; his brothers agreed. Meanwhile some passing Midianite merchants drew

Joseph up out of the cistern and sold him for twenty pieces of silver to the Ishmaelites; they brought Joseph to Egypt. When Reuben came back to the cistern, he found Joseph had gone. He tore his clothes and going to his brothers he said, 'The boy is not there. Whatever shall I do?'

Joseph's brothers took the long robe with sleeves, and dipped it in the blood of a goat which they had killed. After tearing the robe, they brought it to their father and said, 'Look what we have found. Do you recognize it? Is this your son's robe or not?' Jacob recognized it. 'It is my son's,' he said. 'A wild beast has devoured him. Joseph has been torn to pieces.' Jacob tore his clothes; he put on sackcloth and for many days he mourned his son. Though his sons and daughters all tried to comfort him, he refused to be comforted. He said, 'No, I shall go to Sheol mourning for my son.' Thus Joseph's father wept for him. The Midianites meanwhile had sold Joseph in Egypt to Potiphar, one of Pharaoh's court officials, the captain of the guard.

Comments on the Story

With chapter 37 begins the longest cycle of stories in Genesis, and by most accounts the longest sequence of stories written by one hand. It seems virtually certain that chapters 37–47, with the possible exception of chapter 38, are the work of one author. Chapter 50 may also be this person's work. Because that is so, the Joseph story has been looked at as a whole much more often than the other cycles of Genesis.

The family of Jacob now "dwells in the land of his father's sojournings"—that is, whereas Isaac and Abraham had lived temporarily in the promised land, Jacob and his heirs are now living there permanently. The story of the rape of Dinah (Gen. 34) warned of the dangers of living in the land with the long-time inhabitants, but this is the land of promise, the land chosen by God as the place from which the world's blessings will arise. In the ongoing story of the gift of that blessing and the almost continual threats to it, we now turn to the family of Jacob.

Immediately, the narrator focuses in a startling way on Joseph, the child of Rachel, Jacob's best-loved wife. All the sons of Jacob are shepherds, but the youngest one's chief distinction is that he is a tattle-tale. That "evil report" on his brothers is precisely what the people seeking to spy out the land of promise bring back to the waiting wandering tribes, "an evil report" (Num. 13:32, 14:36). This evil report is the very symbol of the faithlessness of the people of Israel as they face their future. Why Joseph is telling tales about his brothers is not fully clarified here, but it offers a glimpse into his character.

Directly after we hear that Joseph is some sort of spy among his brothers, we learn that Joseph is given a "long-sleeved robe" because Jacob loves him more than any of his other sons. Martin Luther, following the Septuagint and the Latin Vulgate, then later, and more influential for English readers, the King James Version, has made the "coat of many colors" a part of our language, but *kethoneth passim* has nothing to do with colors. It is a very distinctive and luxurious garment (II Sam. 13:18), however, and as the brothers watch their spying younger brother parade around wearing the very symbol of Jacob's obsessive love toward the little twit, they can only harbor the greatest ill-will for him. Their anger is so great that they cannot "speak peaceably to him" (37:4)—that is, they could not greet him with the customary and expected *shalom*. One can hardly blame them.

But it gets worse, because Joseph begins to dream, and can hardly wait to reveal the content of these dreams to his brothers. The result, as any clear-thinking person would imagine, is that "his brothers hated him all the more" (37:5). The first dream is that sheaves of grain are standing in a field, but Joseph's sheaf stands up very straight, while the sheaves of his brothers gather around his and bow down to it. Now *there* is a dream designed to cool the anger of some jealous brothers! "Are *you* really going to rule over us?" they shout in disgust. But the young fool cannot leave it alone. He has another dream, and again rushes out to blab it to the raging brothers. This time, "the sun, moon, and eleven stars were bowing down to me" (37:10). This dream is even too much for his doting father, who "rebukes him." The verb for "rebuke" is used several times to describe God's shouts to the sea or at the nations (Isa. 17:13; Nah. 1:4; Ps. 106:9), so it is a powerful locution. Jacob, the patriarch, can hardly believe that he and the boy's mother are actually going to "bow ourselves to the ground before you." Of course, it will happen, just as the dreams say, but at this point in the story, Joseph is portrayed for us as an arrogant, overly indulged megalomaniac. We are not surprised that his brothers hatch a rather elaborate plot to kill him.

They go to pasture the flock near Shechem, a long distance (some sixty miles) from the sight of the story at Hebron. The name *Shechem* rings with ominous memories of the assault on Dinah and the subsequent slaughter by deceit of the Shechemites. Joseph, apparently on another spying mission from his father, goes toward Shechem to discover whether or not it is *shalom* with these brothers, who never speak *shalom* to him anyway. Jacob, in effect, is sending his favorite to his death, whether or not he knows it.

Joseph arrives in Shechem, but the brothers are not at the usual pasturage. Joseph is now quite alone and defenseless; the sheltering arm of his father does not extend this great distance. A stranger (part of the brothers' plan?) meets Joseph and tells him that they have moved the flock even further from Hebron, in fact to Dothan, some eight miles from Shechem by most reckonings. As Joseph stumbles toward Dothan, the point of view moves to the brothers, who "see him from far away" (37:18). The plan is simple. They will kill him and say that a wild beast has eaten him; his repulsive dreams will die with him.

But in the midst of the sinister plotting, the voice of Reuben, the firstborn son of Jacob, breaks in to "deliver him out of their hands, saying, 'Let's not take his life. Shed no blood. Throw him into this pit in the wilderness, but don't lay a hand on him' " (37:21-22). He said this, the narrator tells us, because he wanted to "rescue him out of their hands, to restore him to his father" (37:22). Why? Within the bounds of the chapter itself no answer is given for Reuben's behavior, but the tradition of the story has offered one that makes superb narrative sense.

In 35:22, a small piece of information suggests reasons for Reuben's actions: "While Israel [Jacob] lived in that land, Reuben went and slept with Bilhah, his father's concubine; and Israel heard about it." To sleep with the concubines and wives of the leader of the community is far more than a sexual act; it is a political one (see especially II Sam. 16:20-22), and announces the desire of the perpetrator to take control of the community. Reuben's act with Bilhah has made him odious to his father. Thus out of his desire to save Joseph, or because of his responsibility as firstborn, he sees Joseph as his meal ticket back into the favor of his father.

The brothers accept Reuben's advice; they strip the hated robe off of their brother and throw him into a dry pit. Then, in the midst of their picnic they see a passing caravan of Ishmaelites on their way down to Egypt. Judah is improvising, so he tests another plan before the brothers: "What profit is it if we kill our brother and hide his blood? Let's sell him to the Ishmaelites, and let's not put our hand on him. He is, after all, our brother, our own flesh" (37:26-27). The narrator does not break in to tell us any reason for Judah's speech; it seems to be a sharp bit of business. Why kill the little jerk, when we can make a buck off of him?

But in a wonderful bit of drollery, while the brothers are arguing about what to do with the hated Joseph, some other traders, Midianites this time, come by and pull Joseph out of the pit. *They* sell him to the Ishmaelites for twenty silver shekels (a relatively paltry sum), and they take him off to Egypt. Meanwhile, Reuben returns to the pit and discovers, to his horror, that Joseph is gone. In anguish he tears his clothes and shouts "where shall I go?" Where indeed? His way back to his father's favor is gone.

But the brothers, deprived of the profit for the sale of Joseph, still have his hated robe. They dip it in animal blood and hold it up before their father for his identification, making no comment. Of course, the old man immediately recognizes the torn and bloody robe and concludes that his beloved son has been dismembered and devoured by wild beasts. He begins a process of extreme mourning and refuses to be comforted, wailing, "No, I will go down to Sheol to my son, mourning" (37:35).

Joseph is far from dead. A bit of confusion appears in the text concerning just who it was who sold Joseph into Egyptian slavery (we read "Midianites" in 37:36), but the fact is that he is very much alive and has been sold, not to work in the quarries or on the great building projects, but as a household slave to a rich and powerful man, Potiphar, a captain of Pharaoh's personal bodyguard. Though the brothers may think that they have seen the last of their arrogant sibling, their relationship with him is by no means over. And those of us who silently applauded when the self-centered jerk got his comeuppance may have reason to read on; Joseph's remarkable story has just begun.

Retelling the Story

You may have had a brother or sister just like her, or you may know someone who has. You know the kind I mean. Every Christmas you would count the presents under the tree, as you always did, and your brother would have the most. Every birthday your sister would always get exactly what she wanted, while you got another package of underwear or socks, and no ice cream cake either. After getting her longed-for dress, she would come out of her always neat room wearing the stupid thing, and your parents would call her the most beautiful girl since Elizabeth Taylor in *National Velvet,* a stupid movie that you wouldn't watch if the only other choice was "All Star Wrestling."

She always got the biggest piece, the nicest bed, the last Coke, and the most love. It was just not fair! Mom and Dad simply loved her more, while I got what was left, the stale crumbs, the lumpy pillow, the flat root beer, and precious little love. Then there were her dreams and plans. "I want to be a doctor when I grow up," she used to say, and Mom would say, "Wonderful,

> The tradition is that the reason the story of the coat of many colors (or with long sleeves) is told is to remind later generations not to make a difference when they demonstrate their love for their children. (*Genesis Rabbah* 85.8)

GENESIS

dear! You can be anything you set your mind to be!" And I would say, "I want to be governor of Georgia," and Mom would say, "That's nice," with that sort of other-worldly sound in her voice, you know the one I mean, where the person who said it isn't really listening.

> The rabbis tell that when Joseph would bring back a bad report about his brothers, even God would take him aside and warn him against such behavior. In fact, the tales he told on his brothers became the determining factors in the kinds of trials he suffered later. (*Genesis Rabbah* 84.7)

Well, when she wasn't dreaming about being God's gift to medicine, she would dream about being a great ballerina or an opera diva or an astronaut or the savior of India's lepers. Whatever she thought of being, Mom and Dad would cluck and coo over her like giant brooding birds. They would exchange glances of pure delight and exclaim that their daughter was the smartest and most beautiful girl in the whole world. I, their son, wore mismatched clothes.

One day she went too far. She loudly announced, wearing still another gorgeous dress, a further sign (as if one were needed) that they loved her shamelessly, that *she* wanted to be the governor of Georgia. Mom said, "Wonderful! You can be whatever you want to be. You are so talented and so beautiful, who would not want to vote for you, probably more than once?" But that was *my* dream! She couldn't even leave me my dream. Well, I had to get her. I'm sure you can understand that. I just had to get her, and so I did.

I saved all my allowance for a year and hired a hit man. Now, don't get me wrong. I didn't want her dead, just knocked off her high horse. Well, he did a great job. He broke into her room one night, grabbed her, tore all her dresses into shreds, and spirited her away. I didn't even know where he was going to take her, and I didn't care. I thought that was the last I would ever see of her. And my parents? They were heartbroken, but instead of shifting all that love to me, they just sat around and moped about her. It was awful, worse than ever.

But that isn't the worst. The guy I hired took her to Georgia. They fell in love, married, and last month she was elected governor of Georgia! Life is just not fair. You ever know anybody like that?

Joseph in Potiphar's House

Joseph, a handsome young slave in the house of one of Pharaoh's offi-
cials, makes his master's wife angry when he refuses her advances.
Though innocent, Joseph finds himself in prison.

The Story

When Joseph was taken down to Egypt by the Ishmaelites, he was bought from them by an Egyptian, Potiphar, one of Pharaoh's court officials, the captain of the guard. Joseph prospered, for the LORD was with him. He lived in the house of his Egyptian master, who saw that the LORD was with him and was giving him success in all that he undertook. Thus Joseph won his master's favour, and became his attendant. Indeed, his master put him in charge of his household, and entrusted him with everything he had. From the time that he put Joseph in charge of his household and all his property, the LORD blessed the household through Joseph; the LORD's blessing was on all that was his in house and field. Potiphar left it all in Joseph's care, and concerned himself with nothing but the food he ate.

Now Joseph was handsome in both face and figure, and after a time his master's wife became infatuated with him. 'Come, make love to me,' she said. But Joseph refused. 'Think of my master,' he said; 'he leaves the management of his whole house to me; he has trusted me with all he has. I am as important in this house as he is, and he has withheld nothing from me except you, because you are his wife. How can I do such a wicked thing? It is a sin against God.' Though she kept on at Joseph day after day, he refused to lie with her or be in her company.

One day when he came into the house to see to his duties, and none of the household servants was there indoors, she caught him by his loincloth, saying, 'Come, make love to me,' but he left the loincloth in her hand and ran from the house. When she saw that he had left his loincloth and run out of the house, she called to her servants, 'Look at this! My husband has brought in a Hebrew to bring insult on us. He came in here to rape me, but I gave a loud scream. When he heard me scream and call for help, he ran out, leaving his loincloth behind.' She kept it by her until his master came home, and then she repeated her tale: 'That Hebrew slave you brought in came to my room to make me an object of insult. But when I screamed for help, he ran out of the house, leaving his loincloth behind.' Joseph's master was furious when he heard his wife's account of what his slave had done to her. He had Joseph seized and thrown into the guardhouse, where the king's prisoners were kept; and there he was confined. But the LORD was with Joseph and kept faith with him, so that he won the favour of the governor of the guardhouse. Joseph was put in charge of the prisoners, and he directed all their work. The governor ceased to concern himself with anything entrusted to Joseph, because the LORD was with him and gave him success in all that he did.

Comments on the Story

The story in chapter 38 about Judah, his sons, and his resourceful daughter-in-law Tamar is a surprising intrusion into the ongoing story of Joseph. It could easily be dropped, and no one would miss it in the least. However, it does illustrate two of the themes that the Joseph saga is addressing. The first is the issue of deception and trickery and the significant results of such behaviors on the relationships in a family. Just as Judah is caught in a lie by Tamar's deception of him (38:14-19), so also the brothers of Joseph will be revealed as deceivers, deceived by the deceptions of Joseph himself. The second theme is the fact that although the cultural tradition suggests that the eldest child is the one to inherit the promises and blessing of the family, the stories of Genesis consistently demonstrate that in the realities of human greed and passion, such cultural traditions are not always fulfilled. At the end of chapter 38, Tamar, pregnant by her own father-in-law, gives birth to twins, but the order of their birth says again that the elder will not have the right of inheritance (38:27-30).

There is another reason for this strange story. Prior to the beginning of the Joseph cycle in chapter 37, negative stories have been told about the eldest sons of Jacob. The story of the rape of Dinah indicts Simeon and Levi as outrageous killers (34), and Reuben, as we have already seen, "slept with Bilhah," in an apparent attempt to usurp the role of head of the clan from his father (35:22). Now with this story of Judah, at best a morally and culturally problematic one, all four of Jacob's eldest children are tainted by their actions. It might almost appear that the narrator is clearing the decks of those who precede Joseph in the line of succession. However, there may even be surprises in store about the one who does actually succeed.

With the beginning of chapter 39 the story resumes where it ended in chapter 37. We learn that Joseph has been purchased from the Ishmaelites (37:36 claimed it was the Midianites who did the selling) by Potiphar, the captain of Pharaoh's personal guard. The phrase "the Lord was with Joseph" will appear again and again in the story. One of this narrator's major concerns is to portray the providence of God at work in the life of Joseph. But, as always in the Hebrew Bible, that portrayal will not be a simple one; God is with Joseph, but that does not prevent Joseph from being pictured as a complex human being.

Potiphar notices right away that "the Lord was with him," because everything that Joseph touches "prospers in his hands" (39:3). As a result, Potiphar "made him overseer in his house and over *all* that he had." The emphasis in

39:3-5 is on the inclusiveness of Joseph's increasing power and importance in the house of Potiphar and on the remarkable ways in which Joseph bestows a blessing wherever he turns. Joseph is so trusted by Potiphar that "he abandoned [a strong verb; see Ps. 22:1] all that he had into the hand of Joseph; with him around, Potiphar thought of *nothing* but the food he ate" (39:6). At least Joseph does not touch or handle the food of his master, but he does do *everything* else in the house.

Joseph's complete mastery of the affairs of Potiphar soon brings a crisis, because the narrator only now tells us that "Joseph was handsome, really good-looking" ("good-looking" is a quite literal reading of the Hebrew; see the identical phrase in the description of Rachel at 29:17). "So after a time, his master's wife cast her eyes on Joseph, and she said, "Sleep with me." The next speech is important as a delineation of the character of Joseph. The narrator quickly says that "he refused," using the same verb with which Jacob "refused" to be comforted after the "death" of Joseph (37:35). Yet, the reasons for his refusal are not very simple.

He first says, "Look! My lord, having me, does not know what is happening in the house, and *all* that he has given into my hand. He is not greater in this house than I am" (39:8-9). This is a most intriguing way to respond first to the urgent request of a woman panting for sexual intercourse! Note the remarkable number of first-person pronouns in these lines. It is the claim of a supremely confident man, a man completely aware of his enormous authority. Yet, his final claim to be as great as Potiphar himself could be heard as the boast of an over-reaching arrogant slave; it reminds us of the Joseph of chapter 37. Joseph wants Potiphar's wife to know beyond the shadow of a doubt that he is a *very* important man who handles everything in the house, except Potiphar's food.

He continues, "He has withheld *nothing* from me, except you because you are his wife. How could I do this great wickedness and sin against God?" (39:99). Concern for God finally appears, but it comes only at the end of the speech. Joseph is not concerned primarily with the moral sin of adultery; his primary interest is in jeopardizing his position in the house of Potiphar, the man who has elevated him to a position of enormous responsibility. It is concern for trust that motivates him rather than fear of transgressing a sexual taboo. But also Joseph orders his speech in such a way as to indicate *first* his great power and importance to the woman, lording over her the fact that he very well *could* give in to her desires, but chooses not to do so. It is a refusal, but one that does not cool the passion of the woman; he inflames it all the more.

Day after day she speaks to Joseph, but he will not listen to her, either to sleep with her or even to be with her. But one day, when no one else is in the house, the desperate woman grabs Joseph by his clothes and demands, "Sleep with me!" But Joseph leaves his clothes in her hand and rushes out of the house. The rejected woman then cries rape. She first blames her husband for the insult: "See how he has brought a Hebrew man to make fun of us; he came to me to sleep with me, but I cried out with a loud voice. When he heard my loud cry, he left his clothes with me and ran out of the house" (39:14-15). The poor unfulfilled woman then "rests with his clothes near her until his master came home" (39:16). If she cannot have his body, the only thing she can have is his clothing, which she cuddles in the privacy of her own anguish.

She repeats the story to her husband, and it is no surprise that Potiphar is enraged, so he throws Joseph into prison, "the place where the king's prisoners were confined." Joseph is not immediately killed, nor is he sent to labor out his life in some obscure Egyptian mine or quarry. The prison to which he goes is only for the most famous of prisoners. Still, it is a prison, and perhaps this time Joseph really will disappear from history. However, the familiar line appears again: "But the Lord was with Joseph, showing him steadfast love, and giving him favor in the eyes of the keeper of the prison." Soon, as we now expect from this golden boy, Joseph has charge of *"all* the prisoners who were in the prison; *everything* that was done there was done by him" (39:22). Just like Potiphar before him, the keeper of the prison paid no attention to anything that was in Joseph's hands, "because the Lord was with him" (39:23). Joseph has once again fallen into a pit, but has once again come out smelling like a rose.

The structure of this story is similar to the one that precedes it in chapter 37 in several ways. Jacob is tricked by his sons by means of Joseph's clothing; here Potiphar is tricked by his wife by means of Joseph's clothing. Joseph is thrown into a pit from which he is never expected to exit; here he is also thrown into a pit, after being falsely accused of rape. If the parallel holds, the reader can expect him to escape this pit, too. Joseph remains the arrogant one we saw in chapter 37. He is more than ever convinced of his enormous worth and power, and he hurls it at whomever he meets. And, of course, God is with him in all that he does. It is once again a mystery that the divine choice has come to such a one as this, so like Abraham, Isaac, and his father, Jacob, before him. Just how will God work through this one?

Retelling the Story

Potiphar paces about his study and speaks aloud to himself. "On the one hand, he is the best, most trustworthy worker I've ever employed. He took care of everything but feeding me and would have done that, if I had asked him.

"On the other hand he is young and handsome, and his body hasn't gone soft in the middle like so many men my age. And in truth I am not in the same shape I was when I was his age.

"On the one hand, she is my wife, and I trust and love her. Before this Hebrew came, she had no rival for my affections. Nor did I have a rival for hers.

"On the other hand, she is still young and lovely. A woman has needs, and I travel so much on Pharaoh's business.

"On the one hand he has never lied to me or stolen from me. I would trust him with anything or anyone in my house, including my wife. In fact, I did.

"On the other hand, he is a foreigner and a slave. I have always heard that what they really wanted was our women.

"On the one hand, she has been faithful to me, as far as I know.

"On the other hand, I cannot know everything that goes on in my house.

"Shall I have him killed or put to work under the hot Egyptian sun in a quarry cutting stone? I dare not let him go or sell him to another after this accusation. Perhaps the minimum security prison for the government's favored inmates. Then, if he is truly honest, he can find his way back into the world again."

Potiphar's wife was said to have chased Joseph through the house until she cornered him in the bedroom. Above the bed was an idol, and when she came into the room she threw a sheet over it. Seeing this, Joseph said, "Why do you cover the face of your god, if you are not ashamed of what you are about to do? And how will you keep it hidden from the One who sees us even in secret?" (*Genesis Rabbah* 87.5)

Someone asked one of the rabbis if Joseph (who would have had all the desires of a young man) might not be guilty of having committed the crime of which he was accused. The rabbi brought forth the Torah and read the story of Reuben and Bilhah and that of Judah and Tamar. Then he said, "If the Scripture can be so honest as to tell these stories, would it hesitate to tell the truth about Joseph?" (*Genesis Rabbah* 87.6)

The rabbis suggest that Joseph, in addition to being handsome, was vain about his looks. They compare him to someone who sat looking in a mirror, fixing his hair and face. But when he got up he had to face a she-bear, which was a common rabbinic image for Potiphar's wife. (*Genesis Rabbah* 87.3)

Joseph the Interpreter of Dreams

Joseph is brought from prison to be an interpreter of Pharaoh's dreams and winds up being second only to Pharaoh.

The Story

Some time after these events it happened that the king's cupbearer and the royal baker gave offence to their lord, the king of Egypt. Pharaoh was displeased with his two officials, his chief cupbearer and chief baker, and put them in custody in the house of the captain of the guard, in the guardhouse where Joseph was imprisoned. The captain appointed Joseph as their attendant, and he waited on them.

They had been in prison in the guardhouse for some time, when one night the king's cupbearer and his baker both had dreams, each with a meaning of its own. Coming to them in the morning, Joseph saw that they looked dispirited, and asked these officials in custody with him in his master's house, why they were so downcast that day. They replied, 'We have each had a dream, but there is no one to interpret them.' Joseph said to them, 'All interpretation belongs to God. Why not tell me your dreams?' So the chief cupbearer told Joseph his dream: 'In my dream', he said, 'there was a vine in front of me. On the vine there were three branches, and as soon as it budded, it blossomed and its clusters ripened into grapes. I plucked the grapes and pressed them into Pharaoh's cup which I was hold-ing, and then put the cup into Pharaoh's hand.' Joseph said to him, 'This is the interpretation. The three branches are three days: within three days Pharaoh will raise your head and restore you to your post; then you will put the cup into Pharaoh's hand as you used to do when you were his cup-bearer. When things go well with you, remember me and do me the kindness of bringing my case to Pharaoh's notice; help me to get out of this prison. I was carried off by force from the land of the Hebrews, and here I have done nothing to deserve being put into this dungeon.

When the chief baker saw that the interpretation given by Joseph had been favourable, he said to him, 'I too had a dream, and in my dream there were three baskets of white bread on my head. In the top basket there was every kind of food such as a baker might prepare for Pharaoh, but the birds were eating out of the top basket on my head.' Joseph answered, 'This is the interpretation. The three baskets are three days: within three days Pharaoh will raise your head off your shoulders and hang you on a tree, and the birds of the air will devour the flesh off your bones.'

The third day was Pharaoh's birth-day and he gave a banquet for all his officials. He had the chief cupbearer and the chief baker brought up where they were all assembled. The cupbearer was restored to his position, and he put the cup into Pharaoh's hand; but the baker was hanged. All went as Joseph had said in interpreting the dreams for them. The cupbearer, however, did not bear Joseph in mind; he forgot him.

Two years later Pharaoh had a dream: he was standing by the Nile, when there came up from the river seven cows, sleek and fat, and they grazed among the reeds. Presently seven other cows, gaunt and lean, came up from the river, and stood beside the cows on the river bank. The cows that were gaunt and lean devoured the seven cows that were sleek and fat. Then Pharaoh woke up.

He fell asleep again and had a second dream: he saw seven ears of grain, full and ripe, growing on a single stalk. Springing up after them were seven other ears, thin and shrivelled by the east wind. The thin ears swallowed up the seven ears that were full and plump. Then Pharaoh woke up and found it was a dream.

In that morning Pharaoh's mind was so troubled that he summoned all the dream-interpreters and wise men of Egypt, and told them his dreams; but there was no one who could interpret them for him. Then Pharaoh's chief cupbearer spoke up. 'Now I must mention my offences,' he said: 'Pharaoh was angry with his servants, and imprisoned me and the chief baker in the house of the captain of the guard. One night we both had dreams, each requiring its own interpretation. We had with us there a young Hebrew, a slave of the captain of the guard, and when we told him

our dreams he interpreted them for us, giving each dream its own interpretation. Things turned out exactly as the dreams had been interpreted to us: I was restored to my post, the other was hanged.'

Pharaoh thereupon sent for Joseph, and they hurriedly brought him out of the dungeon. After he had shaved and changed his clothes, he came in before Pharaoh, who said to him, 'I have had a dream which no one can interpret. I have heard that you can interpret any dream you hear.' Joseph answered, 'Not I, but God, can give an answer which will reassure Pharaoh.' Then Pharaoh said to him: 'In my dream I was standing on the bank of the Nile, when there came up from the river seven cows, fat and sleek, and they grazed among the reeds. After them seven other cows came up that were in poor condition, very gaunt and lean; in all Egypt I have never seen such gaunt creatures. These lean, gaunt cows devoured the first cows, the seven fat ones. They were swallowed up, but no one could have told they were in the bellies of the others, which looked just as gaunt as before. Then I woke up. In another dream I saw seven ears of grain, full and ripe, growing on a single stalk. Springing up after them were seven other ears, blighted, thin, and shrivelled by the east wind. The thin ears swallowed up the seven ripe ears. When I spoke to the dream-interpreters, no one could tell me the meaning.'

Joseph said to Pharaoh, 'Pharaoh's dreams are both the same; God has told Pharaoh what he is about to do. The seven good cows are seven years, and the seven good ears of grain are seven years—it is all one dream. The seven lean and gaunt cows that came up after them are seven years, and so also are the seven empty ears of grain blighted by the east wind; there are going to be seven years of famine. It is as I have told Pharaoh: God has let Pharaoh see what he is about to do. There are to be seven years of bumper harvests throughout Egypt. After them will come seven years of famine; so that the great harvests in Egypt will all be forgotten, and famine will ruin the country. The good years will leave no trace in the land because of the famine that follows, for it will be very severe. That Pharaoh has dreamed this twice means God is firmly resolved on this plan, and very soon he will put it into effect.

'Let Pharaoh now look for a man of vision and wisdom and put him in charge of the country. Pharaoh should take steps to appoint commissioners over the land to take one fifth of the produce of Egypt during the seven years of plenty. They should collect all food produced in the good years that are coming and put the grain under Pharaoh's control as a store of food to be kept in the towns. This food will be a reserve for the country against the seven years of famine which will come on Egypt, and so the country will not be devastated by the famine.'

The plan commended itself both to Pharaoh and to all his officials, and Pharaoh asked them, 'Could we find another man like this, one so endowed with the spirit of God?' To Joseph he said, 'Since God has made all this known to you, no one has your vision and wisdom. You shall be in charge of my household, and all my people will respect your every word. Only in regard to the throne shall I rank higher than you.' Pharaoh went on, 'I hereby give you authority over the whole land of Egypt.' He took off his signet ring and put it on Joseph's finger; he had him dressed in robes of fine linen, and hung a gold chain round his neck. He mounted him in his viceroy's chariot and men cried 'Make way!' before him. Thus Pharaoh made him ruler over all Egypt and said to him, 'I am the Pharaoh, yet without your consent no one will lift hand or foot throughout Egypt.' Pharaoh named him Zaphenath-paneah, and he gave him as his wife Asenath daughter of Potiphera priest of On. Joseph's authority extended over the whole of Egypt.

Comments on the Story

We left Joseph in the king's prison, not languishing in a filthy dungeon, but literally in charge of everything in the place. Just as he grew to be in charge of everything in the house of Potiphar, so in prison he also comes to be in control. Movement toward mastery of any situation seems to a hallmark of the life of Joseph, and we can expect more of the same as his story continues.

Chapter 40 tells of two former servants of Pharaoh who offend their lord and are thrown into the prison where Joseph is. The two are the chief cupbearer—that is, Pharaoh's personal servant—and the chief baker. They are, of course, placed under the care of Joseph, the real master of the prison. On the same night both of these men have dreams, "each one with its own meaning" (40:5). When Joseph comes to see them in the morning after the dreams, he sensitively sees that they are troubled. They tell him that they have dreamed, but that no one is capable of interpreting the dreams. Joseph quickly responds, "Do not interpretations belong to God? Please tell them to me" (40:8). The verb translated as "interpret," and the noun that arises from it, are found only in the Joseph story in the Hebrew Bible, and marks it as a unified narrative. Joseph's response to the troubled expressions of the two servants tells him that they do not necessarily need professional dream interpreters to help them, that apparently being the expected procedure in the ancient world. If interpretation belongs to God, then God can bestow the skill on anyone, even Joseph. Of course, the reader already knows that this Joseph has a special way with dreams.

The butler first recounts his dream of a three-branched vine that first blossomed then brought forth grapes. The cupbearer quickly squeezed the grapes right into Pharaoh's cup and handed it to him. Joseph immediately interprets the dream as one predicting speedy restoration to the service of Pharaoh for the imprisoned servant.

Joseph, however, also adds a request. He wants the rulers of Egypt to know that he is innocent and has done nothing wrong to deserve this pit and thus gain his release. There is irony here. It is, in a sense, true that Joseph has done nothing to deserve being thrown into a pit. Yet, in the first story, Joseph's own arrogance led to the fury of his brothers, which caused them to put him in the dry pit in the wilderness. And in the later story, Joseph's taunting of Potiphar's wife, rather than a simple refusal of her sexual advances, led to her lies about rape and Joseph's second trip to a pit. Joseph is hardly completely innocent in either event, and that lack of innocence will be a question later on in the story as well.

Pharaoh's baker, seeing the wonderful future predicted for the cupbearer, urges Joseph to interpret his dream, too. In his dream, three baskets of bread were on his head, and the bread was for Pharaoh. However, birds were eating the bread out of the baskets. The baker would have been better off not to have mentioned this dream, because, as Joseph interprets it, within three days Pharaoh will cut off the baker's head, hang his body on a tree, and the birds will make a great feast on it (40:16-19).

All happens just as Joseph had said; the cupbearer is restored, and the baker is hanged. "But the cupbearer did not remember Joseph, but forgot him" (40:23). Two whole years pass. Then it is Pharaoh's turn to dream, but his dreams are especially rich and suggestive. In the first, seven very healthy cows rise out of the Nile to graze in the grass; then seven diseased cows come up and stand next to the healthy ones. Suddenly, the sick ones eat the fat ones. Pharaoh awakens, probably in a cold sweat. But he dreams a second time: Seven healthy ears of grain are growing on one stalk, but seven blighted ears appear on the same stalk. Suddenly, the thin ears swallow up the healthy ears. Pharaoh awakens again, and now is troubled (41:1-7).

He anxiously calls "the magicians of Egypt and its wise men," and tells them the dream. "But no one could interpret them for Pharaoh" (41:8). The cupbearer finally "remembers his sins [or "faults"] today," and is reminded of the Hebrew prisoner who could so well interpret dreams (41:9-13). Pharaoh hurriedly calls Joseph to be brought to him. "He shaved himself, changed his clothes, and came in before Pharaoh" (41:14). Just as clothes have played a role in every individual story in the cycle up to now (37:32; 39:12), so also Joseph's change of clothes now signifies that an important event is once again about to occur.

Pharaoh recounts his dreams for Joseph, saying first that none of his wise men could interpret it and that he has heard that Joseph is a great interpreter. But Joseph responds, "Not I! God will answer *shalom* to Pharaoh" (41:16). The *shalom* that the brothers could not feel toward their arrogant brother Joseph (37:4), God now offers to Pharaoh through the interpretations of that same Joseph. The word *shalom* has multiple connotations here. It can mean "complete," "whole," "sound," or "peaceful," and it often has the sense of "reward." God will provide *shalom,* and the *shalom* will extend itself into more lives than Pharaoh's alone.

Joseph wastes no time telling the meaning of the dreams; the Egyptian magicians may not have been able to solve them, but Joseph has no trouble at all. Joseph reveals to Pharaoh that the land will have a seven-year famine following seven years of bumper crops. That is the interpretation, which is all that Joseph was asked to do. However, the dream interpreter does not stop there; he now offers specific advice to the most powerful monarch on earth: "So now let Pharaoh look around for a wise and intelligent man, and set him over the land of Egypt" (41:343). Can there be any real doubt about whom Joseph has in mind? Of course, he means himself! This becomes clearer when he enumerates precisely what this "unknown" "wise and intelligent man" should do in this crisis (41:34-36). Listening to the eloquent and resourceful Hebrew, Pharaoh says, "Can we find such a man as this in whom is the spirit of God?" My, my, who could it be? Finally, Pharaoh sees the light. "Since God has shown you all this, there is no one wise and intelligent as you are" (41:39). I imagine Joseph's eyes were wide with mock astonishment as he said with exaggerated tone, "Who, *me?*" Of course, you, Joseph! Here is a man who never lets an opportunity go by for self-promotion, and this was a great opportunity. The result is that he is promoted from forgotten foreign prisoner to secretary of agriculture for the entire kingdom of Egypt.

Once again his clothes are changed (41:42), this time into the fine linen garments of Egypt. He is to ride in the second chariot, preceded only by the pharaoh himself. His power is almost limitless; only Pharaoh has a greater authority (41:44). From dry pit to near absolute power in the greatest kingdom on earth, exactly what manner of man is this?

Retelling the Story

The kingdom was in an uproar! Old Pharaoh had another one of his dreams, and we were being called back to offer an interpretation. These were the times that I dreaded! Even though I was only an apprentice magician, far down the pole of responsibility, I was not so far removed from the situation that, if heads began to roll, mine would rest easily on my shoulders. Pharaoh was prone to these startling night visions, and as he grew older they seemed to increase in intensity and frequency.

He had gone to sleep very early last night, but in less than an hour was screaming for the magicians to be brought to him. We came at a gallop. As we entered the royal bedchamber, we saw that he was trembling uncontrollably and sweating profusely. He spun out in fits and gasps a weird story of sleek cows being gobbled up by diseased cows. That was it. I could make nothing of it, and I looked at my mentor, the chief magician, who was always quite good at this sort of thing. One glance at his eyes, however, told me that this time he was stumped. Pharaoh threw us out, cursing us by all the gods of Egypt.

At least we thought we could sleep the rest of the night, but how wrong we were. About two hours later we were summoned again. Pharaoh was more agitated and drenched in sweat. He screamed something about fat ears of grain being swallowed by some skinny ears. Any fool could see that the dreams were related to each other, but exactly how and what they meant was beyond me. Unfortunately, they were beyond my colleagues, too. Pharaoh was livid; at his age, I had thought, he was not capable of the rage I witnessed. The veins on his neck stood out like cords. I silently prayed to the now-forbidden Aten for safety, for I feared my precious head was about to be separated from my equally well-loved body.

Then, the Aten answered my prayers in a most unlikely manner. Pharaoh's chief butler whispered something in his master's ear, and the ruler of upper and lower Egypt visibly calmed. After a few minutes the door was opened to reveal a Hebrew slave, but hardly a typical one. He strode into the room as one who was supremely confident, in absolute control of the situation. We magicians moved out of his way to avoid contamination by the heathen, but I must admit to a certain admiration as he walked toward Pharaoh without any visible sign of fear.

> The rabbis say that there were other interpretations of Pharaoh's dreams by his own wise people. One said that they meant Pharaoh would have seven daughters and that they would all die. Another said that they meant Pharaoh would conquer seven new provinces but that they would all rebel against him. But Pharaoh did not accept any of these interpretations as true. (*Genesis Rabbah 89.6*)

> The tradition reminds us that what Joseph suffered was for the sake of the world. He was brought to Egypt so that all might have bread in a time of famine. (*Genesis Rabbah* 84.17)

Pharaoh repeated his two dreams, and with no hesitation the slave spun out an interpretation that was really quite brilliant. I saw the jealousy in my mentor's eyes as the slave talked, but I felt relief as Pharaoh seemed to have forgotten us and was single mindedly attentive to the Hebrew. But the slave did not stop with interpretation, he went on to suggest a plan of action based on his interpretations. I saw immediately what this clever man was about. He urged Pharaoh to select a wise man to oversee the policies needed to save the country, then he detailed a plan for that salvation. The man was setting himself up as savior! And Pharaoh picked right up on it and appointed the slave master of Egypt's agriculture. It was a dizzying social rise and a devilishly clever bit of business. As we magicians left the bedchamber, I glanced again at the new man of power. Here was a man to be watched!

Joseph Reveals Himself

Joseph, who is now second only to Pharaoh in Egypt, meets his brothers again but conceals his identity from them for a time.

The Story

When Jacob learned that there was grain in Egypt, he said to his sons, 'Why do you stand staring at each other? I hear there is grain in Egypt. Go down there, and buy some for us to keep us alive and save us from starving to death.' So ten of Joseph's brothers went down to buy grain from Egypt, but Jacob did not let Joseph's brother Benjamin go with them, for fear that he might come to harm.

Thus the sons of Israel went with everyone else to buy grain because of the famine in Canaan. Now Joseph was governor of the land, and it was he who sold the grain to all its people. Joseph's brothers came and bowed to the ground before him, and when he saw his brothers he recognized them but, pretending not to know them, he greeted them harshly. 'Where do you come from?' he demanded. 'From Canaan to buy food,' they answered. Although Joseph had recognized his brothers, they did not recognize him. He remembered the dreams he had had about them and said, 'You are spies; you have come to spy out the weak points in our defences.' 'No, my lord,' they answered; 'your servants have come to buy food. We are all sons of one man. We are honest men; your servants are not spies.' 'No,' he maintained, 'it is to spy out our weaknesses that you have come.' They said,'There were twelve of us, my lord, all brothers, sons of one man back in Canaan; the youngest is still with our father, and one is lost.' But Joseph insisted, 'As I have already said to you: you are spies. This is how you will be put to the test: unless your youngest brother comes here. I swear by the life of Pharaoh you shall not leave this place. Send one of your number to fetch your brother; the rest of you will remain in prison. Thus your story will be tested to see whether you are telling the truth. If not, then by the life of Pharaoh you must be spies.' With that he kept them in prison for three days.

On the third day Joseph said to them, 'Do what I say and your lives will be spared, for I am a godfearing man: if you are honest men, only one of you brothers shall be kept in prison, while the rest of you may go and take grain for your starving households; but you must bring your youngest brother to me. In this way your words will be proved true, and you will not die.' They consented, and among themselves they said, 'No doubt we are being punished because of our brother. We saw his distress when he pleaded with us and we refused to listen.

That is why this distress has come on us.' Reuben said, 'Did I not warn you not to do wrong to the boy? But you would not listen, and now his blood is on our heads, and we must pay.' They did not know that Joseph understood, since he had used an interpreter. Joseph turned away from them and wept. Then he went back to speak to them, and took Simeon from among them and had him bound before their eyes. . . .

. . . Then Judah went up to him and said, 'Please listen, my lord, and let your servant speak a word, I beg. Do not be angry with me, for you are as great as Pharaoh himself. My lord, you asked us whether we had a father or a brother. We answered, "We have an aged father, and he has a young son born in his old age; this boy's full brother is dead, and since he alone is left of his mother's children, his father loves him." You said to us, your servants, "Bring him down to me so that I may set eyes on him." We told you, my lord, that the boy could not leave his father; his father would die if he left him. But you said, "Unless your youngest brother comes down with you, you shall not enter my presence again." We went back to your servant my father, and reported to him what your lordship had said, so when our father told us to go again and buy food, we answered, "We cannot go down; for without our youngest brother we cannot enter the man's presence; but if our brother is with us, we will go." Then your servant my father said to us, "You know that my wife bore me two sons. One left me, and I said, 'He must have been torn to pieces.' I have not seen him since. If you take this one from me as well, and he comes to any harm, then you will bring down my grey hairs in misery to the grave. Now, my lord, if I return to my father without the boy—and remember, his life is bound up with the boy's—what will happen is this: he will see that the boy is not with us and he will die, and your servants will have brought down our father's grey hairs in sorrow to the grave. Indeed, my lord, it was I who went surety for the boy to my father. I said, "If I do not bring him back to you, then you can blame me for it all my life." Now, my lord, let me remain in place of the boy as my lord's slave, and let him go with his brothers. How can I return to my father without the boy? I could not bear to see the misery which my father would suffer.'

Joseph was no longer able to control his feelings in front of all his attendants, and he called, 'Let everyone leave my presence!' There was nobody present when Joseph made himself known to his brothers, but he wept so loudly that the Egyptians heard him, and news of it got to Pharaoh's household. Joseph said to his brothers, 'I am Joseph! Can my father be still alive?' They were so dumbfounded at finding themselves face to face with Joseph that they could not answer. Joseph said to them, 'Come closer to me,' and when they did so, he said, 'I am your brother Joseph, whom you sold into Egypt. Now do not be distressed or blame yourselves for selling me into slavery here; it was to save lives that God sent me ahead of you. For there have now been two years of famine in the land, and there will be another five years with neither ploughing nor harvest. God sent me on ahead of you to ensure that you will have descendants on earth, and to preserve for you a host of survivors. It is clear that it was not you who sent me here, but God, and he has made me Pharaoh's chief counsellor, lord over his whole household and ruler of all Egypt. Hurry back to my father and give him this message from his son Joseph: "God has made me lord of all Egypt. Come down to me without delay. You will live in the land of Goshen and be near me, you, your children and grandchildren, your flocks and herds, and all that you have. I shall provide for you there and see that you and your household and all that you have are not reduced to want; for there are still five years of famine to come." You can see for yourselves, and so can my brother Benjamin, that it is really Joseph himself who is speaking to you. Tell my father of all the honour which I enjoy in Egypt, tell him all you have seen, and bring him down here with all speed.' He threw his arms round his brother Benjamin and wept, and Benjamin too embraced him weeping. He then kissed each of his brothers and wept over them; after that his brothers were able to talk with him.

Comments on the Story

At one level, Joseph quite literally reveals himself to his astonished brothers in chapter 45; they, who thought he was dead, stand in terror before the great potentate of Egypt, suddenly unmasked. But there is another level at which this material is a revelation of Joseph, if only a partial one. We will learn much more about Joseph as a man as we watch him interact with his brothers, who come to Egypt to buy food for the family. It is a long story, and I urge you to read all of it. I will look specifically at those portions printed above.

As a result of the careful agricultural practices of the wise Joseph, Egypt is spared the worst ravages of the famine. During the seven years of plenty, Joseph has stockpiled grain against the evil days to come. When the famine arrives, the people ask Pharaoh for food, and he sends them all to Joseph, who now controls all of the grain in the land (41:55). Moreover, the famine spreads over all the earth so that "all the earth came to Egypt to Joseph to buy grain" (41:57).

The family of Jacob, still living in the southern part of Israel, are soon forced to go to Egypt to buy grain. But Benjamin, the youngest and new favorite of Jacob, did not go with them; Jacob was afraid that some harm might come to him, in the same way some terrible beast had supposedly torn his other favorite to pieces so long ago. Already, we can anticipate the confrontation that is certain to come.

As the ten brothers come face to face with the terrible Egyptian, whom we know to be Joseph, they bow down "with their faces to the ground" (42:6). And with that action, Joseph's arrogant dreams of so long ago are fulfilled (37:5-11). The narrator now slows the action of the scene to allow the reader to reflect on the possible response of Joseph to his prostrate brothers.

"Joseph saw his brothers and he knew them." There is no doubt who they are; Joseph recognizes them immediately. "But he spoke to them harshly,

187

'Where do you come from?' " (42:7). "Thus Joseph knew his brothers, but they did not know him. And Joseph remembered the dreams that he had dreamed about them, and said, 'You are spies! To search out the weakness of the land you have come!'" (42:8-9).

The sequence of this scene is very important. The brothers bow down, and Joseph knows them immediately, while they do not know that their long-lost brother is before them. But his first response to them is called "harsh." The very dreams he remembers cause a true explosion of anger as he accuses them, quite falsely, of being spies who have come to examine the land of Egypt for its defensive weak spots. And we need to ask why. Here we have a true gap in the text. Joseph's behavior is in one sense unexpected, and the text has not given us many direct clues by which we might understand it. We know he is full of himself, and we know that the actions of the brothers earlier have been truly callous. Is this a clear attempt at revenge? After all, he has them right where he wants them. Or is he maneuvering them toward some sort of repentance of their evil deed?

The brothers claim to be "honest," but, of course, we know them to be far from that. They claim to be "twelve brothers," the youngest being at home with their father, although they admit that "one is no more" (42:13). But the cruel potentate will hear none of these excuses. The disguised Joseph then demands that they choose one of them to go get the younger brother while the rest of them must remain behind in prison. If they refuse the test, they will prove themselves to be spies.

But after three days, the cruel one changes the rules of the test. Now he demands that *one* remain behind in prison, while the *rest* return to get Benjamin. This inconsistency in rules for those imprisoned is a classic example of psychological warfare, designed to create fear and uncertainty in the minds of the captives.

The result of the shifting test is a discussion among the brothers about their guilt. If the goal of the test is to engender an admission of guilt, it has worked. But Joseph does not reveal himself yet; surely we can conclude that an admission of guilt is not all that Joseph is after. Reuben then says, in effect, I told you so (42:22), but we know from our earlier discussion of Reuben's actions that his reason for wanting to save Joseph was not mere selflessness (see the discussion of Gen. 37).

Joseph, of course, is listening to this entire conversation. The brothers assume that this mighty Egyptian cannot understand Hebrew, because there is a translator standing between them, all the better to make Joseph's charade more believable. But as he listens, "he turned away from them and wept," but then returns to tie Simeon up before their eyes. He is the hostage who will forfeit his life if Benjamin does not return with the other brothers.

Joseph further upsets the brothers by putting the food money back into their sacks, and they fear that the angry Egyptian will accuse them of theft. In this, they are quite right, but not just yet. The brothers return home safely and tell their father about the demands of the Egyptian. At first, Jacob refuses to allow Benjamin to go back to Egypt; he seems ready to sacrifice Simeon to save his youngest son (42:29-38). But the famine remains severe, and the brothers are forced to return to Egypt and to the harsh Egyptian. Jacob accuses his sons of revealing the existence of Benjamin to the terrible man for no reason (43:6), but his sons claim that "the man questioned us closely" (43:7), something that the reader knows did not happen (42:9-13).

Jacob finally agrees, but in typical fashion prepares a huge gift for the Egyptian to assuage his anger. The reader remembers a similar ploy when Jacob was trying to appease the fury of Esau (Gen. 33). The brothers, accompanied by Benjamin, return to the presence of the Egyptian. When Joseph sees Benjamin, he weeps for a second time (43:30). Though his desire to be with his brother is so overwhelming that he weeps for him, it is not strong enough yet for him to end the game. He offers them a meal, but serves the plates in the order of their birth (how would an Egyptian know that?) but gives Benjamin five times as much as the rest of them (43:32-34).

He then bids them return to their land, but instructs his servant again to replace the food money in their sacks, and this time to hide his favorite cup in Benjamin's sack. The servant is then instructed to overtake them, accuse them of theft, and then bring them back to Joseph (44:1-5). The plan works beautifully, and they all return to Egypt, expecting to be killed by the mysterious and heartless Egyptian.

Judah then utters what may be the only heartfelt speech in the entire story (44:18-34). In moving phrases, he offers his own life for the life of Benjamin and his other brothers, and for his father, the old and lonely man, anxiously waiting word from his youngest son.

This speech finally breaks the spell of the game for Joseph. He sends his servants away so that no one will hear when he reveals himself to his brothers. However, he weeps so loudly that the Egyptians hear it anyway (45:2). Finally, he says, "I am Joseph; is my father still alive?" The brothers are literally struck dumb by this incredible revelation. He continues by saying, "Do not be distressed or angry with yourselves, because you sold me here. Surely, God sent me before you to preserve life" (45:5). Everything has been in the hands of God, says Joseph, and he tells his brothers that they can come to live with him in Egypt (45:6-13). He weeps again and kisses both Benjamin and his other brothers, and finally they can talk to him (45:15).

This scene is *not* the complete reconciliation that Joseph might desire, which will become clear in the last chapter of the story. Still, is it enough to claim that *all* was finally in the hand of God? Can we so quickly forget that

Joseph played a cruel game with his brothers and his father? If engendering remorse and repentance was his only motivation, the game went on far too long, for remorse was reached at 42:21. No, Joseph also wanted revenge for his ill treatment at the hands of his brothers, and he achieves it. But the cost of that revenge is high, as the final scenes of the saga of Joseph unfold.

Retelling the Story

Joseph's translator speaks:

"I couldn't imagine why he had asked me to be there. He speaks Hebrew as well as I can; better even. He may have forgotten where he came from, but believe me there are those of us who haven't. He may have an Egyptian name and wife, and he may have a position of power, but he is still a foreigner.

"Also, I couldn't figure out why he took such an interest in this particular rag-tag gaggle of Hebrews with their hands out. Most of the time he just signed the papers approving food rations without so much as a question. Just because those other governments had not the foresight that we (rather, Joseph) had to store up food during the good years, they think now that it is Egypt's responsibility to feed the whole world. And the way Joseph acted, he must have thought so, too.

"But this group was different. He questioned them and accused them of being spies. I, for one, was glad he was taking a harder line with these beggars. They would talk among themselves in their language and never had a clue that he could understand every word.

"Finally, he kept one and sent the rest back home with food and orders to bring their youngest brother with them when they returned. Don't ask me why. It didn't make any sense to me either.

"Well, when they did come back, more out of hunger than concern for their brother, if you ask me, this time he seemed upset about something. He

> The rabbis say that Joseph hoped to be reunited with his brothers. Some say that he put guards at all the gates with a list of his brothers' names. He knew when they entered the city, but he didn't know that they were looking for him. Since he was good looking the last time they saw him, they went looking for him in the red-light district. They thought because of his looks he would be running with a fast crowd. When his guards found them, they confessed to what they had done to their brother. Even so, he did not reveal himself immediately.
>
> Others say that he simply left instructions for everyone entering the land to give the name of his or her father and grandfather. That way he knew when his brothers were on their way. (*Genesis Rabbah* 91.4, 6)

190

would go back into his chamber and return with eyes red and swollen. I hope he hasn't taken to using those illegal potions sold by unscrupulous herbalists.

"After toying with them further, Joseph invited them home for dinner. I can't tell for sure what happened after that, since I was not one of the dinner guests. But I heard from one of his servants that when they left, Joseph had one of his own cups placed in the sack of the youngest brother, then had his people stop and search them for it. When they returned, one of the brothers begged Joseph to keep him instead of the youngest one. It would kill their father to lose him, since he had lost his other favorite years ago. A rather nice speech from what I heard. Then Joseph told them that he was their brother, whom they had tried to get rid of years earlier. Then he told them to go home and bring the whole family back to settle in Egypt.

"Well, things may look fine now, but just wait until their protector is gone. Then they'll learn what we Egyptians think of foreigners."

> Once there was a well full of clear, cold water, but no one could get the water out of it. Finally someone tied pieces of rope and cord and twine and thread together until the bucket could reach the water and bring it up. Just so, Judah put together words like rope, cord, twine, and thread until they reached the depths of Joseph's heart and drew forth the refreshment of compassion. (*Genesis Rabbah* 93.4)

GENESIS 50:1-26

Jacob and Family Come to Egypt

Joseph's brothers bring Jacob and the entire family to Egypt to settle in one of the better parts of the land. Here Jacob dies and is buried back in Canaan.

The Story

Then Joseph threw himself upon his father, weeping over him and kissing him. He gave orders to the physicians in his service to embalm his father, and they did so, finishing the task in forty days, the usual time required for embalming. The Egyptians mourned Israel for seventy days. When the period of mourning was over, Joseph spoke to members of Pharaoh's household: 'May I ask a favour—please speak for me to Pharaoh. Tell him that my father on his deathbed made me swear that I would bury him in the grave that he had bought for himself in Canaan. Ask Pharaoh to let me go up and bury my father; and afterwards I shall return.' Pharaoh's reply was: 'Go and bury your father in accordance with your oath.' So Joseph went up to bury his father, and with him went all Pharaoh's officials, the elders of his household, and all the elders of Egypt, as well as all Joseph's own household, his brothers, and his father's household; only their children, with the flocks and herds, were left in Goshen. Chariots as well as horsemen went up with him, a very great company.

When they came to the threshing-floor of Atad beside the river Jordan, they raised a loud and bitter lamentation; and Joseph observed seven days' mourning for his father. When the Canaanite who lived there saw this mourning at the threshing-floor of Atad, they said, 'How bitterly the Egyptians are mourning!' So they named the place beside the Jordan Abel-mizraim.

Thus Jacob's sons did to him as he had instructed them: they took him to Canaan and buried him in the cave on the plot of land at Machpelah, the land which Abraham had bought as a burial-place from Ephron the Hittite, to the east of Mamre. After burying his father, Joseph returned to Egypt with his brothers and all who had gone up with him for the burial.

Now that their father was dead, Joseph's brothers were afraid, for they said, 'What if Joseph should bear a grudge against us and pay us back for all the harm we did to him?' They therefore sent a messenger to Joseph to say, 'In his last words to us before he died, your father gave us this message: "Say this to Joseph: I ask you to forgive your brothers' crime and wickedness; I know they did you harm." So now we beg you: forgive our crime, for we are servants of your father's God.' Joseph was moved to tears by their words. His brothers approached and bowed to the ground before him. 'We are your slaves,' they said. But Joseph replied, 'Do not be afraid. Am I in the place of God? You meant to do me harm; but God meant to bring good out of it by preserving the lives of many people, as we see today. 'Do not be afraid. I shall provide for you and your dependants.' Thus he comforted them and set their minds at rest.

Joseph remained in Egypt, he and his father's household. He lived to be a hundred and ten years old, and saw Ephraim's children to the third generation; he also recognized as his the children of Manasseh's son Machir. He said to his brothers, 'I am about to die; but God will not fail to come to your aid and take you from here to the land which he promised on oath to Abraham, Isaac, and Jacob.' He made the sons of Israel solemnly swear that when God came to their aid, they would carry his bones up with them from there. So Joseph died in Egypt at the age of a hundred and ten, and he was embalmed and laid in a coffin.

Comments on the Story

One climax in the story of Joseph and his brothers has apparently been reached. Joseph's shocking revelation of himself to his brothers was intended by him to reconstitute the family unity. On the surface, this appears to happen. However, tension in the family is still very real, as subsequent events reveal, so this so-called climax is no final climax at all. Joseph's lengthy manipulation of his brothers, with the apparent twin purposes of engendering repentance and gaining revenge, has scarred the family deeply.

Pharaoh urges Joseph to invite his family to live in Egypt, where they will be given the finest land in the kingdom (45:16-20). Joseph supplies his brothers with wagons to return to Israel, to load up the family belongings, and to come back to Egypt to live. If the family is so well reconciled, why then does Joseph warn them: "Do not fight with one another on the way" (45:24)? It is obvious that Joseph's control of the family situation is far from complete, no matter what the external circumstances seem to indicate.

At 46:1-4, God appears to Jacob once again (see Gen. 28 and Jacob's belief that God had appeared to him in Gen. 32 and 33) and reissues the promise to him, saying that the promise will be in force even if they are living in Egypt. Upon Jacob's arrival in Egypt, he twice blesses Pharaoh himself (47:7, 10), indicating that the promise and the blessing are indeed operative. However, it is Joseph who makes the blessing work, due to his agrarian policies that literally save the Egyptians from disaster (47:13-26). First, the people spend all their money for the grain that Joseph has stockpiled during the seven years of bumper crops (41:56). Next, as their money disappears, they exchange all their livestock for food. Last, they offer themselves and their land to Pharaoh for food. The result of these policies is that Pharaoh comes to control all of the land of Egypt, to have access to the people's labor, and is also entitled to one-fifth of the production of the fields. In short, Pharaoh becomes very rich and powerful indeed, and the cause of all of it is Joseph, the Hebrew. Yet, the irony may cut even deeper. Because of Joseph's policies, the possibility of Pharaoh's control of labor comes into being; later, another, less generous, Pharaoh will use this policy to enslave the Hebrews. Thus one could say that Joseph, of all people, made the bondage of Israel possible!

"Thus Israel lived in the land of Egypt, in the land of Goshen. They grew strong in it, were fruitful and multiplied exceedingly" (47:27). With those words the promise and blessing are again evident, and the reader is returned to Genesis 1:28. The God who created the world is the same God who is present with the Israelites even during their time in Egypt.

Finally the old patriarch Jacob dies (49:33), after seemingly blessing the wrong son of Joseph (the old younger-elder problem again; 48:17-19), and after offering a long poetic predictive blessing for all of his sons (49:1-27). One notable feature of that blessing is the claim that from the family of *Judah* will spring the messiah, not from the tribe of Joseph at all (49:10; unfortunately, the text here is extremely difficult). Once more the biblical story is characterized by surprise and the dashing of our expectations.

At his death, the Egyptians accord Jacob's body the singular gift of embalming, for which they take forty days, and they weep for him for seventy days (50:1-3). The numbers are round ones, the former being the typical "long-time" number in the Hebrew Bible, and the latter indicating the approximate length of official mourning in ancient Egypt (Diodorus, an early historian, says that the official time for mourning a king in Egypt was seventy-two days, although his information may not be fully trustworthy). After the official period of mourning ends, Joseph asks the pharaoh, "Let me go up and bury my father [in the land of Canaan], and I will return" (50:5). This is an ironic prefiguring of the demand a later leader will make to another pharaoh, "Let my people go! (Exod. 5:1 and others). But this pharaoh readily agrees, and even sends "both chariots and horsemen" with him for protection on the journey (50:9). Later, of course, a pharaoh will send chariots and horsemen, but then the goal will be Israelite destruction, not protection (Exod. 14:9). Thus this small story of Joseph's trip to Israel to bury his father is a mirror image of the later story of Israel's exodus from Egypt.

The great procession of lamenting Israelites and Egyptians arrives in the land of Canaan. The Egyptians are weeping so loudly that the Canaanites are moved to name one of their stopping places *Abel Mizraim,* the "mourning of Egyptians." All the company go to "the field at Machpelah" to the cave purchased by Abraham from Ephron the Hittite long ago (Gen. 23).

The family returns to Egypt, and immediately the brokenness of the group is made manifest. The death of Jacob has been sorrowful, but now the brothers of Joseph see it as dangerous. "Joseph will hate us and pay us back for all the evil that we did to him" (50:15). Even after the so-called reconciliation in chapter 45 and the invitation to live together in the land of Goshen, the brothers do not at all believe that Joseph has really forgiven them. And who can blame them? Joseph's carefully planned and cruelly employed games and tricks have left deep scars on his brothers that are not so easily wiped away.

They send a message to Joseph, wherein they lie, using the now-dead Jacob as the source of the deception. "Your father gave a command [to us] before he died, 'say to Joseph, Please forgive the transgression of your brothers and their sin, because they did evil to you' " (50:16-17). There is profound irony in the fact that even in death, Jacob the deceiver is used in an act of deception. He, of course, said no such thing to his sons, but they use him to express their fears of a brother they still do not trust.

And one last time, "Joseph wept when they spoke to him" (50:17). He knows now that they do not trust him and that the reconciliation has not occurred. And when his brothers then "fall on their faces and say, 'Look! We are your slaves,' " Joseph realizes that the breach between them is very wide indeed. Once again, he attempts to effect reconciliation. "Don't be afraid! Am I in the place of God?" That is a very good question for the brothers; as far as they have seen, Joseph's power and manipulation of their lives has been nearly god-like. And, they might ask, how can we *not* be afraid in the face of this still mysterious brother?

Joseph concludes his speech with famous lines: "You planned evil against me, but God planned it for good, so that today many people might live. So, don't be afraid! I will provide for you and for your little ones" (50:20-21). Perhaps Joseph still has not understood the depths of their fear. He still emphasizes *their* sin against him, as in 45:4-5, but says nothing about *his* cruel sin against them as master puppeteer in Egypt. To this concluding speech, the brothers say nothing at all. The book ends with the death of Joseph, after his charge that his bones not be left in Egypt, but be taken back to the family ground in the promised land.

Thus the great story of Genesis ends with a promise fulfilled and unfulfilled. The family of Israel has survived and prospered against all kinds of dangers, from both within and without. In that sense, God's promise is still alive. However, the unfinished business of the family of the chosen ones is quite real; their fears and internal squabbling have not been rounded off despite God's and Joseph's best efforts. Much remains to be done; much is left to be addressed. Still, Genesis is the great first act of the Bible. To read it carefully is to establish the themes of the whole, to appreciate the threads that remain to be woven into the complex tapestry that will be the two testaments of the ongoing tradition, to capture the very real hope that pervades that whole. And the best of all, through it all, is that God is with us. If I may paraphrase the wily Jacob, "Seeing your face (in this case the face of Genesis) is like seeing the face of God."

Retelling the Story

I simply do not trust him. I know perfectly well what he said, how he would provide for us in his adopted land of Egypt. And, I must admit, he has. We live comfortably enough on some of the finest land in the country. And our family is together, although he continues to spend a great deal of time at the seats of power; he is still responsible for the agricultural policies of the whole country. My little brother, the secretary of state of the land of Egypt! It still seems scarcely possible. When we threw him into that dry hole in the wilderness, anxious to be rid of him and his arrogant dreams, not one of us could ever have thought in our wildest nightmares that we would meet him again and that he would save our lives, just as his dreams had promised so long ago.

I suppose I sound ungrateful. Without him, we would all have starved to death long ago. Well, I can be grateful to him without trusting him, without loving him, can't I? You were not there when he played his tricks on us. If you had been, perhaps you would not have been so ready to welcome his help with open arms.

We had come to Egypt literally starving to death. Our father, Jacob, had remained at home to care for our youngest brother, Benjamin. Like many other foreigners we made our plea before this mighty Egyptian, or so we assumed he was. After we had made our simple request, the man had accused us of espionage and had demanded that we choose one of us to return to Israel, while the rest of us were to be tossed into prison. It was all absurd! The man had demanded that Benjamin be brought to Egypt by the one who returned. What in the world could this Egyptian want with Benjamin?

Then after three days he changed his mind. Now *one* of us was to be thrown into prison, while the rest went to retrieve Benjamin. The Egyptian was acting capriciously, to terrify us into doing his bidding. We did, believe me! But when we returned home, we found that the money we had given him to buy the food had mysteriously reappeared in our sacks. When the food ran out, we knew we had to return to Egypt to get more, but we also knew that if we did not bring Benjamin with us the crazy Egyptian would not even see us. So with great pain our father let him go with us.

All went well at first, but after we got the food and began to return home, the Egyptian's servant caught up with us and accused us of theft. His charges were ridiculous, but after a thorough search of our goods, to our horror, the Egyptian's favorite cup fell out of Benjamin's sack. Our lives are ended, we thought.

And they might have been if brother Judah had not pled with the Egyptian to save us, offering himself for all of us. Then, to our utter amazement, the Egyptian revealed himself to be none other than our brother Joseph! We were all stunned into silence. But while I was shocked, I was also angry as I thought of the cruel games that he had played with us, causing us constant anguish and bringing our father enormous grief.

So when Jacob died, I was terrified that Joseph would take final revenge on us, finishing the job he had begun earlier. So we lied. We claimed that Jacob, before he died, had demanded that Joseph not hurt us. Of course, we lied! We were scared of Joseph; he was not to be trusted. When he heard our lie, he wept, and I think I know why. He now realized that his cruel game was coming home to roost. He can say all he wants to about "God meaning it for good," but bringing God into it is not going to sweep his games from my memory. Oh, no. I will never trust Joseph completely again.

The tradition states that peace is so important that a person is allowed to make up a story to keep it, just as the brothers made up their father's wish to keep peace between Joseph and themselves. (*Genesis Rabbah* 100.8)

The rabbis said that those who show compassion show that they are true children of their honored forebears (Abraham and Sarah, Isaac and Rebekah, Jacob and Rachel, and others whose stories you have heard here). Those who are cruel prove that they are not the children of the honored dead. (Plaut, p. 318)

Index of Readings
from the *Revised Common Lectionary*

Gen. 1:11–2:4a	Trinity Sunday	A
Gen. 1:1–2:4a	Easter Vigil	A (c)
Gen. 1:1–2:4a	Easter Vigil	B (c)
Gen. 1:1-5	Baptism of the Lord	B (c)
Gen. 1:1–2:4a	Easter Vigil	C (c)
Gen. 2:4b-9, 15-17, 25–3:7	Lent 1	A (c)
Gen. 2:18-24	Proper 22 [27]	B (c)
Gen. 3:8-15	Proper 5 [10]	B (c)
Gen. 6:9-22	Proper 4 [9]	A
Gen. 7:1-5, 11-18; 8:6-18; 9:8-13	Easter Vigil	A, B, C (c)
Gen. 9:8-17	Lent 1	B (c)
Gen. 11:1-9	Pentecost (Alt.)	C (c)
Gen. 12:1-9	Proper 5 [10]	A
Gen. 12:1-4a (4a-8)	Lent 2	A (c)
Gen. 15:1-12, 17-18	Lent 2	C (c)
Gen. 15:1-6	Proper 14 [19]	C
Gen. 17:1-10, 15-19	Lent 2	B (c only)
Gen. 18:1-15 (21:1-7)	Proper 6 [11]	A
Gen. 18:1-10a	Proper 11 [16]	C
Gen. 18:20-32	Proper 12 [17]	C
Gen. 21:8-21	Proper 7 [12]	A
Gen. 22:1-18	Proper 8 [13]	A
Gen. 22:1-18	Easter Vigil	A, B, C (c)

Gen. 22:1-14	Lent 2	B
Gen. 24:1-4, 20-21, 50-51, 62-67	Proper 9 [14]	A
Gen. 25:19-34	Proper 10 [15]	A
Gen. 28:10-19a	Proper 11 [16]	A
Gen. 29:15-19	Proper 12 [17]	A
Gen. 32:22-32	Proper 13 [18]	A (c)
Gen. 32:22-31	Proper 24 [29]	C (c)
Gen. 37:1-4, 12-36	Proper 14 [19]	A
Gen. 45:4-20	Proper 15 [20]	A
Gen. 45:3-11, 15	Epiphany 7 [7]	C (c)
Gen. 50:15-21	Proper 19 [24]	A

(c) appears in the current *Common Lectionary*

Index of Midrashim
from *Genesis Rabbah*